Allied Convoys to
Northern Russia 1941–1945

Allied Convoys to Northern Russia 1941–1945

Politics, Strategy and Tactics

William Smith

Pen & Sword
MARITIME

First published in Great Britain in 2023 by
Pen & Sword Maritime
An imprint of Pen & Sword Books Limited
Yorkshire – Philadelphia

Copyright © William Smith 2023

ISBN 978 1 39905 473 7

The right of William Smith to be identified as
Author of this Work has been asserted by him in accordance
with the Copyright, Designs and Patents Act 1988.

A CIP catalogue record for this book is
available from the British Library

All rights reserved. No part of this book may be reproduced or
transmitted in any form or by any means, electronic or mechanical
including photocopying, recording or by any information storage and
retrieval system, without permission from the Publisher in writing.

Typeset by Mac Style
Printed in the UK by CPI Group (UK) Ltd, Croydon, CR0 4YY.

Pen & Sword Books Limited incorporates the imprints of After
the Battle, Atlas, Archaeology, Aviation, Discovery, Family History,
Fiction, History, Maritime, Military, Military Classics, Politics,
Select, Transport, True Crime, Air World, Frontline Publishing, Leo
Cooper, Remember When, Seaforth Publishing, The Praetorian Press,
Wharncliffe Local History, Wharncliffe Transport, Wharncliffe True
Crime and White Owl.

For a complete list of Pen & Sword titles please contact

PEN & SWORD BOOKS LIMITED
47 Church Street, Barnsley, South Yorkshire, S70 2AS, England
E-mail: enquiries@pen-and-sword.co.uk
Website: www.pen-and-sword.co.uk
or
PEN AND SWORD BOOKS
1950 Lawrence Rd, Havertown, PA 19083, USA
E-mail: uspen-and-sword@casematepublishers.com
Website: www.penandswordbooks.com

*For my wife Valerie and daughter Deborah
with thanks for their understanding and support.*

Contents

Chapter 1	Aid for Russia June 1941 to February 1942	1
Chapter 2	The German Military Response	17
Chapter 3	The May 1942 Shipping Debate	31
Chapter 4	Convoy PQ 17	47
Chapter 5	Future Convoys' Competing Operational Priorities	67
Chapter 6	September 1942 Convoy Suspension PQ 19 Independent Sailings	77
Chapter 7	Treatment of British Service Personnel in North Russia	89
Chapter 8	November 1942: Resumption of Convoys	96
Chapter 9	Operation GRENADINE and Anglo-Russian Diplomatic Relations	113
Chapter 10	March 1943 Convoy Suspension	141
Chapter 11	Continuing British Service Personnel Problems in North Russia	162
Chapter 12	Russian Pressure for Resumption of Convoys	179
Chapter 13	Negotiation on Renewal of the Convoy Programme	189
Chapter 14	Churchill's Preconditions for Resumption	193
Chapter 15	Resumption of Convoy Cycle: November 1943 to April 1944	210
Chapter 16	Suspension of Convoys Before OVERLORD	218

Chapter 17 The Final Convoy Cycle   225

Chapter 18 Retrospection and Reflection   238

Appendix
Analysis and Conclusions   244
Convoy Sailing Programme   251
Notes   255
Bibliography   265
Index   266

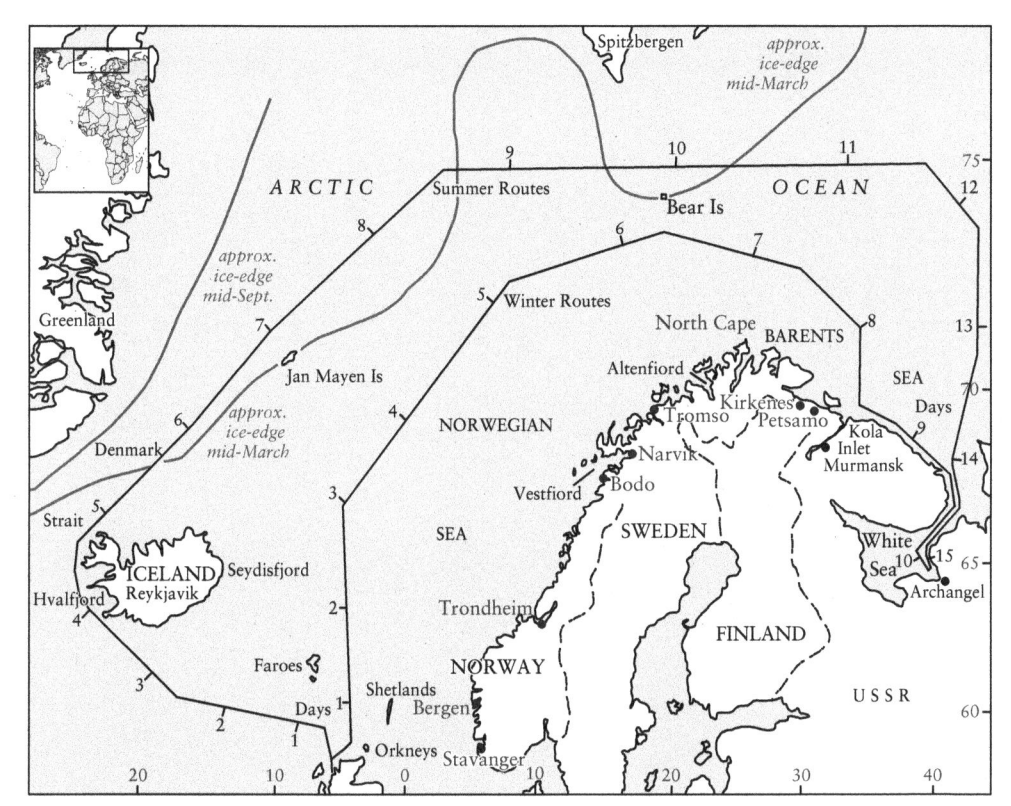

Map 1. Arctic Convoy Routes.

Chapter One

Aid for Russia
June 1941 to February 1942

The Invasion of Russia: Operation BARBAROSSA

At 4.00 am on the morning of 22 June 1941, Hitler launched Operation BARBAROSSA: the German attack on and invasion of Russia. When Churchill awoke at 8.00 am, the news of Hitler's invasion of Russia was brought to him. He later wrote: 'I had not the slightest doubt where our duty and our policy lay. Nor indeed what to say. There only remained the task of composing it.'

Churchill asked that notice be given to the BBC that he would broadcast at 9.00 pm that night and spent the day composing his statement. The War Cabinet was not consulted in advance as Churchill judged that they all felt the same on the issue.

In a somewhat lengthy and dramatic speech, Churchill announced: 'At 4 o'clock this morning Hitler attacked and invaded Russia.' In the course of his lengthy speech he declared: 'Any man or State who fights against Nazism will have our aid.'

He continued: 'We shall give whatever help we can to Russia and to the Russian people. We shall appeal to all our friends and Allies in every part of the world to take the same course and pursue it as we shall, faithfully and steadfastly to the end', and announced: 'We have offered to the Government of Soviet Russia any technical or economic assistance which is in our power and which is likely to be of service to them.'

The implications of the invasion were discussed in the War Cabinet the following day when the line taken by Churchill in his broadcast was endorsed.[1] Interestingly, it would appear that Churchill had acted independently, announcing Britain's commitment to support Russia without prior Cabinet discussion or agreement. It was then left to the Foreign Secretary, Anthony Eden, to brief the House of Commons the following day on Churchill's decision.[2] In his opening remarks he stated:

> The Prime Minister, on Sunday night, told the world after his own unrivalled fashion of the decisions at which His Majesty's Government

had arrived as a consequence of the German invasion of Soviet Russia. To-day, I would wish to give the House a brief account of the diplomatic events which preceded that giant act of aggression and of the developments which have followed upon it.

After delivering the account, the Foreign Secretary ended his statement, noting:

> As the outcome of the events of the last few days, conversations have, of course, been proceeding between the Russian Government and ourselves. The House will appreciate that I am not able to reveal the full results of those discussions, but I can tell the House that I have now heard from His Excellency the Soviet Ambassador that his Government have accepted our offer to send military and economic missions to Russia to co-ordinate our efforts in what is now, beyond doubt, a common task – the defeat of Germany. The Soviet Government have made it plain to us that in the period of military collaboration which now lies ahead, help will be upon a mutual and a reciprocal basis. His Majesty's Government accept and endorse that view.

A similar statement was made in the House of Lords by the Secretary of State for Dominion Affairs (Lord Cecil, Viscount Cranborne).[3]

Having received no response from the Soviet government to his broadcast, Churchill expressed in a message to Stalin on 7 July the 'intention to bring all aid in our power to the Russian people'. He added: 'We shall do everything to help you that time, geography and our growing resources allow. The longer the war lasts the more help we can give.'[4]

On 14 July, Harry Hopkins, President Roosevelt's friend and emissary, arrived in London. The reason for the visit was to work out the operating procedures for the Lend-Lease programme. At the end of a meeting with Churchill in the garden at No. 10 during which they discussed the British war situation, Hopkins suggested that Churchill should meet in person with Roosevelt for wide-ranging talks on their strategy for the future conduct of the war. Churchill immediately agreed to the meeting, code-named 'Riviera', which was to take place at Argentia, Placentia Bay, Newfoundland.

Assistance to Russia

During the subsequent days and weeks, Churchill sent a steady stream of messages to Stalin informing him of the steps Britain was taking to help the Soviet cause. Most went unacknowledged, until in his first reply on 18 July sent via the Russian Ambassador in London, Stalin called for the opening of a Second Front, commenting:

> Your messages have initiated agreement between our two Governments. Now, as you with every justification put it, the Soviet Union and Great Britain have become fighting Allies in the struggle against Hitler's Germany. I have no doubt that our two countries are strong enough to defeat our common enemy in the face of all difficulties.

Stalin then went on to call for the establishment of a Second Front against Hitler in the west, in France and in the north in the Arctic, stating:

> It would be easier still to open a front in the North. This would call for action only by British naval and air forces, without landing troops or artillery. Soviet land, naval and air forces could take part in the operation. We would be glad if Great Britain could send thither, say, one light division or more of Norwegian volunteers, who could be moved to Northern Norway for insurgent operations against the Germans.

Churchill later commented in his *History of the Second World War*: 'This theme was to recur throughout our subsequent relations with monotonous disregard for physical facts.'[5]

In his reply of 20 July Churchill attempted to offer Stalin some crumbs of comfort, saying:

> It is however to the North that we must look for any speedy help that we can give. The Naval Staff have been preparing for three weeks past an operation by sea-borne aircraft upon German shipping in Northern Norway and Finland, hoping thereby to destroy the enemy's power of transporting troops by sea to attack your Arctic flank.[6] We have asked your Staff to keep a certain area clear of Russian vessels between July 28th and August 2nd when we shall hope to strike. Secondly, we are sending forthwith some cruisers and destroyers to Spitzbergen,[7] whence they will be able to raid enemy shipping in concert with your naval forces. Thirdly, we are sending submarines to intercept German traffic on the Arctic coast, although owing to perpetual daylight this service is particularly dangerous. Fourthly, we are sending a mine-layer with various supplies to Archangel.[8] This is the most we can do at the moment. I wish it were more. Pray let the most extreme secrecy be kept until the moment when we tell you that publicity will not be harmful.

We are also studying, as a further development, the basing of some British fighter air squadrons on Murmansk.[9] This would require first of all a consignment of anti-aircraft guns, in addition to ground staff and equipment, then the arrival of the aircraft, some of which could be flown off carriers and others crated. When these were established our Spitsbergen squadron might possibly come to Murmansk. As soon as our naval forces are known to be in the North, we are under no delusion but that the Germans will immediately follow their invariable practice of opposing our forces with a strong force of dive-bombers, and it is therefore necessary to proceed step by step. All this, however, will take weeks.

Churchill cabled to Roosevelt on 25 July: 'Cabinet has approved my leaving. Am arranging, if convenient, to sail 4 August, meeting you some time 8th-9th-10th.'

Hopkins, meanwhile, had flown to Moscow to establish from Stalin detailed knowledge of the Russian situation and military aid he required. He later joined Churchill on board the *Prince of Wales* at Scapa Flow to sail to Newfoundland for the conference.

Churchill Pledges Military Aid

On 25 July in a personal message to Stalin, following discussions in the War Cabinet the previous day, Churchill wrote:

> I am glad to inform you that the entire War Cabinet have decided, despite the fact that this will seriously deplete our fighter resources, to send to Russia as soon as possible two hundred Tomahawk fighter aeroplanes. One hundred and forty of these will be sent from here to Archangel, and sixty from our supplies in the United States of America. Details as to spare parts and American personnel to erect the machines have still to be arranged with the United States Government.
>
> From two to three million pairs of ankle boots should shortly be available in this country for shipment. We are also arranging to provide during the present year large quantities of rubber, tin, wool and woollen clothes, jute, lead and shellac.[10] All your other requirements for raw materials are receiving careful consideration. Where supplies are impossible or limited here, we are discussing matters with the U.S.A. Details will of course be communicated through the usual official channels.
>
> We are watching with admiration and emotion all your armies magnificent fight, and all our information shows the heavy losses and

concern of the enemy. Our air attack on Germany will continue with increasing strength.

He followed this up three days later with a message which read:

As regards your request for rubber, we will deliver the goods from here or the U.S.A. by the best and quickest route. Please say exactly what kind of rubber, and which way you wish it to come. Preliminary orders are already given.

Mr Harry Hopkins has been with me these days. Last week he asked the President to let him go to Moscow. I must tell you that there is a flame in this man for democracy and to beat Hitler. A little while ago, when I asked him for a quarter of a million rifles, they came at once. He is the nearest personal representative of the President. The President has now sent him full instructions, and he leaves my house tonight to go to you. You will be advised of his arrival through the proper channels. You can trust him absolutely. He is your friend and our friend. He will help you to plan for the future victory and for the long-term supply of Russia.

When Hopkins met Stalin at the Kremlin on 30 July, he told him that he came as personal representative of the president who considered Hitler the enemy of mankind and therefore wished to aid the Soviet Union in its fight against Germany and was determined to extend all possible aid to the Soviet Union at the earliest possible time. Stalin then provided a list of his immediate and longer-term requirements. He believed the Archangel route was probably the most practicable by which to send supplies. Both he and Molotov stated that Archangel Harbour could be kept open in the winter with the aid of icebreakers. Stalin pointed out that the only two completely ice-free ports in the north were Murmansk and Kandalaksha.

Churchill briefed the War Cabinet on 31 July[11] on the content of the telegram he had dispatched to Stalin, informing him that steps were being taken to send 10,000 tons of rubber to Russia from Britain and invited the First Sea Lord to make suitable arrangements for the escort of the convoy carrying this.

The telegram to Stalin read:

Following my personal intervention, arrangements are now complete for the despatch of ten thousand tons of rubber from this country to one of your northern ports. In view of the urgency of your requirements we are taking the risk of depleting to this extent our metropolitan stocks, which are none too large and will take time to replace.

The British ships carrying this rubber and certain other supplies will be loaded within a week, or at most ten days, and will sail to one of your northern ports as soon as the Admiralty can arrange a convoy.

The Atlantic Conference

Churchill met President Roosevelt aboard the USS *Augusta* at Placentia Bay (Newfoundland) between 9 and 12 August to discuss the implications of the Soviet Union's entry into the war against Germany for the United States and British foreign policy and conduct of the war. During the conference Harry Hopkins, the president's emissary who had just returned from Moscow, briefed them on the Russian requirements and they discussed the supply of arms and matériel to the Soviet Union. Following this discussion, Churchill and Roosevelt pledged the supply of aid to Russia and on 12 August sent a joint letter to Stalin proposing a conference in Moscow to discuss long-term arrangements as to how future Russian requirements might be met and promising in the meantime to continue sending supplies and matériel as quickly as possible. The message read:

> We have taken the opportunity afforded by the consideration of the report of Mr Harry Hopkins on his return from Moscow to consult together as to how best our two countries can help your country in the splendid defence that you are putting up against the Nazi attack. We are at the moment cooperating to provide you with the very maximum of supplies that you most urgently need. Already many shiploads have left our shores and more will leave in the immediate future.
>
> The war goes on upon many fronts and before it is over there may be yet further fighting fronts that will be developed. Our resources, though immense, are limited and it must become a question of where and when those resources can best be used to further to the greatest extent our common effort. This applies equally to manufactured war supplies and to raw materials.
>
> The needs and demands of your and our armed services can only be determined in the light of the full knowledge of the many facts which must be taken into consideration in the decisions that we take. In order that all of us may be in a position to arrive at speedy decisions as to the apportionment of our joint resources, we suggest that we prepare a meeting which should be held at Moscow, to which we would send high representatives who could discuss these matters directly with you.

If this conference appeals to you, we want you to know that pending the decisions of that conference we shall continue to send supplies and material as rapidly as possible. Hitlerism is the brave and steadfast resistance of the Soviet Union, and we feel therefore that we must not in any circumstances fail to act quickly and immediately in this matter of planning the programme for the future allocation of our joint resources.
Franklin D. ROOSEVELT, Winston S. CHURCHILL

The First Convoy

The first supply convoy to North Russia, code-named 'Dervish' and made up of six merchant ships and a fleet oiler, set out from Liverpool on 12 August, departed Reykjavik on 21 August for North Russia and arrived in Archangel on 31 August. More convoys would sail with supplies shortly after the return of the Beaverbrook-Harriman Mission from the Moscow Conference (see below).

In a radio broadcast of 24 August, Churchill, reporting on his meeting with Roosevelt, included the following:

> Now Hitler is striking at Russia with all his might, well knowing the difficulties of geography which stand between Russia and the aid which the Western democracies are trying to bring. We shall strive our utmost to overcome all difficulties and to bring this aid. We have arranged for a conference in Moscow between the United States, British and Russian authorities to settle the whole plan. No barrier must stand in the way.

Churchill-Stalin Correspondence

Five days later, prior to the visit of Beaverbrook and Harriman to Moscow to arrange the long-term supply of military assistance, Churchill wrote to Stalin:

> I have been searching for any way to give you help in your splendid resistance pending the long-term arrangements which we are discussing with the United States of America and which will form the subject of the Moscow Conference. M. Maisky has represented that fighter aircraft are much needed in view of your heavy losses.

Churchill went on to describe in detail the arrangements for an interim supply of fighter aircraft. Stalin, while expressing thanks for the promise to supply more fighter aircraft, in his reply of 3 September once again appealed for the opening of a Second Front.

Prior to the Moscow Conference,[12] Churchill telegraphed Stalin on 4 September promising to try before the conference to let him know the numbers of tanks, aircraft and other supplies the US and the UK could send each month. He said:

> About supplies. We are well aware of the grievous losses which Russian industry has sustained, and every effort has been and will be made by us to help you. I am cabling President Roosevelt to expedite the arrival here in London of Mr Harriman's Mission, and we shall try even before the Moscow Conference to tell you the numbers of aircraft and tanks we can jointly promise to send each month, together with supplies of rubber, aluminium, cloth, etc. For our part we are now prepared to send you, from British production, one-half of the monthly total for which you ask in aircraft and tanks. We hope the United States will supply the other half of your requirements. We shall use every endeavour to start the flow of equipment to you immediately.

The subsequent exchanges of correspondence between Stalin and Churchill during September were dominated by Stalin's repeated demands for the opening of a Second Front. As Churchill would later write:

> All of this placed a new burden on the Royal Navy. The need to aid Russia focussed attention on the sea routes to Archangel and Murmansk. On August 12th the 1st PQ convoy of six ships for Russia sailed from Liverpool via Iceland to Archangel.[13] The plan thereafter was to run convoys to North Russia regularly once or twice a month. Initially they were not attacked by the Germans. When Archangel was ice-bound the convoys sailed to Murmansk.[14]

The Anglo-American Mission

Received on 19 September 1941:

PERSONAL MESSAGE FROM MR CHURCHILL TO MONSIEUR STALIN
Many thanks for your message. The Harriman Mission has all arrived, and is working all day long with Lord Beaverbrook and his colleagues. The object is to survey the whole field of resources, so as to be able to work out with you a definite programme of monthly deliveries by every available route and thus help to repair as far as possible the losses of

your munition industries. President Roosevelt's idea is that this first plan should cover up till the end of June, but naturally we shall go on with you till victory. I hope that the Conference may open in Moscow on the 25th of this month, but no publicity should be given till all are safely gathered. Routes and methods of travel will be signalled later.

On 22 September the Anglo-American supply mission set off in the cruiser HMS *London* from Scapa Flow to Archangel and from there flew to Moscow. Churchill provided the following letter for Beaverbrook to hand to Stalin:

My dear Premier Stalin,
The British and American Missions have now started, and this letter will be presented to you by Lord Beaverbrook. Lord Beaverbrook has the fullest confidence of the Cabinet, and is one of my oldest and most intimate friends. He has established the closest relations with Mr Harriman, who is a remarkable American, wholeheartedly devoted to the victory of the common cause. They will lay before you all that we have been able to arrange in much anxious consultation between Great Britain and the United States.

President Roosevelt has decided that our proposals shall, in the first instance, deal with the monthly quotas we shall send to you in the nine months period from October 1941 to June 1942 inclusive. You have the right to know exactly what we can deliver month by month in order that you may handle your reserves to the best advantage.

The American proposals have not yet gone beyond the end of June 1942, but I have no doubt that considerably larger quotas can be furnished by both countries thereafter, and you may be sure we shall do our utmost to repair as far as possible the grievous curtailments which your war industries have suffered through the Nazi invasion. I will not anticipate what Lord Beaverbrook will have to say upon this subject.

You will realise that the quotas up to the end of June 1942 are supplied almost entirely out of British production, or production which the United States would have given us under our own purchases or under the Lease and Lend Bill. The United States were resolved to give us virtually the whole of their exportable surplus, and it is not easy for them within that time to open out effectively new sources of supply. I am hopeful that a further great impulse will be given to the production of the United States, and that by 1943 the mighty industry of America will be in full war swing. For our part, we shall not only make substantially increased contributions from our own existing forecast production, but also try to obtain from our people an extra further effort to meet our common needs. You will understand, however, that our Army and its supply which has been planned is perhaps only one-fifth or one-sixth as large as that of yours or Germany's. Our first duty and need is to keep open the seas, and our second duty is to obtain decisive superiority in the air. These have the first claims upon the man-power of our 44,000,000 in the British Islands. We can never hope to have an Army or Army munitions industries comparable to those of the great Continental military Powers. None the less, we will do our utmost to aid you.

General Ismay, who is my personal representative on the Chiefs of the Staffs Committee, and is thoroughly acquainted with the whole field of our military policy, is authorised to study with your Commanders any plans for practical cooperation which may suggest themselves.

There is no doubt that a long period of struggle and suffering lies before our peoples, but I have great hopes that the United States will enter the war as a belligerent, and if so, I cannot doubt that we have but to endure to conquer.

I am hopeful that as the war continues, the great masses of the peoples of the British Empire, the Soviet Union, the United States and China, which alone comprise two-thirds of the entire human race, may be found marching together against their persecutors; and I am sure the road they travel will lead to victory.

With heartfelt wishes for the success of the Russian Armies, and of the ruin of the Nazi tyrants,

Believe me,
Yours sincerely,
Winston S. CHURCHILL
September 21, 1941

The PQ/QP Convoys

The first convoy of the PQ/QP series after 'Dervish', QP 1 comprising the six merchant ships of 'Dervish' plus seven Russian merchant ships, left Archangel at 12.00 pm on 28 September. The first eastbound PQ convoy to North Russia, PQ 1 of eleven merchant ships, sailed from Hvalfiord, Iceland one day later.

The Moscow Conference

The Moscow Conference began on 29 September and concluded on 1 October with the signing of a protocol[15] listing those items of material aid to be supplied to Russia over the period up to 30 June 1942.

Premier Stalin at first seemed suitably pleased with the outcome of the Moscow Conference but, always looking for more, commented in his reply to Churchill of 3 October:

> I admit that our present requirements in military supplies, arising from a number of unfavourable circumstances on our front and the resulting evacuation of a further group of enterprises, to say nothing of the fact that a number of issues have been put off until final consideration and settlement in London and Washington, transcend the decisions agreed at the conference. Nevertheless, the Moscow Conference did a great deal of important work. I hope the British and American Governments will do all they can to increase the monthly quotas and also to seize the slightest opportunity to accelerate the planned deliveries right now, since the Hitlerites will use the pre-winter months to exert the utmost pressure on the U.S.S.R.

President Roosevelt informed Stalin on 3 October that he had seen the protocol of the Three-Power Conference in Moscow and discussed with the members of the American Mission the data set forth therein, approved all the items of military equipment and munitions, directed the raw materials to be provided as rapidly as possible, and given orders that the deliveries were to begin at once and were to be continued in the largest possible volume.

Churchill replied to Stalin on 6 October:

> I am glad to learn from Lord Beaverbrook of the success of the Tripartite Conference at Moscow. '*Bis dat qui cito dat*' ['He who gives swiftly gives twice'].[16] We intend to run a continuous cycle of convoys leaving every ten days. The following are on their way and arrive at Archangel on October 12th: 20 heavy tanks, 193 fighters (pre-October quota). The following will sail on October 12th, arriving October 29th: 140 heavy tanks, 100 Hurricanes, 200 Bren carriers, 200 anti-tank rifles and ammunition, 50 2-pounder guns and ammunition. The following will sail on October 22nd: 200 fighters, 120 heavy tanks. The above shows that the total October quota of aircraft and 280 tanks will arrive in Russia by November 6th. The October quota of Bren carriers, anti-tank rifles and 2-pounder tank guns will all arrive in October. 20 tanks have been shipped to go via Persia and 15 are about to be shipped from Canada via Vladivostok. Total of tanks shipped will therefore be 315 which is 19 short of our full quota. This number will be made up in November. Above programme does not take into account goods from the United States.

In arranging this regular cycle of convoys we are counting on Archangel to handle the main bulk of deliveries. I presume this part of the job is in hand.

October 6th, 1941

The overall outcome of the Moscow Conference as discussed in the War Cabinet on 6 October[17] was regarded as 'highly satisfactory'.[18] However, Churchill advised that it was clear from the Russian point of view that the only thing which really counted (with Stalin) was the early arrival in Russia of supplies under the agreement. Following a meeting of the Defence Committee (Supply) the previous afternoon to set in motion the dispatch of supplies under the agreement, Churchill had sent a further telegram to Stalin which he read out to the Cabinet.

It was not until 12 October that Churchill acknowledged Stalin's message of the 3rd, saying:

I thank you for your letter of October 3rd.

I have given incessant directions to accelerate the deliveries at Archangel, as reported to you in my telegram of October 6th.

The Initial German Military Response

The German Naval Staff announced on 13 October: 'U-boats were to be sent to the Arctic to operate against the British and Russian supply convoys to Murmansk with the proviso that should the British strengthen their forces in the Arctic, U-boats would have to be withdrawn from the Atlantic for the offensive against them.'

Parliamentary Debates

In the House of Commons debate on Russia (British Aid)[19] of 23 October the Foreign Secretary, commenting on the German invasion of Russia, noted:

On the day that the attack took place the Prime Minister himself, as Prime Minister and as Chairman of the Defence Committee of the Cabinet, gave instructions that every possible means should be examined of giving help to Russia in every sphere. That was the instruction given on the very day that the attack took place. From that day the preparations to send help began.

He then went on to report that Lord Beaverbrook had, in the name of the government and with the full assent of the government, promised in tanks and aircraft exactly what Stalin himself had asked for.

That same day Lord Beaverbrook spoke in the House of Lords in the Debate on Aid For Russia[20] on the outcome of the joint mission to Moscow:

> Forthwith, after some consultation together, the Americans and our Mission promised to Stalin, to Russia, that we would at once restore to them from the supplies in this country and in America, from British and American exports, everything required.
>
> Mr Harriman opened up the first meeting with Stalin by declaring that the American assistance to Russia would only become a possibility if Britain would give up American production ear-marked for this country. At once I said that I was authorized by the Prime Minister to say that we would give up such production.

Problems at Archangel

Although Stalin had nominated the port of Archangel as the northern terminus for the supply convoys, there were early indications that the facilities there were struggling to cope. Although only small numbers of merchant ships carrying supplies had by now arrived in North Russia, there was already concern that their cargoes were not being unloaded in Archangel as quickly as expected (despite earlier Russian assurances), and so Churchill telegraphed Stalin on 4 November:

> I hope our supplies are being cleared from Archangel as fast as they come in. A trickle is now beginning through Persia.[21] We shall pump both ways to our utmost. Please make sure that our technicians who are going with the tanks and aircraft have full opportunity to hand these weapons over to your men under the best conditions. At present our Mission at Kuibyshev[22] is out of touch with all these affairs. They only want to help. These weapons are sent at our peril, and we are anxious that they shall have the best chance. An order from you seems necessary.

Churchill's message was not received until 7 November. Stalin's response the following day, while offering appropriate assurances, also contained what proved to be in the event a well-justified complaint. He replied:

You may rest assured that everything is being done to ensure that the arms delivered to Archangel from Britain reach their destination in time. The same would be done with regard to Iran. I must add, however, even though it is a trifling matter, that the tanks, guns and aircraft are badly packed, some parts of the guns come in different ships and the aircraft are so badly crated that we get them in a damaged state.[23]

Further German Military Response

Despite the force of the Führer's directives, there were indications as early as 1 November 1941 that the German Naval War Staff remained unconvinced that U-boat operations in the Arctic offered much prospect for success given the long winter nights, poor weather, navigational conditions and strength of the enemy defences, while the volume of the sea traffic between Britain and Archangel was not regarded at the time as great enough to warrant any large-scale U-boat offensive. These doubts would continue to persist through the early months of 1942.

Meantime, despite the Führer's directives, there were still only two U-boats operating in Arctic waters in mid-November 1941. With one outbound and one returning, only three were in the operational area at any one time. The German Naval Staff still regarded operating conditions for U-boats in the area as unfavourable and the prospects of success limited.

German Reinforcement of Northern Norway

The strengthening of German naval forces in Northern Norway began on 30 November when three destroyers[24] from Bergen and two U-boats[25] from Kiel sailed for Kirkenes and a third U-boat[26] was assigned for duty in the northern area.

Shortage of Royal Navy Escorts

Initially the supply convoys to North Russia had been escorted throughout their passage. Early in December the Admiralty decided that the long hours of darkness and prevailing bad weather offered sufficient protection after the convoys had passed Bear Island, and they should therefore disperse in those longitudes and proceed to their destinations unescorted. This reduced the strain on the Home Fleet as it enabled the escorts to fuel in the Kola Inlet instead of at Archangel and then to return westward.[27]

The United States Enters the War

On 11 December 1941, Germany declared war on the United States, opening the way for the US merchant fleet to participate in the supply convoys to North Russia. One of the first American merchant ships sailed with PQ 8 on 8 January 1942: the Panamanian-registered *El Almirante*.

German Military Intervention

The C-in-C Home Fleet had become aware, from intelligence intercepts during December, of the presence of German destroyers in northern waters and the potential threat they posed. With the deployment of the German surface fleet together four days after its arrival at Kirkenes, the 8th Destroyer Flotilla sailed on an operation along the Murman coast. In the course of this operation, during the evening of 17 December four German destroyers[28] of the flotilla[29] engaged in mine-laying operations 14 miles north-east of Cape Gorodetski[30] encountered and attacked the minesweepers *Hazard* and *Speedy*, which had sailed from Murmansk on 15 December (as the Eastern Local Escort) to meet PQ 6. In the ensuing engagement *Speedy* was badly damaged by the destroyers' gunfire, but both minesweepers managed to break off contact, turn away and make off under a smokescreen and the cover of fog for Murmansk. This engagement is claimed by some sources as the *Kriegsmarine*'s first attempt to intercept a convoy to North Russia, but there is no evidence in German records to confirm that the destroyers were aware of the convoy's presence or that they had been in contact with Royal Navy warships, having mistaken the minesweepers for much larger Russian destroyers.

The defence of Norway was raised again in the 29 December Führer Conference on Naval Affairs in which Admiral Raeder argued that the battleship *Tirpitz* should go to Trondheim as soon as possible as a strategic measure aimed at countering British attacks on Norway and provide opportunities for attacks on the convoy routes between Britain and North Russia as well as on enemy warships. Hitler, however, deferred his decision on the redeployment of the *Tirpitz* until the next conference on 12 January. Hitler considered that the best place for the *Scharnhorst*, *Gneisenau* and *Prinz Eugen* was Norway from where they could attack White Sea convoys. Failing this, Hitler would decommission the ships and use their guns and crews for coastal defence in Norway.

Continuing Problems at Archangel

By the end of December 1941, as later official accounts made clear, it became evident that the infrastructure in the Russian ports had been inadequate from the outset to cope with the volume of cargo, despite Stalin's earlier assurances. In his monthly report for December[31] SBNO North Russia described the handling of convoys at Archangel as having become very difficult and slow. Apart from the delay to ships and risk of damage, the delay to cruisers and destroyers of the ocean escorts was a serious matter. It was difficult to estimate when a convoy would be ready to sail as the date depended entirely on the ice conditions and availability of ice-breakers, the former varying considerably according to wind and temperature. Once clear of the ice, however, convoys could not wait. A plan was therefore proposed whereby PQ convoys would be routed to a rendezvous off the Kola Inlet and ships diverted to the White Sea only if ice conditions were favourable and ice-breakers were ready to meet them in clear water, with the remainder of the ships proceeding to Murmansk. QP convoys would assemble in the Kola Inlet and be instructed by SBNO to sail when sufficient ships were collected to form a convoy and ocean escorts were available. Ships would be escorted from the White Sea to the Kola Inlet by the local escort; the local fog in the Kola Inlet would undoubtedly cause delays but these should not be comparable to those caused by ice. The risk of air attack in the Kola Inlet was always present but the anti-aircraft defences were good and the weather for the most part unsuitable for flying. The plan was seen to have many advantages. It was thought the Russian authorities might see in it a way out of their difficulties and be glad to agree to a plan which they could say was only accepted to oblige the British. Otherwise SBNO feared convoys would cease to function during January, February and March. Thus from January to June 1942, Murmansk would become the principal convoy terminus.

Between October and December 1941, little apparent effort had been made by the German forces, despite the weight of Hitler's Directives (which were taking time to implement) to attack the convoys to North Russia. It appears, given the operational challenges faced by their Naval Staff and a lack of resources, that action was limited simply to noting and recording the passage of the PQ convoys with no offensive action taken against them. By the end of December, the first seven convoys had delivered 750 tanks, 800 planes, 2,300 vehicles and more than 100,000 tons of military and general supplies unchallenged by German forces.

This then was the context in which the events of late 1941 and 1942 would be played out.

Chapter Two

The German Military Response

The Strengthening of German Forces in Norway

The initial deployment of destroyers and U-boats to North Norway in December 1941 was reinforced in January and February 1942 by the transfer of a number of the *Kriegsmarine* heavy surface ships. Previously, on 13 November 1941 at their Conference on Naval Affairs, Grand Admiral Raeder proposed to Hitler that the *Tirpitz* be redeployed to Norway from where she would be able to attack the convoys bound for the Soviet Union and serve as a 'fleet in being'[1] to tie down British naval assets and deter any Allied invasion of Norway. Hitler, who had forbidden an Atlantic sortie after the loss of the *Bismarck*, approved the proposal. This would take time to implement, with the *Tirpitz* requiring a number of modifications to operate in Norwegian waters and not being ready to move until early January 1942.

By the end of 1941, the *Kriegsmarine* was beginning to focus attention on the convoys to North Russia. We again find an account of the Naval Staff's intentions in their War Diary for 1 January 1942 which contains the following entry: 'Group North advised the German Naval Staff of its intention to send the *Tirpitz* on a three to four-day raid against the presumed PQ convoy route immediately after the battleship has left the North Sea.'

In the event the shortages of fuel, lack of destroyer escorts and a perceived unacceptable degree of risk resulted in this plan being dropped.

The First Convoy Loss

The first seven convoys[2] to North Russia all arrived safely without encountering any German opposition, but this was about to change. The first loss of a merchant ship from a convoy to North Russia occurred on 2 January 1942 when the merchant ship *Waziristan*, a straggler from PQ 7A, was attacked and sunk by a U-boat about 20 miles south of Bear Island. This sinking was significant, as was recognized in the German Naval Staff War Diary for 2 January: 'Submarine *U-134* reports the sinking of an eastbound unescorted ship about eighteen miles south of Bear Island. This furnishes the first practical data on the location of the Russian supply route.'

The Deployment of German Heavy Ships from France to Norway

On 8 January while the *Scharnhorst*, *Gneisenau* and *Prinz Eugen* were still docked at Brest, proposals were again submitted to Hitler for their transfer to Norway. Admiral Raeder reported:

> The great value of assembling a strong Naval force in northern Norway is recognized in view of that area's decisive importance to the outcome of the war and the need to protect it; particularly the presence of a massed force of battleships in the Arctic Ocean has great possibilities from an operational as well as a strategic point of view.

Raeder then requested a decision on transfer of the ships from Brest and the *Tirpitz* and *Admiral Scheer* from the port of Kiel in the Baltic.

At a conference with Grand Admiral Raeder on 12 January, Hitler reiterated his views on the importance of defending Norway and the case for moving the heavy ships from Brest, comparing the latter to 'a patient with cancer who is doomed unless he submits to an operation.' The passage up-channel would, he considered, 'constitute such an operation and had therefore to be attempted'. Raeder now agreed to the Führer's proposal and outline plans for the move were drafted at the conference. Since surprise was essential, Hitler ordered that the squadron must not leave Brest until after dark, accepting that this would mean the ships passing through the Dover Strait in daylight. Hitler also authorized the transfer of the *Tirpitz* to Trondheim: 'Every ship,' he declared, 'which is not stationed in Norway is in the wrong place.'

The Strengthening of the U-boat Force in Norway

Meanwhile the measures to strengthen the German forces in Norway continued. The commander of the U-boat force, Grand Admiral Dönitz, received a totally unexpected order on 25 January to send eight U-boats to the waters between Iceland, the Faeroes and Scotland to protect Norway from the anticipated invasion. The final German defence plan envisaged the disposition of no fewer than twenty medium-sized U-boats for this task. Though Dönitz personally protested vigorously against this diversion of resources, the German Naval Staff appears to have made no serious attempt to counter Hitler's obsession by arguing the probability of invasion or the potential consequences for operations in the Atlantic.

The Threat from the *Tirpitz*

Churchill appears to have shown little obvious recent direct interest or involvement in the progress of the convoys to North Russia, but on 25 January, recognizing the threat presented by the presence of the *Tirpitz* in Norway, he wrote to General Ismay of the COS Committee:[3]

> The presence of *Tirpitz* at Trondheim has now been known for three days. The destruction or even the crippling of this ship is the greatest event at sea at the present time. No other target is comparable to it. She cannot have ack-ack protection comparable to Brest or the German home ports. If she were even only crippled, it would be difficult to take her back to Germany. No doubt it is better to wait for moonlight for a night attack, but moonlight attacks are not comparable with day attacks. The entire Naval situation throughout the world would be altered and the Naval command in the Pacific would be regained.
>
> There must be no lack of co-operation between Bomber Command and the Fleet Air Arm and aircraft carriers. A plan should be made to attack both with carrier-borne torpedo aircraft and with heavy bombers by daylight or at dawn. The whole strategy of the war turns at this period on this ship, which is holding four times the number of British capital ships paralysed, to say nothing of the two new American battleships retained in the Atlantic. I regard the matter as of the highest urgency and importance. I shall mention it in Cabinet to-morrow and it must be considered in detail at the Defence Committee on Tuesday night.

Churchill's concerns were addressed in the War Cabinet the following day when the First Sea Lord and Chief of the Air Staff[4] reported that the possibility of attacking the *Tirpitz* in Trondheim Fiord had been exhaustively examined and hoped an attack would be made as soon as weather conditions were favourable. Churchill stressed that it was of the utmost strategic importance that the *Tirpitz* should, if possible, be disabled or sunk. A bombing plan approved on 28 January would be carried out on the night of 29/30 January. This would prove unsuccessful, with repeated attempts made to disable the *Tirpitz* until she was finally sunk by RAF bombing on 12 November 1944.

Deficiencies in German Capability

While the redeployment of the heavy ships to Norway and the Strategy for the Defence of Norway were being progressively implemented, the

German Naval Staff War Diaries reflect persistent concern about continuing deficiencies in the quantity, quality and utility of the available resources which would have serious implications for both tactics and operational efficiency and effectiveness. These issues would continue to be debated at some length by the Naval Staff during the following months, as we shall see later.

The Admiralty for its part appears to have been largely unaware of the nature and extent of these issues and their significance and as a result seems to have overestimated the actual capabilities and state of readiness of the German naval units in terms of their training, availability of sufficient experienced personnel, especially U-boat crews, and the persistent shortages of fuel for the surface units that continued to limit their operations. Conversely, the *Kriegsmarine* had at the same time concluded that the Royal Navy's capabilities exceeded theirs in a number of key areas.[5]

The Deployment of German Forces in Norway

Until February 1942, the Germans still had no immediate intention of employing the heavy ships directly against the convoys, in part because the ongoing fuel oil shortage limited their operational endurance. There were, however, now twenty U-boats available and the German Fifth Air Force had built up a combat strength of sixty twin-engine bombers, thirty dive-bombers, thirty single-engine fighters and fifteen naval floatplane torpedo-bombers. In addition to the strengthened surface ships and U-boat fleet now relocated to Norway, two specialized Luftwaffe anti-shipping units, KG/26 and KG/30, were transferred to the air bases at Bardufoss and Banak.

German Knowledge of Convoy Routes

German intelligence on convoy movements was progressively improving. By 11 February, the Naval Intelligence Division had correctly established an emerging pattern, as confirmed by the War Diary entry for the day:

> PQ convoys left Iceland (they thought probably Seydisfjordur), sailing to the southern point of Bear Island, then to the east to about 38° 40 E, then south to about 70° N, where they split before approaching Archangel and Murmansk; the returning QP convoys seemed to be routed further south or east, the ships bound for the British Isles possibly steering directly for Scotland. The PQ and the QP convoys seemed to leave their ports of departure simultaneously.[6] The eight- to ten-day rhythm observed at first seemed to have been slowed up and was now believed to be fifteen

days. The time required for the voyage between Iceland and Murmansk or Archangel was said to be nine to ten days. The convoy strength was presumed to be an average of ten to fifteen ships.

By the end of February 1942, eleven supply convoys had sailed to North Russian ports for the loss of only one merchant ship. All that, however, was now about to change dramatically as the *Kriegsmarine* and Air Forces embarked on a determined attempt to cut the supply line once and for all.

The Battle for the Arctic

March 1942 marked the beginning of what would prove to be the most dangerous and costly phase of the convoy programme as the *Kriegsmarine* and Luftwaffe began a determined effort to disrupt the flow of supplies by sea to North Russia. The convoy route around the coast of German-occupied Norway had become particularly dangerous due to the proximity of German air, submarine and surface forces and the likelihood of severe weather: high winds, rough seas, frequent fog and strong currents. The perpetual darkness of winter months made navigation and station-keeping in convoy formation difficult. Snow, ice and the freezing conditions represented significant hazards, both to the seamen exposed to the elements and to the safety of the ships as spray froze on the decks, superstructures and rigging. The weather during the coming summer months would become more benign, but would bring increased risk of attack around the clock in constant daylight.

Now on 9 March the German Naval Staff Operations Division War Diary, referencing a review by the Plans Division, noted: 'Enemy traffic to Murmansk-Archangel, very important to Allied war strategy, is as yet undisturbed.'

The War Diary also noted:

a. One of the principal tasks of the Navy is to disrupt enemy supplies to Murmansk and Archangel in order to safeguard northern Norway and support Army operations against the Soviet Union. This task is not being fulfilled at the present time. Supplies are being shipped to Russia almost undisturbed.
b. According to available reports, British convoys to Russia leave northern or western Scotland and sail west of the Faeroes, east of Iceland, south of Jan Mayen, in the vicinity of the ice border, south of Bear Island until approximately 40° E, and from there to the Russian coast. This traffic is of great importance for enemy warfare.

Apart from the *Tirpitz*'s unsuccessful sortie, the only damage inflicted on the convoys to North Russia to date had been the sinking of one merchant ship on 2 January 1942. Following Hitler's latest intervention, the convoys would now face an increasing level of attacks.

Hitler issued a Führer Directive on 14 March,[7] which stated:

1. Most of the reports about the British and American intentions agree that the enemy considers it most important to maintain Russia's power, of resistance by means of the largest possible amount of supplies of war matériel and food, and in addition to set up a second front in Europe in order to force us to withdraw forces from Russia. The regular, heavy convoy traffic from Scotland to Murmansk or Archangel can serve both purposes. Thus one can expect enemy landing operations on the Arctic coast; the enemy objective most dangerous for us, and therefore the most probable one is the nickel mines in northern Finland which are vital for Germany.
2. For this reason it is necessary to cut the sea communications between the Anglo-Americans and Russia in the Arctic Ocean, which up to the present time have been practically undisturbed, and to eliminate the naval supremacy of the enemy, which reaches into our own coastal waters. All available means must be employed in the battle in this sea area, which at this time is more important than the area off the West African coast.
3. I order in detail as follows:
    a. The Navy is to increase submarine operations in the Arctic Ocean to such an extent that we can count on successes against the enemy convoys in spite of difficulties brought on by the weather conditions in the Arctic Ocean.
    b. The Air Force is to increase the planes in the Arctic area, particularly by using more long-range reconnaissance and bomber units. The bulk of the torpedo plane Squadrons is to be transferred far enough to the north that they can be employed off the particularly endangered Arctic coast. The most important tasks of the Air Force are as follows: to attack persistently the enemy unloading ports on the Murman coast, increase reconnoitring of the area between Bear Island and the Murman coast and to attack the convoys and enemy naval forces which are reported, particularly enemy Aircraft Carriers.
    d. In order to reinforce the forces in the Arctic Ocean we will have to reduce operations in other areas. In particular sea reconnaissance

in the Atlantic, the range of which is no longer adequate for submarine operations there in any case, must be greatly reduced. However, blockade-runners must be brought to and from the French west coast as before.

This directive resulted primarily from the conference between Admiral Raeder and the Führer on the 12th. Two days later, Group North was tasked to direct the operations of the twenty U-boats now assigned for the defence of Norway:

So as to disrupt both enemy supply lines in the Arctic Ocean and outside the ports of destinations along with enemy transport movements outside of the ports of departure, and also to detect and hamper enemy landing plans in the Norway area, with the disruption of enemy supply lines the first priority.

On the same day the Commander-in-Chief, Air issued instructions to the 5th Air Force for the continuation of operations with attacks on PQ convoys to be given prime importance. These were to be undertaken both in co-operation with the navy and independently by the 5th Air Force; the orders also contained special provisions for co-operation with the navy.

There was also to be a change of tactics, as the War Diary now observed:

The most favourable spot for intercepting the PQ convoys lay between Bear Island and North Cape (between the Norwegian and Barents Seas) which offered greater prospects of success in this narrow strait between the coastal waters and the ice border than near the ports of arrival, it would be necessary to extend the operations area to the west, especially when an ice-free route north of Bear Island entered the picture.

On 17 March Churchill, concerned by the threat from the *Tirpitz*, asked Roosevelt to provide US warships to supplement the Home Fleet. The message read:

No. 28, March 17th
Former Naval Person to President

1. Your numbers one one nine (119) and one two zero (120). If *Tirpitz* comes out only the fastest heavy ships are of any use. We must therefore keep two (2) *King George Fifth* and *Renown* in north working with our only remaining fast aircraft carrier on this station. *Tirpitz* has gone

north to strike at our joint munition convoys to Russia and action may easily arise. *Texas*-class could not play any part in such fighting. They could not therefore release corresponding force to go to Gibraltar.
2. In view of your help we could send to Gibraltar one eight (8)-inch cruiser and four (L) destroyers (British) from the home fleet and makeshift with that while force Hypo is away.
3. We should greatly welcome your sending to home fleet one or two heavy cruisers, not less than four (4).
4. We assume any ships you will send will be under operational orders of C in C, home fleet.
5. Your points about sinkings and Atlantic convoys are being gone into separately, and a further signal will be made from Pound to King.

Prime.

The presence of the *Tirpitz* in Norway continued to preoccupy Churchill. On 27 March, in an exchange of correspondence on the deployment of US and RN warships in various theatres of the war[8] Churchill advised Roosevelt that if the *Tirpitz* put to sea, only the fastest heavy warships would be of any use. It would therefore be necessary to keep two battleships and a fast aircraft carrier available as the *Tirpitz* had gone north to strike at their joint munitions convoys to Russia and action might easily arise. He went on to ask Roosevelt to send to the Home Fleet one or two heavy cruisers, no fewer than four destroyers and above all a fast carrier invaluable to join *Victorious* in catching the *Tirpitz*.

The German Naval Staff once again emphasized the strategic tasks assigned to the German naval forces in Northern Norway as 'To help defend the coast against Allied invasion, interrupt the flow of supplies to the Russian front via Murmansk and Archangel, and tie down, by their mere presence, heavy enemy forces in the northern Atlantic so they could not be made available elsewhere.'

German Review of Deployment of Heavy Surface Forces

The deployment of the German Heavy Surface Forces came under review yet again at the end of March, with the War Diary confirming 'Units of the fleet in the northern area served to exert strategic pressure and to prevent landings; strategic pressure, due to lack of oil, was exerted merely by the presence of the ships.'[9]

Between 1 February and 20 March 1942, five convoys[10] sailed from Scotland and Iceland to Murmansk; a total of fifty-eight merchant ships, of which six were lost from the last two convoys.

Declaration of Battle for the Arctic

Hitler's directive of 14 March was followed by Admiral Raeder's declaration on the 31st of the commencement of an all-out offensive against convoys carrying vital British and American war goods to Russia. His statement immediately followed the British Admiralty announcement that a strongly-escorted convoy (PQ 13) had reached Murmansk despite three air and sea attacks. German newspapers promised that the *Kriegsmarine* and Air Force would take necessary steps to close the Murmansk route. A German naval spokesman said the attack was the first act in the Battle for the Arctic.

The Royal Navy Response: Review of Convoy Protection

In the face of the increasing threat, the C-in-C Home Fleet made further representations to the Admiralty[11] seeking additional resources and was promised additional destroyers and corvettes from the Western Approaches Command. Early in April a number of destroyers, corvettes and trawlers were transferred to build up the anti-submarine escort for each convoy to ten ships. Requests were again made to the Russian naval authorities to co-operate by reinforcing the escort at the eastern end of the route, providing long-range fighter or anti-submarine air escort, bombing the enemy aerodromes and deploying submarines south of the convoy route to discourage surface attacks east of Bear Island. The Russians also agreed to receive a mission from Coastal Command to help in organizing their maritime reconnaissance and fighter protection; the overall results, however, were once again disappointing.

The C-in-C Home Fleet also recommended that the number of convoys be reduced during the summer months when operating conditions at the German airfields in Norway would allow increased air reconnaissance; this would improve while the convoy routes were still restricted by ice.

Limitations on German Naval Operations

During April 1942, the fuel oil situation continued to critically limit German operational planning. The early March operation by the *Tirpitz* had consumed 7,500 tons of fuel oil. As a result, for all future operations the targets were first to be clearly located and identified prior to surface ship deployments, a restriction difficult to meet in Arctic conditions. In fact, decreasing oil supplies plagued the Naval Staff from the outset, and by late 1941 the monthly allotment had been reduced by 50 per cent. The delivery of 90,000 tons of fuel oil to the Italian navy in January 1942 during the reluctance of Romanian producers to deliver oil except for payment in gold further compounded the problem.

Problems with the Volume of Aid Shipments

At the Defence Committee (Operations) Meeting on 8 April[12] the First Sea Lord, noting that there had been several proposals to increase the flow of supplies from the UK and the USA to Russia via Murmansk, or Archangel when ice-free, drew attention to the limits imposed by the naval situation. He summarized the reasons that the Royal Navy was unable to do more to meet the demand for an increase in the flow of supplies, noting that following the deployment of the German reinforcements, convoys were now threatened with surface attacks by battleships based at Trondheim, cruisers based at Narvik or Tromsø and modern destroyers based in North Norway. They were also at risk of attack from U-boats based in Norway, air attack from the numerous Luftwaffe bases in Norway and from sea mines laid in the approaches to the North Russian ports. In addition, the convoy route was restricted by the ice conditions, which put it within range of enemy air reconnaissance throughout, providing targeting information for enemy surface, submarine and air forces. All this meant that it was necessary for the convoys to be protected by major units of the Home Fleet as well as being closely escorted by an anti-submarine screen and, in addition, an escort of adequate strength was required to protect the convoys against enemy cruiser and destroyer attack during the easterly portion of their passage in waters where the main Home Fleet could not operate.

This commitment, combined with the many other calls being made on the fleet at the time, had become so demanding in relation to the number of fleet units available that the Naval Staff judged they would be unable to sail more than three Russian convoys every two months with the size of each limited to twenty-five ships, otherwise the number of anti-submarine escorts required would become prohibitive. The earlier RN reinforcement measures requested during March had enabled the Admiralty to increase the scale of close anti-submarine escorts by transferring ships from other very important tasks, while the main strength of the Home Fleet was required to provide the necessary cover for each convoy. The Russian naval forces had up to this point provided very limited assistance. The First Sea Lord argued for the Russian Air Force to provide both air escort and striking forces to destroy the enemy's air bases, but it was recognized that protection of the convoys by Russian aircraft in the northern and most dangerous part of their route would not be easy. In an additional complication, during March and April both Murmansk and Archangel had been heavily bombed and it was feared that their cargo-handling capacity might be seriously reduced and ships lost if the Russians were unable to counter this threat effectively. Up until April Murmansk had been kept working practically to full capacity and with the opening up of Archangel after the winter a greater flow of shipping could be dealt with by the two ports, but the deciding factor remained not the amount of supplies or number of ships available but the provision of adequate protection for the convoys.

Taking all these factors into account, the First Sea Lord argued for the number of merchant ships included in convoys to be limited to fifty a month; i.e. two convoys of twenty-five ships each, subject to the Home Fleet not being committed to other operations. He added that geographical conditions also so greatly favoured the Germans that losses – both in merchant ships and escorts – might become so great as to make the running of convoys uneconomical. (These were prescient words, as would be seen in Churchill's weighing up of the outcome of PQ 18.)

In the event the next convoy – PQ 14, a larger one of twenty-four ships – sailed that day from Iceland, and QP 10 of sixteen merchant ships from the Kola Inlet two days later.

The First Sea Lord's concerns were discussed in the War Cabinet on 13 April.[13] This was at the time that PQ 14 was reported as being in difficulty, having unexpectedly run into ice. Four damaged merchant ships and three escorts had returned to Iceland, while the remainder continuing on passage faced attack from enemy submarines. The convoy returning from Russia (QP 10) had been attacked: first from the air with one ship being sunk,[14] and then by U-boats with two ships known to have been sunk. Churchill now thought it important that the Russian government be made aware of the extent of the risks being taken and efforts being made to maintain the northern supply route to Russia. The Foreign Secretary was tasked to make representations, through diplomatic channels, explaining the seriousness of these risks and the importance of securing the fullest co-operation from Russian air and naval forces in the protection of the convoys. Churchill undertook to send a telegram in the same vein to Stalin, although there is no evidence to suggest that he actually did so.[15]

This strengthened German resolve to disrupt the convoys and sink as many merchant ships as possible was articulated in the German Naval Staff War Diary of 14 April: 'It was of decisive importance to sink as much Allied shipping as possible in order to hamper their offensive operations; Hitler considered attacks on Murmansk convoys especially important at that moment.'

Bottleneck in Shipments

The War Cabinet learned on 14 April[16] that the American authorities were making arrangements to send large numbers of merchant ships via Britain or

Iceland to Russia without prior consultation (forty a month), which, with twelve British ships, made a total of fifty-two. It looked as though the availability of the necessary numbers of convoy escorts would prove to be the bottleneck and, to further complicate matters, of the forty ships from the United States, thirty-two did not carry protocol materials but foodstuffs and other commodities which, though no doubt acceptable to the Russians, were not essential imports, while the quantity of heavy tanks loaded, which were essential, was constrained by the very limited lifting facilities on board these ships.

In the meeting the First Sea Lord continued to argue that twenty-five ships was the maximum for a convoy on the North Russian route, although in a few days' time he would have more evidence on which to judge the size of convoys that could be managed into North Russia. In any case, it would now be necessary to employ a much heavier scale of convoy protection on the route than before, which had resulted in a reduction in strength of the escorts to convoys on the North American route. Two convoys of twenty-five ships a month therefore probably represented the absolute maximum that could be sent to Russia; indeed, he would have preferred to sail a convoy of twenty-five ships once a month with a stronger escort. This would also involve fewer risks to the vessels of the Home Fleet employed in covering the convoys. Serious losses were likely to be incurred if the effort required in order to sail the convoys to Russia on the present scale continued throughout the summer months. It was again argued that it was unsatisfactory for Britain to be making great efforts to send materials in these strongly-escorted convoys to North Russia at considerable risk without any real knowledge of the Russian rate of production or of the extent of their needs for such supplies. The Minister of Production Lord Beaverbrook was invited to produce a report setting out the maximum supplies Britain could afford to send to Russia from the point of view of availability of shipping (including convoy escorts) and of production from July to December 1942 and January to June 1943 and to consult the Service Chiefs of Staff on the strategic aspect.

Shortage of Convoy Escorts

By the middle of April 1942 the North Cape route to North Russia had become so dangerous that the C-in-C Home Fleet was unable to provide enough escorts for the convoys. Sixteen out of eight-four eastbound merchant ships and eleven out of seventy-eight westbound merchant ships – in four convoys each way – had been sunk, not including those that had suffered serious damage in Murmansk itself. These losses were far greater than those on any other convoy route. Meantime, in Reykjavik dozens of ships were awaiting the formation of a convoy and others had to turn back from the Murmansk run or be routed to Scotland instead of Iceland because of the congestion in Reykjavik. At the same time, the Russians continued to press for faster delivery of the badly-needed weapons and ammunition. In view of the heavy losses suffered by the convoys, US Navy Admiral King suggested that the Russians conduct bombing missions on the German air and sea bases in Northern Norway, especially those of Narvik and Kirkenes, and provide air coverage for the convoys as they approached Murmansk, but in the event the Russians made no move to comply with these requests. In an attempt to relieve the pressure on the Royal Navy, at the beginning of April the United States sent Task Force 39 under the command of Rear Admiral John W. Wilcox, Jr. This included the battleships *Washington* and *North Carolina*, aircraft carrier *Wasp*, heavy cruisers *Wichita* and *Tuscaloosa*, and a destroyer squadron arrived at Scapa Flow on 4 April to join the Home Fleet.[17]

The VCNS reported to the War Cabinet on the 20th[18] that only eight ships of PQ 14 had arrived in Murmansk; one had been sunk near the port and fifteen returned on account of damage from ice. Those not too badly damaged would sail in the next convoy, but serious congestion was likely to occur if the Americans continued to send over ships regardless of the Royal Navy's capacity to convoy them to their destination. These convoys now involved a substantial naval operation, and it was necessary for the American authorities to realize that it was the number of ships for which escorts could be provided rather than the capacity of the ports determining the volume of supplies that could be sent to Russia. Further, the Americans were again reported to be sending ships loaded with cargoes not of the first priority.

The War Cabinet invited the Foreign Secretary to consult with the Minister of Production and the First Lord of the Admiralty as to the representations that should be made to the United States' authorities with a view to regulating the sailing from America of ships bound for Russia and ensuring, so long as present conditions lasted, that these ships carried only high-priority supplies. There was recognition that 1942 was also going to be a bad year for ice and some effort needed to be made to distribute the more valuable cargoes across more ships. Now, in addition to the ships returned from PQ 14, another sixty-five were already loaded or on their way and the backlog was building up, particularly in Iceland. The Russian ambassador had got wind of the problem and was worried about the delay. The position had been explained to him and he had been told it might be possible to include thirty-five ships in the next convoy, PQ 15, which the Russians had said could go to Archangel.

U-Boat Deployments: Shift in Strategy

The German Naval Staff were now formulating a new strategy to deal with the threat posed by the convoys. A German Naval Staff report of 23 April on operations against PQ convoys included the following comment:

> The enemy, regarding the Bear Island/North Cape area as being greatly threatened, had increased his defences there, and suggested the focal point of U-boat attacks be moved further west, where convoy protection might be weaker and attacks could be made by large numbers of U-boats despite the possibility the convoy might be more scattered.

Chapter Three

The May 1942 Shipping Debate

The Need for Regulation of American Shipments

The Secretary of State for Foreign Affairs briefed the Cabinet on 24 April[1] on the results of his consultations with ministers and the Admiralty on the need to regulate the sailing from America of ships bound for Russia, and ensuring, so long as present conditions lasted, that these ships carried only high-priority supplies. The Admiralty had already concluded that the existing convoy cycle would have to be reduced to three convoys in two months with the number of ships in each convoy restricted to twenty-five and a request should be made, at a very high level, for increased Russian assistance in the defence of the convoys.

Two measures were proposed to deal with the backlog: first, a considerable number of United States' ships in Iceland should be brought to the UK, unloaded and the high-priority goods restowed to maximize the greatest volume of cargo in the smallest number of ships so as to deliver greater economy in shipping; and secondly, the flow of ships from North America should be slowed down until the backlog in Iceland had been cleared. United States government agreement to both these measures would be required and it would be necessary to explain the reasons for the above measures to the Russian authorities.

The Foreign Secretary also pointed out that the shipments of tanks, aircraft and other high-priority material from Britain would, if properly stowed, occupy not more than twenty-four ships every two months; this would leave fifty-one, which should suffice to take all the protocol commitments from the United States with an ample margin. The Cabinet approved that the proposal convoys should continue at the rate proposed by the Admiralty and invited the Foreign Secretary to consult the Russian and United States' authorities on the proposals.

Changes in German U-Boat Tactics

There was a further shift in German tactics on 25 April when U-boats were now ordered

To attack both PQ and QP convoys at every opportunity, in conjunction with the G.A.F, especially the PQ convoys running between Iceland and Murmansk. It was estimated PQ convoys ran from Reykjavik through the Denmark Strait south of Jan Mayen near the ice barrier to Bear Island and from there to Murmansk every 14 to 21 days, the convoys generally consisting of 10 to 15 steamers escorted by one cruiser and four to eight destroyers, corvettes and aircraft-carrying craft of varying sizes, with Heavy units disposed at a distance from the convoy. Russian submarines were active near the coast but enemy submarines could be expected at all times.

The first serious attempt at pursuing Murmansk convoys had been made in late April.[2] It was reported that although light nights and strong air cover prevented successful operations in summer, it had been possible for single boats to remain for a considerable time off Reykjavik. As opportunity offered, it was proposed that single boats should operate again in the next new moon period. On receipt of reliable news of the departure of a PQ convoy, several boats were to be sent; as many as were available of those on passage from Germany.

Regulation of American Shipments

On 26 April Churchill wrote to Hopkins:

London
Apr. 26, 1942

Prime Minister to Harry Hopkins Personal and Secret.
   Thank you for your personal telegram about shipping accumulations for Russia.
   We have been considering this question very carefully in the light of the serious convoy situation and Harriman was given today full information on number of convoys we are able to send by Northern route, number of cargo ships in each convoy and our proposals for dealing with accumulation of shipping. I hope you will feel able to agree. We are asking Russians to help with increased measures of protection for convoys.
   All good wishes.

The Backlog of Shipments

The subject of supplies for Russia was raised yet again in the War Cabinet on 26 April[3] when the Minister for Production set out a number of recommendations and priorities for delivery of supplies. Key to his recommendations were the proposals that the Americans should be informed the Naval Staff did not expect to be able to sail more than three convoys in two months to Russian northern ports and considered that these be limited to twenty-five ships each and, as ships were arriving at Russia's northern ports with little more than half of their potential cargo, the Anglo-American supply programme should be jointly planned in such a way that the ships were fully loaded. This could be done either by bringing bulk materials and foodstuffs to Britain to be transhipped and loaded with priority cargo (aeroplanes and tanks), or by supplying more of the priority cargos directly from North America; Britain could not cope with the arrival of sixty ships a month.

The Admiralty note read:

ANNEX III to W.P. (42)178 Dated April 26, 1942
Notes by the Vice-Chief of Naval Staff on the limitations imposed by the availability of naval protection.

1. The North Russian convoys are now threatened by:-
   (a) Enemy heavy ships and cruisers stationed in Norway.
   (b) Enemy destroyers based on North Norway.
   (c) German U-boats.
   (d) A concentration of German air striking forces based in Norway.
   (e) Enemy minelaying in vicinity of Northern Russian ports.
2. The convoy route is restricted at present by ice conditions and is easily covered by enemy air reconnaissance throughout its passage, and it is on information provided by this reconnaissance that the enemy's surface, submarine and air forces can strike.
3. In view of the above it will now be necessary for the convoys to be covered by major units of the Home Fleet as well as being closely escorted by an anti-submarine screen. In addition an escort of adequate strength must be provided to protect the convoys against cruiser and destroyer attack during the easterly portion of their passage in waters where the main Home Fleet cannot operate.
4. The above commitment, combined with the many other calls now being made on the Fleet, is so heavy that the Naval Staff do not anticipate that they will be able to sail the Russian convoys with reasonable security more often than three convoys in two months; moreover, they consider that the size of the convoys should be limited to 25 ships, as otherwise the number of A/S escorts required would become prohibitive.

(Signed) II. R. MOORE.
April 17, 1942.

On 26 April Roosevelt cabled Churchill:[4]

> I have seen your cable to Harry this morning relative to the shipments to Russia. I am greatly disturbed by this because I fear not only the political repercussions in Russia but even more the fact that our supplies will not reach them promptly. We have made such a tremendous effort to get our supplies going that to have them blocked except for the most compelling reasons seems to me a serious mistake.
>
> I realise in talks I have had with Pound and again with Little this morning and my own naval advisers that the matter is extremely difficult and I do not want for a moment to underrate those difficulties. On the other hand would it not be better for us to make all our plans in the immediate future on the basis of further experience? It may be that the next convoy will move through easier than we expect and that the difficulties which we now foresee may not be insurmountable and the losses which we may have to undergo may well be worth the risk.
>
> I do hope particularly that you can review again the size of the immediate convoys so that the stuff now backed up in Iceland can get through and I hope that in any conversation that Eden may have with the Russian Ambassador they be confined to telling him the difficulties and urging their cooperation in bringing the convoys in rather than any firm statement about the limit on the number of ships that can be conveyed.
>
> I can and will make some immediate adjustments at this end but I very much prefer that we do not seek at this time a new understanding with Russia about the amount of our supplies in view of the impending assault on their armies. It seems to me that any word reaching Stalin at this time that our supplies were stopping for any reason would have a most unfortunate effect.

Churchill responded to Roosevelt two days later:

> Eden has been dealing with this for me in consultation with First Sea Lord and Leathers. Following is the position. Voyage of each of these convoys now entails major fleet operation. With the best will in the world cycle of convoys cannot be more than 3 in 2 months. One convoy (PQ 15), limited to 25 merchant ships, has just sailed. In view of what you tell me we are ready to consider, in the light of the experience gained in this convoy, whether the number of merchant ships in future convoys can be increased to as many as 35. Convoy should reach North Russian ports in about 10 days' time. Meanwhile we are arranging for 35 merchant

ships to be loaded for the next convoy (PQ 16), due to leave Iceland (C) on the 14th May. But 35 is the absolute maximum number which it is safe to risk without further experience of the scale of enemy attack.

It is not clear from your telegram whether you have seen the contents of Leathers' letter to Harriman of 25th April which were telegraphed to Hopkins the same day. This explains that even if size of the convoys is limited to 25 merchant ships each there will be 75 ships carrying supplies to Russia every 2 months of which 24 are sufficient to lift protocol supplies from the United Kingdom, leaving 51, including tankers, available to carry supplies from the USA in each 2-monthly period. We estimate that, apart from food, the protocol calls for about 130,000 short tons per month from the USA. Deducting 10,000 tons from this for deliveries via the Persian Gulf, and proceeding on the assumption that each ship will carry on the average 6,000 short tons, not more than 24 ships per month (i.e. 48 in the 2 months) would be required to lift your quotas, leaving a margin of 2 or 3 for tankers and food supplies.

But the assumption that each ship can carry an average 6,000 short tons presupposes that the cargo is stowed in such a way as to ensure that the highest-priority goods are loaded into a much smaller number of ships than is now employed. Hitherto ships have been carrying about half this tonnage. This is a waste we can neither of us afford. The only possible course to adopt in order to work off the present accumulation at Iceland (C) is therefore to bring to the United Kingdom most of the 16 ships now waiting there, and also some of the 50 American and Russian ships which are on their way across the Atlantic. These would be discharged and restowed. In our view this is the only possible course if the most important cargo is to reach Russia in the largest possible volume at an early date.

I hope this may meet your views.

We are at our utmost strain for convoys escorts,
PRIME

Roosevelt's message of the 26th was followed by a further telegram on the 30th, which read:

Admiral King[5] is communicating with Pound today about the urgent necessity of getting off one more convoy in May in order to break the log jam of ships already loaded or being loaded for Russia. I am very anxious that ships should not be unloaded and reloaded in England, because I believe it would leave an impossible and very disquieting impression on

Russia. Our problem is to move 107 ships now loaded or being loaded in the United Kingdom and the United States prior to June 1. I hope you would agree to the proposal King is making, because I think on balance that this is the most important thing we can use our escorts for.

We would watch our loadings from here out so that the agreed upon number leaving Iceland after June 1 would fall within the possibilities of our convoy system. I know that this is a difficult enterprise, but I think it is so important that I hope you would examine King's proposal with Pound carefully.

Churchill later wrote: 'It was impossible to meet these [Roosevelt's] requests, great as was our desire to do so.'[6]

Shortfalls in German Military Capability

The German Naval Staff Operations Division War Diary entries of Friday, 1 May 1942 illustrate the challenges and conflicts of interest their Naval Staff faced in judging how best to allocate scarce resources to meet the perceived threats in the northern theatre of operations. All the areas under review would have direct or indirect implications for convoy operations. The first problem faced by the Chief of the Naval Staff was the requirement for U-boats to conduct operations against the convoys:

> The situation might require an increase of the number of our submarines operating in the Arctic Ocean, especially since the chances of success by the Air Force are limited, and our surface forces are greatly handicapped by lack of fuel oil.
>
> So far experience has shown that the present operational possibilities of the submarines would be greatly reduced as the days become longer and consequently the coastal waters are more carefully patrolled and shipping more heavily escorted. An increase in the number of submarines could therefore not be expected to increase our chances and is therefore not justified. On the contrary, the present situation warrants investigating whether it would not be advisable to withdraw submarines from the Norwegian theatre of operations in order to strengthen the forces in other areas.

The evidence pointed to reduced prospects of success and possible better utilization of existing numbers of U-boats in other areas of operations. The diary then went on to address the situation in the northern theatre of operations in a number of key areas of concern. The first of these was the transfer of additional heavy ships to Northern Norway, the benefits of a 'fleet in being' and the risks involved: 'Units of the fleet in the northern area serve to exert strategic pressure and to prevent landings. Strategic pressure, due to lack of oil, is exerted merely by the presence of the ships.'

Continuing Debate over Shipping Backlog

Returning to the previous correspondence with Roosevelt, Churchill was neither impressed nor intimidated by the American lobbying over the running of the convoys, replying somewhat forcefully on 2 May[7] (note there is a discrepancy between Churchill's own memoirs which quote 2 May and the FDR Archive which quotes 1 May):

1. With very great respect, what you suggest is beyond our power to fulfil. Admiral King has expressed opinion that our transatlantic escorts are already too thin. Reduction proposed would dislocate convoy system for eight weeks. During which, if enemy switched from your east coast to mid-ocean, disastrous consequences might follow to our main life-line.
2. Moreover, difficulty of Russian convoys cannot be solved merely by anti-submarine craft. Enemy heavy ships and destroyers may at any time strike. Even on this present convoy we have been attacked by hostile destroyers, which were beaten off with damage to one of ours. *Edinburgh*, one of our best 6-inch cruisers, has been badly damaged by U-boats and is being towed to Murmansk, where *Trinidad*, damaged last convoy, is still penned. Just now I have received news that *King George V* has collided with our destroyer *Punjabi*, *Punjabi* being sunk, and her depth-charges exploding have damaged *King George V*. Difficulty of Russian convoy escorts is therefore at least as much surface ships of high fighting quality as anti-submarine craft. We have made desperate attacks on *Tirpitz* in Trondheim, but, alas, although near the target, we have not achieved any damage.
3. I beg you not to press us beyond our judgement in this operation, which we have studied most intensely, and of which we have not yet been able to measure the full strain. I can assure you, Mr President, we are absolutely extended, and I could not press the Admiralty further.
4. Six ships from Iceland have already arrived at the Clyde, and their reloading ought to begin forthwith. Three convoys every two months, with either thirty-five or twenty-five ships in each convoy, according

to experience, represent extreme limit of what we can handle. Pound is cabling separately to Admiral King.

Confronted with Churchill's argument, Roosevelt conceded defeat on 3 May and gave his consent to the reduction of the convoys with the proviso that they should contain thirty-five (merchant) ships each,[8] if at all possible:

> It is now essential for us to acquiesce in your views regarding Russian convoys, but I continue to hope that you will be able to keep convoys at a strength of thirty-five ships. I propose to press Russians to reduce requirements to absolute essentials, on grounds that preparations for BOLERO will require all possible munitions and shipping.
> 3 May 1942

On 4 May[9] the War Cabinet received an account of the attacks on both the outgoing and the returning Russian convoys (PQ 15-QP 11 in which four ships had been sunk) and was informed by Churchill of his exchange of telegrams with Roosevelt on the aggregation of United States' ships loaded for Russia which could not all be included in convoys sailing from this country. Churchill advised that the position had been fully explained and the president accepted the British proposals.

Russian Pressure for Clearance of Convoy Backlog

The Russians continued to press for an improvement in the rate of delivery of supplies and returned to the charge. On 6 May Stalin requested Churchill to take action to clear the backlog of ninety shiploads of supplies, accumulated in and on the approaches to Iceland, from America. Stalin understood the ships to have been delayed for a long time owing to the difficulty British naval forces had in running a convoy, and while expressing himself conscious of the real difficulty involved and the sacrifices Britain had made in this matter, demanded delivery of the supplies to Russia during May. It would not, however, be uncharitable to suggest that Stalin, accustomed as he was to land-centric warfare, had little appreciation of the difficulties and dangers of maritime warfare, especially as he was again offering little assistance by way of merchant shipping to carry the supplies or military forces to defend the approaches to the Kola Inlet.

As we have seen, Churchill had, some weeks previously, indicated an intention to write to Stalin about the size and frequency of convoys, but had not yet done so. Now, on the 9th, he wrote to Stalin at some length:

I have received your Telegram of May 6 and thank you for your message and greetings. We are resolved to fight our way through to you with the maximum amount of war materials. On account of the *Tirpitz* and other enemy surface ships at Trondheim the passage of every convoy has become a serious fleet operation. We shall continue to do our utmost.

No doubt your naval advisers have pointed out to you the dangers to which the convoys are subjected from attack by enemy surface forces, submarines and the air from various bases in enemy hands, which flank the route of a convoy throughout its passage.

Owing to adverse weather conditions the scale of attack, which the Germans have so far developed, is considerably less than we can reasonably expect in future.

We are throwing all our available resources into the solution of this problem, have dangerously weakened our Atlantic convoy escorts for this purpose, and as you are no doubt aware have suffered severe naval casualties in the course of these operations.

I am sure that you would not mind my being quite frank and emphasising the need of increasing the assistance given by the USSR naval and air forces in helping to get these convoys through safely.

If you are to receive a fair proportion of the material which is loaded into ships in the United Kingdom and the USA, it is essential that the USSR naval and air forces should realise that they must be largely responsible for convoys, whether incoming or outgoing, when to the east of meridian longitude 28 degrees east in waters which are out of sight of the Murmansk coast.

The ways in which further assistance is required from the USSR forces are as follows:

(a) Increased and more determined assistance from the USSR surface forces;
(b) Provision of sufficient long-range bombers to enable the aerodromes used by the Germans to be heavily bombed during the passing of convoys in the North Cape areas;
(c) Provision of long-range fighters to cover convoys for that part of their voyage when they are approaching your coasts;
(d) Anti-submarine patrols both by aircraft and surface vessels.

When broadcasting tomorrow (Sunday) night I propose to make a declaration warning the Germans that if they begin gas warfare upon the Russian armies we shall certainly retaliate at once upon Germany.

Failure of German Operations against Convoys

The German Naval Staff were, however, dissatisfied with the outcome of operations against the convoys, as stipulated in an assessment of 8 May:

> Of a total of about 25 to 28 enemy tankers and ships carrying war matériel approximately 21 to 24 vessels had reached Russian ports safely. This was a similar percentage to that of previous convoys and proved it had not yet been possible to cut off, or reduce decisively, enemy supply operations in the Arctic Ocean.
>
> The failure to achieve this strategic aim was attributed to the superior strength of the Royal Navy's close and distant naval and air cover and anti-submarine protection; the extremely unfavourable weather conditions (heavy seas or low visibility), which the British exploited to get convoys through; the continuous daylight, throughout day and night, which, depriving U-boats of the tactical advantages of night attacks as due to destroyer and air defences an underwater attack was rarely successful, the light conditions making it impossible to take up positions for an attack. Until about the end of August only occasional successes could be expected. But in view of the great importance of checking the Murmansk traffic, the Naval Staff saw no possibility of completely terminating submarine warfare in the Arctic Ocean. On the contrary, since there was no more justification for keeping submarines in central or southern Norway for the prevention of possible landing attempts, all available submarines must be used against convoys in the Arctic Ocean.

The assessment recognized that the Germans could not hope to prevent landing operations or to be successful against fast naval forces and transport ships; only against supply traffic once a landing had been made, and it continued:

> Against such traffic it would always be possible to commit our submarines at sea in good time. The disastrous fuel situation had also interfered badly with the operations of Heavy Surface Forces. At the time it was no longer possible to move *Tirpitz* and the *Hipper* with their destroyer escorts, except in the event of an immediate threat to the Norwegian coast. Destroyer operations offered few chances, since destroyers always encountered superior enemy forces, besides the fuel situation interfered with such action.

Finally it concluded that the navy's means to achieve sinkings in the Arctic Ocean during the summer months were very limited, particularly due to the oil situation. Air Force operations afforded the principal means of attack and as long as the ice border limited the open water off the Arctic coast the Air Force would be able to achieve good results in systematic attacks as recently shown. It was therefore of the utmost importance that the Air Forces in the northern area directed their activities against this target.

Promised Increase in Deliveries

Stalin replied in a more conciliatory manner to Churchill in his telegram of 12 May received on the following day:

> I have received your message of May 11 and thank you for the promise to take measures to deliver the maximum war materials to the USSR. We fully realise the serious difficulties which Great Britain has to overcome and the heavy naval casualties involved in carrying out that major task.
>
> As to your proposal for increased assistance by the Soviet air and naval forces in covering the supply ships in the area mentioned by you, rest assured that we should immediately do all we can. It should be borne in mind, however, that, as you know, our naval forces are very limited and by far most of our air forces are engaged in action at the front.[10]

Churchill wrote to General Ismay of the COS Committee on 17 May:

> Not only Premier Stalin but President Roosevelt will object very much to our desisting from running the convoys now the Russians are in heavy action and will expect us to run the risk and pay the price entailed by our contribution. The United States ships re queuing up, my own feeling, mingled with much anxiety, is the convoy ought to sail on the 8th. The operation is justified if half gets through. Failure on our part to make the attempt would weaken our influence with both our major allies. There are always the uncertainties of weather and luck, which may aid us. I share your misgivings, but I feel it is a matter of duty.

Roskill later noted:[11] 'Admiral Tovey fully endorsed Admiral Bonham-Carter's recommendation that unless the airfields in north Norway could be neutralised, or some cover obtained from darkness, the convoys should be stopped. If, he went on, they must continue for political reasons, very serious and heavy losses must be expected.'

Nor did the First Sea Lord disagree. On 18 May Admiral Pound, the First Sea Lord, wrote to Admiral King, USN (Chief of Naval Operations): 'The whole thing is a most unsound operation with the dice loaded against us in every direction. These Russian convoys are becoming a regular millstone round our necks, and cause a steady attrition in both cruisers and destroyers.'

Review of U-Boat Deployments in the Arctic

The German Naval Staff's lengthy ongoing deliberations between March and May on whether or not to increase the number of submarines operating in the Arctic Ocean led to the decision on the 20th that the fight against the convoys to Russia was of such importance that submarine operations should continue despite the unfavourable conditions and efforts should be made to send at least eight submarines against each convoy.

The German Naval Command then issued a directive to the Commanding Admiral, Submarines, Group North and Admiral, Arctic Ocean emphasizing the paramount importance of the fight against the PQ convoys. Although it continued to recognize that submarine operations had only slight chances of success, during the light Arctic summer nights and particularly against strong escorts of the PQ convoys the operations were considered of great importance in the occasional successes achieved. More particularly, their value in shadowing the convoys and guiding the Air Forces to their targets was sufficient to justify the assignment of a sufficiently large number of submarines against PQ convoys, even although this involved withdrawals from the Atlantic zone of operations. In order to permit operations by five to eight submarines against each convoy and on the other hand to withdraw from other areas as few submarines as possible for the Norwegian area, submarines were ordered to operate against empty QP convoys sailing west only in combination with operations against PQ convoys. Group North now had twenty-three U-boats at its disposal.

Review of Convoy Programme

Possible Postponement of PQ 16
The War Cabinet met on 18 May[12] to discuss whether in view of the substantially increased risk of air attack from Norway the next convoy to Russia should sail. The Cabinet was informed that with the ice barrier in its present position, the convoy must sail for six to seven days within range of enemy bombers based in Norway. The Germans had about 100 bombers in this area, 69 of which were long-range, and a very good system of air reconnaissance. The scale and duration of the air attack on the next two convoys was likely to be greater than any yet experienced. The chiefs of staff feared that, unless the weather

conditions were particularly unfavourable for air operations, losses were likely to be considerable. In addition to the loss of merchant vessels, account had to be taken of the risks to which the escorting vessels would be exposed.

In these circumstances Churchill questioned whether it would not be expedient to cancel the convoys due to sail in May and June and increase the size of the convoys sailing after the beginning of July when it would be possible to take a more northerly route which, for the greater part of the voyage, would lie outside the range of Ju 87s and Ju 88s.

The main points then raised in the Cabinet discussion were as follows:

(a) If the May and June convoys were cancelled, how far it would be possible to make up the deficit by increasing the quantity of supplies sent thereafter. After the beginning of July the Admiralty would be prepared to take the risk of increasing the size of the convoy to fifty ships. But if no convoys sailed until July, the congestion of shipping destined for Russia would be very large and, if the supplies, which had been dammed up, were released too rapidly, a great strain would be thrown on the port facilities in Russia.

(b) It was recognised the Navy would be relieved of a heavy responsibility, and a substantial risk, if these sailings could be deferred until after the end of June. On the other hand, it would not be easy to convince either Premier Stalin or President ROOSEVELT it was right to interrupt the flow of supplies to Russia.

(c) It was suggested the position should be explained to Premier Stalin, who might be asked to say whether he was in such immediate need of these supplies that he would wish an attempt made to get through the May and June convoys during those months, even though, say, half the amounts shipped might well be lost en route, rather than to face postponement until July, when conditions would be easier.

In reply to this suggestion, it was pointed out the decision was one the Cabinet must take themselves and ought not to place on other shoulders. In any event, Premier Stalin was almost certain, if the point was put to him, to reply an attempt should be made to force through these supplies, at whatever cost.

(d) Churchill expressed the view it was our duty to fight these convoys through, whatever the cost. The Russians were engaged in a life and death struggle against our common enemy. There was little we could do to help them, except by maintaining the flow of supplies by this northern route. In the last convoy twenty-two out of twenty-five ships had got through, in spite of our apprehensions, and this time we might again do better than we feared.

The effect on war comradeship between the United Nations of cancellation of the May convoy would, he feared, be very serious.
(e) It was not thought any appreciable advantage would be gained by confining the convoy to faster vessels. On the whole the First Sea Lord thought if the convoy was to sail, we might as well send thirty-five ships.

The War Cabinet decided:

(1) The May convoy, due to leave that night, should sail as arranged.
(2) Premier Stalin should be informed that we had given orders for this convoy to sail, notwithstanding the additional risk to which it would be subject. He should be strongly urged to send heavy bombers to attack the aerodromes in Norway from which the German aircraft were operating and warned that it might be necessary to cancel the sailing of the June convoys.
(3) The question whether the June convoy should sail should be decided by the War Cabinet in the light of the losses sustained by the May convoy.
(4) The Chiefs of Staff were asked to prepare a draft Telegram, covering the points set out in paragraph (2) for the Prime Minister to send to Premier Stalin.

Resumption of the Convoy Programme

The telegram subsequently sent by Churchill to Stalin on 20 May following the 18 May Cabinet meeting read as follows:

A convoy of thirty-five ships left yesterday[13] with instructions to make its way to you. Having about a hundred bombers, the Germans are on the look-out for these ships and escort. Our advisers believe that unless the weather is again favourable enough to hamper operations by the German air forces we should expect the greater part of the ships and the war materials they carry to be lost.

As I pointed out in my Telegram of May 9th, a very great deal depends on the extent to which your long-range bombers can bomb enemy airfields, including the one at Bardufoss, between May 22nd and 29th. I know you would do all in your power.

The May 1942 Shipping Debate 45

> If we are in bad luck and the convoy suffers very heavy losses, then the only thing we can do would be to hold up the further sailing of convoys until we have greater sea space when the ice recedes northwards in July.

Churchill's telegram of 20 May was acknowledged by Stalin on the 24th. The reply read:

> I have received the message, transmitted in Kuibyshev on May 20, in which you say that thirty-five ships with supplies for the USSR are en route to Soviet ports. Thank you for the message and the steps taken by you in sending the ships. Our air and naval forces would, on their part, do all they can to cover the supply ships in the sector of which you informed me in your message of May 9.

The War Cabinet learned on the 26th[14] that the outward-bound Russian convoy (PQ 16) had been attacked on the previous day by some thirty-two torpedo and dive-bombers, of which one was certainly and four were probably destroyed. The convoy had escaped damage except for one [merchant] ship, which had turned back. Churchill wrote again to Stalin on the following day: 'So far all has been well with the convoy, but it is now at its most dangerous stage. Many thanks for the measures you are taking to help it in.'

In a further telegram of 27 May, Churchill reported to Roosevelt:[15] 'So far all has gone well with the Northern Convoy but the dangers on the next 2 days must necessarily be serious.'

Stalin assured Churchill the following day: 'As to measures for covering the convoy, you may rest assured that we are doing and will continue to do our utmost in this respect.'

Churchill sent Stalin a further telegram the next day,[16] paragraph 3 of which read: 'So far our northern convoy is fighting its way through having lost five ships sunk or turned back out of 35. Tomorrow, 28th, we ought to be getting under the Russian air umbrella if any has been provided. Otherwise, two more days of this.'

The German Military Response

The German Naval Staff War Diary of 28 May records the emphasis placed on the importance of continuing U-boat operations against the convoys despite the difficulties encountered and issued a further directive to the Commanding Admiral, Submarines, Group North and the Admiral, Arctic Ocean, which read:

1. The fight against PQ convoys is of paramount importance.
2. Although submarine operations have only small chances of success at the moment, due to the light Arctic summer nights and to the

particularly strong escorts of the PQ convoys, they are considered of such great importance in the occasional successes and particularly in shadowing the convoys and guiding the air forces to their targets the assignment of a sufficiently large number of submarines against PQ convoys is justified, although this involves withdrawals from the Atlantic zone of operations.
  a. Submarines are to operate against empty QP convoys sailing west only in combination with operations against PQ convoys.

On the 28th, Group North proposed a coordinated attack on the next PQ convoy: PQ 17 involving the Air Force, submarines and surface ships.

Reduced Supplies for Russia

Roosevelt wrote to Churchill on 31 May:[17]

United Staff are now working on proposal to increase shipping for use in BOLERO[18] by cutting out large portion of materials for Russia, other than munitions which can be used in battle this year. This ought not to diminish supplies of munitions like planes, tanks, guns, ammunition, which Russians could use in combat this summer. I think we can cut further on Murmansk Archangel convoys and send more ready-to-use munitions via Basra. This should make your Home Fleet task easier, particularly destroyers.

Convoy Programme to end of May 1942

By the end of May 1942, a total of seventeen convoys[19] comprising 245 merchant ships, 100 of them British, had carried British protocol supplies to North Russia from the United Kingdom. They had sailed at an average rate of eleven per month, but there were wide variations in the intervals between sailings for operational reasons. The time taken between loading ports in the United Kingdom and the port of arrival in North Russia therefore varied between seventeen days and more than two months.

On 1 June the War Cabinet received an account of the latest convoy to Russia [PQ 16]. Of thirty-five ships in the convoy, twenty-seven had reached port. During attacks on the convoy, at least two enemy aircraft had been destroyed by two Hurricanes catapulted from ships in the convoy. Of the two pilots of these Hurricane aircraft, one had been killed and the other injured. Four U-boats had also probably been damaged. The War Cabinet took note.

Chapter Four

Convoy PQ 17

The Postponement of Convoy PQ 17

It was nevertheless now obvious that with the political situation unchanged and so many ships from the US and Britain assembling off Iceland, it would be necessary to run another convoy. The decision to run PQ 17 on 11 June had been taken on the 4th, but the priority requirement for the protection of convoy WS 19Z to Malta[1] left insufficient destroyers in the Home Fleet for the simultaneous running of Russian convoys. The sailings of PQ 17 and QP 13 were postponed until 27 June until sufficient fleet escorts [destroyers] returned from duties in the Mediterranean.

German Naval Staff Analysis of Supplies to Russia

The failure of the German forces to successfully disrupt the flow of matériel to North Russia is illustrated by the concerns expressed in the German Naval Staff Analysis of Supplies to Russia via the Northern Route dated 7 June 1942 which reported:

> Sixteen convoys reached Russian Arctic ports in the period between October 1941 and the end of May 1942. Of the approximately 250 to 300 vessels involved, the Foreign Merchant Marine Branch, Naval Intelligence Division, Naval Staff had been able to identify 62 (including 6 sunk) vessels by name and deduced, based on an average tonnage of 5,000 GRT per vessel, the total tonnage from October 1941 to May 1942 had amounted to approximately 1,500,000 GRT. Of this, 40 ships totalling 218,924 GRT were sunk, and 86 ships totalling 458,493 GRT damaged. It was assumed about 1,250,000 GRT arrived in Russian ports, allowing for some the sinkings and damages being incurred by ships on their return voyage from Russia.
>
> The cargos had consisted of combat vehicles, guns, ammunition, airplanes, medical supplies, wheat, oil seeds and sugar from England, as well as light tanks, trucks, cereals, raw materials, tools and canned goods from the US and Canada. This type of cargo resulted in the ships

being loaded below capacity. In view of the shallow waters in the ports of destination, the majority of the vessels were loaded to draw no more than 21 feet. The analysis assumed 1,250,000 tons, or a monthly supply of about 150,000 tons, has been shipped to Russia. With the exception of 5 tankers, apparently no motor ships were used, but only steamships. The round trip USA-Murmansk-USA lasted on average 3 to 4 months, and from Great Britain via Iceland and back about 6 to 8 weeks.

Review of U-Boat Operations in Northern Waters

The Chief of the German Naval War Staff, commenting on 10 June to FO U-boats on U-boat operations in northern waters, asserted:

> Attack on England-Murmansk convoys was the most important task of naval forces in Norwegian area. Every ton of war material sunk lightened the burden on the Eastern Front. Indeed the Navy should apply all means at its disposal to this task, even at the cost of tasks in other areas.

The following day the War Diary of the Commanding Admiral, Submarines commented on the use of submarines in the northern area and the difficult conditions faced: 'The Naval Staff continued to regard the fight against the Murmansk convoys as the primary task of all naval forces stationed in the Northern Area.'

US/Soviet Mutual Aid Agreement

On 11 June, President Roosevelt signed off a Mutual Aid Agreement between the United States and the Union of Soviet Socialist Republics, Article I of which read: 'The Government of the United States of America will continue to supply the Government of the Union of Soviet Socialist Republics with such defense articles, defense services and defense information as the President of the United States of America shall authorize to be transferred or provided.'

A Temporary Strengthening of Anglo-Russian Relations: Russian Recognition of Operational Difficulties

Even the Russian Foreign Minister M. Molotov had said in his report at the Supreme Soviet of the USSR on 18 June:

> We must, of course, bear in mind that the delivery of armaments and war materials to the Soviet Union was and is a matter of no little difficulty....

Nevertheless, the delivery of arms and materials from the USA and Great Britain has not only not decreased but has increased in recent months. These supplies are an essential and important supplement to those arms and supplies which the Red Army receives, in their overwhelming bulk, from our internal resources ... the fulfilment of these deliveries has played and will play in the future an important part in strengthening friendly relations between the USSR, Great Britain and the USA.

Recognition of Increasing Enemy Threat

The potential increased risk of losses from the Russian convoys was recognized in the War Cabinet discussion of 22 June on the shipping situation:[2]

As the Cabinet are aware, the enemy has concentrated powerful surface, submarine and air forces in Northern Norway. This has made the passage of each convoy a fleet operation, besides forcing us to provide close anti-aircraft and anti-submarine escort for the convoy on a greatly increased scale. It has also meant greatly enhanced risk of losses.

The PQ 17 Convoy Disaster

The next pair of convoys, PQ 17 and QP 13 of thirty-six and thirty-five merchant ships respectively, sailed on 27 and 26 June 1942.[3] After PQ 17 sailed, Group North learned that in addition to the usual escort of cruisers and destroyers there would also be a cover force of two battleships and an aircraft carrier to contend with. The German Naval Staff then amended their operation plan and ordered all their ships to Alta Fjord where German air superiority was judged sufficient to drive off the enemy's heavy ships. While making the transfer, however, the battlecruiser *Lützow* and four of the escorting destroyers ran aground, damaging their hulls and weakening the capability of the strike force.

By 27 June, the *Tirpitz* was at Trondheim with the *Hipper*, and *Lützow* and *Scheer* at Narvik, while the German Fifth Air Force had assembled a force of 264 combat aircraft in the vicinity of the North Cape. When PQ 17 sailed from Hvalfiord the German Naval Staff had already decided to interdict the sea lane to northern Russia with all the forces at their disposal: land-based aircraft, U-boats and surface ships, the latter including the battleship *Tirpitz* and cruiser *Hipper*, with four destroyers at Trondheim, and the battlecruisers *Scheer* and *Luützow*, together with six destroyers at Narvik.

Part of PQ 17 ran into drifting ice in thick weather in the Denmark Strait; two merchant ships were damaged and returned to Iceland. On 1 July the convoy was located by enemy aircraft and U-boats and was shadowed continuously from then onwards except for a few short intervals in fog. On the morning of 4 July, German aircraft and U-boats began to attack the convoy, claiming four sinkings in the first strike. That evening the Admiralty, in the face of the perceived threat from the German heavy ships, ordered the escort force to return westwards, directed the convoy to scatter and ordered the merchant ships to proceed independently to North Russia. In fact no German heavy ships were at sea at that time.

When the order to scatter was received, PQ 17 had already covered more than half its route with the loss of only three merchant ships. Of the thirty-four remaining when the convoy was scattered, twenty-one including a fleet oiler and one rescue ship were later sunk; only thirteen, including one refloated after running aground in Nova Zemlya, eventually reached Archangel. The last would not reach North Russia until 25 July.

Churchill later called the event 'One of the most melancholy naval episodes in the whole of the war.'[4]

The return QP 13 of thirty-five merchant ships sailed in two sections from Murmansk and Archangel: the Archangel section of twelve sailed on 26 June and the Murmansk section of twenty-three on 27 June. The two sections joined up on 28 June; the convoy was not attacked, with the focus of the German effort again being on PQ 17.

PQ 17: German Naval Staff Assessment

The German Naval Staff assessment on 6 July of the overall outcome of the operation against PQ 17 considered it one of the most outstanding successes scored in one blow against enemy supply lines. It continued:

> A convoy carrying a full cargo of war matériel from America was almost completely annihilated in spite of a very strong escort, just as it was approaching its destination. A severe blow had been dealt to Russia's armament enemy shipping tonnage. The strategic, physical and moral effect of this blow was similar to that of a lost battle. Aided by circumstances, the Air Force and the submarines, in 5 days of purposeful and unerring action achieved what was to have been accomplished by the attack of the fleet forces on PQ 17 in Operation *Rösselsprung* ['Knight's Move'].

Despite this success, the following day Admiral Raeder expressed his frustration at the lack of success in the commitment of heavy surface forces in the Norwegian theatre. The entry in the War Diary for 7 July 1942 read:

Two attempts to dispatch the Heavy ships against the Murmansk-Archangel shipping route had now met with no success. Every attempt to bring Heavy Surface Forces into action had been made difficult by the Führer's insistence losses or setbacks must be avoided at all cost. Consequently, it was only possible to undertake such operations in those instances where, as far as human judgement could predict, no serious risk was involved, particularly from enemy Carriers. To a certain extent this condition had been present during Operation Rösselsprung. It was not known ever to have occurred before in connection with PQ convoys and would probably never do so again. Thus it could hardly be expected the Heavy ships would ever undertake a mission against PQ convoys. However, since the commitment of Heavy ships was a matter of fundamental strategy, new tasks would have to be found for them outside of the eventuality of an expected enemy invasion. Such tasks were open to them in operations against Russian shipping along the north Siberian route, in the eastern portion of the Barents Sea and against the QP convoys. The Naval Staff had already ordered Group North to make preparations for the first of these tasks.

Alternative Means of Assistance to Russia

In the meantime Churchill, still seeking ways of providing additional assistance to Stalin, cabled Roosevelt on 8 July:

We are studying very hard the possibility of an operation in Northern Norway or if this should prove impracticable elsewhere in Norway. The difficulties are great owing to the danger of shore-based aircraft attack upon our ships. We are having frightful difficulties about the Russian convoys. All the more is it necessary to try to clear the way and maintain the contact with Russia.

PQ 17: The Aftermath

On 10 July, the Defence Committee (Operations)[5] met to discuss the action to be taken following the losses incurred by PQ 17,[6] noting that of the thirty-six ships[7] that sailed, sixteen were safe, the fate of two others unknown, two returned to Iceland and the remaining sixteen were probably lost. The next convoy, PQ 18, was due to sail from Iceland on the 23rd. Despite the seriousness of the situation, the committee was initially reluctant to cancel the running of PQ 18 given the battles raging on the Russian Front. It was therefore agreed that there should be no interruption in the sailing of convoys to Russia, and the First Sea Lord was invited to present to the committee on the 13th proposals to enable the next convoy to be sailed without prejudicing the arrangements for the convoy to Malta.

However, come the 13th,[8] the Defence Committee (Operations) learned, based on the additional albeit limited information available, that it seemed almost certain only 8 merchant ships of PQ 17 had survived and around 500 tanks and 260 aircraft had been lost, along with 19 American and 8 British merchant ships. The First Sea Lord's prognosis based on these facts was pessimistic; the ice and bad weather conditions in the Arctic would remain the same for PQ 18 as they had for PQ 17 and no additional protective measures to safeguard the passage of the convoy were possible. Although arrangements for the new convoy were still proceeding,[9] he was unable to offer any assurance that even a single ship would get through. The Germans had gradually stepped up their tactics against the convoys, initially relying on U-boats and aircraft, then deploying surface forces westward of Bear Island and finally U-boats westward of Bear Island and surface ships eastward; this arrangement favoured the Germans and was impossible to overcome. The Service Chiefs of Staff felt bound to recommend, in the circumstances, that the sailing of convoys to Russia should for the present be suspended. Churchill said that he had taken the view that if 50 per cent of the ships of a convoy got though it would be justifiable to sail the next one, but if the losses were heavier than that, it would be wrong to continue. The loss of so many ships and so much material meant that the convoy, far from helping Russia, constituted a disastrous loss to the whole Allied cause. Cabinet members unanimously concluded that the convoy should not sail.

Thus, in view of the disastrous outcome of PQ 17, the Admiralty proposed to suspend the Arctic convoy cycle, at least until the northern ice-packs melted and receded and perpetual daylight had passed. Churchill records:[10] 'I felt this would be a very grave decision and was inclined not to lower but on the contrary to raise the stakes, on the principle of "In defeat, defiance."'

The Russian Ambassador M. Maisky called on the Foreign Secretary on 14 July to ask about the latest convoy to Russia. Mr Eden told him that the news was bad and the First Sea Lord considered, if he were on the German side, he could ensure that no ship of the next convoy reached port.[11]

On the same day, Churchill cabled Roosevelt:[12]

Only four ships have reached Archangel with four or five more precariously in the ice off Nova Zemlya out of the thirty-three included in convoy PQ 17. If a half had got through we should have persevered, but with only about a quarter arriving the operation is not good enough. For instance out of nearly six hundred tanks in PQ 17 little over one hundred have arrived and nearly five hundred are lost. This cannot help anybody except the enemy. The Admiralty cannot see what better protection can be devised, nor can they hazard battleships east of Bear Island. Stark agrees with Admiralty view and that all possible was done by us last time. *Washington* has already been withdrawn for her task in the Pacific.

We therefore advise against running PQ 18, which must start 18th at latest. If it were composed only of our Merchant ships we should not send them, but no fewer than twenty-two are your own American ships. We should therefore like to know how you feel about it.

Future prospects of supplying Russia by this northern route are bad. Murmansk has been largely burnt out and there are several signs of an impending German attack upon it. By the time that perpetual daylight gives place to the dark period, Archangel will be frozen. Some additional supplies may be passed over the Basra route. This is being pressed, but it will not amount to much. Thus Russia is confronted at this anxious moment with a virtual cutting off of the Northern sea communications. We wait your answer before explaining things to Stalin. The message which it is proposed to send to him, if you agree that the convoy is not to go, is being sent to you later today. Meanwhile the convoy is continuing to load and assemble.

Allied shipping losses in the seven days ending July 13th including the Russian convoy were reported at not far short of four hundred thousand tons for this week, a rate unexampled in either this war or the last, and if maintained evidently beyond all existing replacement plans.

Roosevelt's reply of 15 July read: 'After consultation with King I must reluctantly agree to the position which the Admiralty has taken regarding the Russian convoy to the north and I think your message to Stalin is a good one. I assume you will send it at once.'[13]

Churchill also sent a memo on 15 July to the First Lord of the Admiralty and the First Sea Lord in which he directed:

Let the following be examined.

Suspend the sailing of PQ 18 as now proposed from 18th instant. See what happens to our Malta operation. If all goes well, bring *Indomitable*, *Victorious*, *Argus* and *Eagle* north to Scapa, and collect with them at least five of the auxiliary Aircraft Carriers, together with all available Didos and at least twenty-five destroyers. Let the two 16 Battleships go right through under the air umbrella and destroyer screen, keeping southwestward, not hugging the ice, but seeking the clearer weather, and thus fight it out with the enemy. If we can move our armada in convoy under an umbrella of at least a hundred fighter aircraft we ought to be able to fight our way through and out again, and if a fleet action results so much the better.

Following Stalin's response of the 13th, on the 17th Churchill wrote to General Ismay of the COS Committee:

Not only Premier Stalin but President Roosevelt would object very much to or desisting from running the convoys now. The Russians are in heavy action, and would expect us to run the risk and pay the price entailed by our contribution. The United States' ships are queuing up. My own feeling, mingled with much anxiety, is that the convoy[14] ought to sail on the 18th. The operation is justified if a half gets through. Failure on our part to make the attempt would weaken our influence with both our major Allies. There are always the uncertainties of weather and luck, which may aid us. I share your misgivings but I feel it is a matter of duty.

However, the Naval Staff, who always had to consider each requirement in relation to the other worldwide commitments, judged that this meant hazarding the navy's entire carrier strength for a purpose that could not justify taking such risks with irreplaceable ships. Churchill's proposal was rejected by the Admiralty and so the idea was quietly dropped and Churchill wrote to Stalin on 17 July:

1. We began running small convoys to North Russia in August 1941, and until December the Germans did not take any steps to interfere with them. From February 1942, the size of the convoys was increased, and the Germans then moved a considerable force of U-boats and a large number of aircraft to Northern Norway and made determined attacks on the convoys. By giving the convoys the strongest possible escort of destroyers and anti-submarine craft, the convoys got through with varying but not prohibitive losses. It is evident that the Germans were dissatisfied with the results which were being achieved by means of aircraft and U-boats alone, because they began to use their surface forces against the convoys. Luckily for us, however, at the outset they made use of their Heavy Surface Forces to the westward of Bear Island and their submarines to the eastward. The Home Fleet was thus in a

position to prevent an attack by enemy surface forces. Before the May convoy was sent off, the Admiralty warned us that losses would be very severe if, as was expected, the Germans employed their surface forces to the eastward of Bear Island. We decided to sail the convoy. An attack by surface ships did not materialise, and the convoy got through with a loss of one-sixth, chiefly from air attack. In the case of the last convoy which is numbered PQ 17, however, the Germans at last used their forces in the manner we had always feared. They concentrated their U-boats to the westward of Bear Island and reserved their surface forces for attack to the eastward of Bear Island. The final story of PQ 17 convoy is not yet clear. At the moment only four ships have arrived at Archangel but six others are in Nova Zemlya harbours. The latter may, however, be attacked from the air at any time. At the best therefore only one-third would have survived.

2. I must explain the dangers and difficulties of these convoy operations when the enemy battle squadron takes its station in the extreme North. We do not think it right to risk our Home Fleet eastward of Bear Island or where it can be brought under the attack of the airmen of German shore-based aircraft. If one or two of our very few most powerful types were to be lost or even seriously damaged while the *Tirpitz* and her consorts, soon to be joined by the *Scharnhorst*, remained in action, the whole command of the Atlantic would be lost. Besides affecting the food supplies by which we live, our war effort would be crippled; and, above all, the great convoys of American troops across the ocean, rising presently to as many as 80,000 in a month, would be prevented and the building-up of a really strong second front in 1943 rendered impossible.

3. My Naval Advisers tell me that if they had the handling of the German submarine, surface and air forces in the present circumstances, they would guarantee the complete destruction of any convoy to North Russia. They have not been able so far to hold out hopes that convoys attempting to make the passage in perpetual daylight would fare better than PQ 17. It is therefore with the greatest regret that we have reached the conclusion that to attempt to run the next convoy, PQ 18, would bring no benefit to you and would only involve a dead loss to the common cause. At the same time I give you my assurance that if we can devise arrangements which give a reasonable chance of at least a fair proportion of the contents of the convoys reaching you, we would start them again at once. The crux of the problem is to make the Barents Sea as dangerous for German warships as they make it for ourselves. This is what we should aim at doing with our joint

resources. I should like to send a senior officer shortly to North Russia to confer with your officers and make a plan.

4. Meanwhile we are prepared to despatch immediately to the Persian Gulf some of the ships which were to have sailed in PQ convoy.

Stalin replied to Churchill on the 23rd with what Churchill later described as a rough and surly answer:

I have received your message of July 18.

I gather from the message, first, that the British Government refuses to go on supplying the Soviet Union with war materials by the northern route and, secondly, that despite the agreed Anglo-Soviet Communiqué on the adoption of urgent measures to open a second front in 1942, the British Government is putting off the operation till 1943.

According to our naval experts, the arguments of British naval experts on the necessity of stopping delivery of war supplies to the northern harbours of the USSR are untenable. They are convinced that, given goodwill and readiness to honour obligations, steady deliveries could be effected, with heavy loss to the Germans. The British Admiralty's order to the PQ 17 convoy to abandon the supply ships and return to Britain, and to the supply ships to disperse and make for Soviet harbours singly, without escort, is, in the view of our experts, puzzling and inexplicable. Of course, I do not think steady deliveries to northern Soviet ports are possible without risk or loss. But then no major task can be carried out in wartime without risk or losses. You know, of course, that the Soviet Union is suffering far greater losses. Be that as it may, I never imagined that the British Government would deny us delivery of war materials precisely now, when the Soviet Union is badly in need of them in view of the grave situation on the Soviet-German front. It should be obvious that deliveries via Persian ports can in no way make up for the loss in the event of deliveries via the northern route being discontinued.

As to the second point, namely, that of opening a second front in Europe, I fear the matter is taking an improper turn. In view of the situation on the Soviet-German front, I state most emphatically that the Soviet Government cannot tolerate the second front in Europe being postponed till 1943.

I hope you will not take it amiss that I have seen fit to give you my frank and honest opinion and that of my colleagues on the points raised in your message.

J. STALIN

As if this telegram, which ignored the fact that Britain had given no undertaking either to ship supplies or to invade the Continent in 1942, were not enough, rumours about the handling of PQ 17 began to circulate in London. These were soon traced to the Soviet Embassy. When the Soviet Ambassador M. Maisky and Admiral Kharmalov, Head of the Soviet Mission to Great Britain were called to consultations with the Foreign Secretary and the First Sea Lord, they took it upon themselves to criticize the Admiralty's controversial decision. Admiral Kharmalov declared that the British Admiralty had made a mistake, the basis of which was that the *Tirpitz*, even if she had come out of the fiord in which she was stationed, could not have caught up with the convoy. The distance from the fiord to the convoy was too great. Consequently there had been no justification for recalling the cruisers and still more the destroyers.

Maisky added with emphasis: 'No one denies the great services of the British Navy in this war … but even British Admirals are not without sin.' His remarks, although tactless, concealed understandable disappointment as the Russian Army's offensive against Kharkov in May had failed and the German Army was advancing after an earlier setback at Kursk. The Russians needed relief, either by the opening of a Second Front in the west or increased supplies, neither of which was to be forthcoming.

Churchill read out to the War Cabinet on the 24th[15] the reply from Stalin which the Russian Ambassador had handed to him the previous night,[16] the content of which was regarded as not entirely unpredictable or unexpected. Churchill told the Russian ambassador he would not have received a message in these terms but for the stern fight that the Russians were putting up against the Germans and would consult the Cabinet, but his present view was that it would be better for Premier Stalin's telegram to be left unanswered and we would, of course, continue to do our utmost to help the Russians. The Cabinet agreed that no reply should be sent.

The question of when to resume the convoys to Russia was revisited by the War Cabinet on the 27th[17] when the First Sea Lord reported that of the ships in convoy PQ 17, only ten had reached Archangel, one was still on the way, one unaccounted for and twenty-one sunk. If the ships still on passage reached port safely, the convoy would have delivered to Russia 164 tanks, 896 vehicles of various kinds and 87 aircraft, in addition to general cargos of considerable size. Churchill accepted that practically one-third of the convoy reaching Archangel was a better outcome than had at one time been expected and thought there was much to be said for attempting to run a further convoy to North Russia in September, by which time the Germans might have withdrawn their naval forces from North Norway.[18] There would be great political advantage if the Russians could be told that this was the plan, and this view was strongly supported by the Secretary of State for Foreign Affairs. The First Lord of the Admiralty reported at the same meeting that a number of loaded ships were being held up in Iceland, the crews of these were giving trouble and the position would certainly deteriorate if they were left there until September. It was therefore a matter for consideration whether the ships should be brought back to Britain.

On the same day the Secretary of State for Foreign Affairs reported to the Cabinet[19] following the decision on 13 July to suspend convoys to North Russia: the United States government had now agreed to the diversion of the next shipments of supplies by the Persian Gulf route. It was proposed that nothing be shipped from the United Kingdom to the Persian Gulf for Russia that could be produced in and shipped direct from the United States, and other supplies would be sent from the United Kingdom as and when the northern route was reopened. Materials shipped from North America to the Persian Gulf would reach Russia as quickly as supplies dispatched from the United Kingdom at the same time. This would also avoid double handling of matériel shipped through the United Kingdom from North America and make for more economical loading of shipping, particularly foodstuffs and raw materials. The exception to this plan was the four ships carrying large cargos of high-priority goods including about 100 Hurricanes that should have sailed in PQ 18 and were now to be routed via the Persian Gulf.

PQ 17: Joint Anglo-Soviet Inquiry

Churchill called for a joint Anglo-Soviet inquiry into the PQ 17 disaster to be held on 28 July in the Foreign Secretary's room in the House of Commons with the Foreign Secretary, the First Lord of the Admiralty and the First Sea Lord present to represent the British case. The First Sea Lord was invited to speak, but before he could do so he was interrupted by the Russian ambassador who demanded to know when the next PQ convoy was to sail. The First Sea Lord countered that Marshal Stalin had not so far replied to Churchill's proposal that a senior Air Force officer should go to Russia to arrange air cover for the convoys. To the Russians, this remark seemed to be just a means of gaining time. According to Maisky's version, the Head of the Soviet Naval Mission criticized the Admiralty's orders that the cruisers were to withdraw and the convoy was to scatter, whereupon the First Sea Lord, his face growing redder and redder, retorted: 'That order was given by me! Me! What else should have been done?' The First Lord of the Admiralty intervened to apologize for the Admiralty's and First Sea Lord's actions, and Maisky commented ingratiatingly 'even British admirals make mistakes'. At this, the First Sea Lord grew even more furious and said 'Tomorrow I shall ask Churchill to appoint you First Sea Lord instead of myself!'

PQ 17: The Political Fall-Out

The following day there was a brief exchange in the House of Commons on the subject of the armament of merchant ships. Several Members of Parliament were evidently extremely disquieted by facts revealed to them in Secret Session two weeks before [about PQ 17 presumably?]. The Financial Secretary to the Admiralty, George Hall, asked by Walter Windsor[20] whether he was satisfied that ships travelling to war areas were receiving adequate protection and had proper protective equipment for defending themselves during air attacks, replied that weapons were provided in all ships for defence against air attack and there was special provision for the protection of personnel, with ships moving in the more dangerous areas given priority and special consideration. The minister was then pressed by Mr Emmanuel Shinwell[21] to say whether he was aware that a recent convoy proceeding in a very important direction was denuded of Admiralty protection almost at the last minute and a large number of vessels were lost. There was mounting uproar as members chanted 'Answer, answer!', but the Financial Secretary to the Admiralty remained seated and silent. Mr Shinwell then gave notice that he would raise the matter during discussion on the Appropriation Bill.[22] The possibility that he might actually do so would be addressed by the War Cabinet on 4 August.

The Possible Resumption of Convoys in September 1942

Churchill wrote again to Roosevelt on the 29th[23] with the news of Stalin's response to his telegram of 18 July:

> Campbell[24] is being instructed to communicate to you Stalin's answer to my message of July eighteenth. I do not propose to embark on an argument, but Stalin will no doubt expect some account of our recent conversations here on the second front. Subject to what you may feel, I propose to refer Stalin to the aide-mémoire explaining our attitude handed to Molotov here just before he left for Moscow, which I showed you, and to say that it still represents our general position, but that we have agreed with you on certain action, although at the present stage nothing can be said about time and place.
>
> We might also say that we hope to resume convoys in September, if the Russians can provide necessary air force to deny German surface ships

use of the Barents Sea and that if the battle in Egypt goes well we should be able to make a firm offer of air support on the Russian southern flank.

What are your views?

In the meanwhile we are explaining to Maisky in detail the nature of problems of Russian convoys and the latest position about bombing attacks on Germany and plans for Commando raids.

Prime

President Roosevelt's response of the 29th was brief and to the point:

> I agree with you that your reply to Stalin must be handled with great care.
>
> While I think you should not raise any false hopes in Stalin relative to the Northern convoys, nevertheless I agree with you that we should run one if there is any possibility of success, in spite of the great risk involved.

On the basis of this agreement with the US, preliminary plans would be made for reopening the northern route during the winter months in order to help the United States' authorities to adjust their production to fit in with the tonnage that could be escorted by that route and the Admiralty was tasked to prepare a programme to be brought into effect as soon as it was possible to forecast, however tentatively, the resumption of the northern convoys.

Churchill chose not to enter into a debate over the content of Stalin's last message, but told him on 31 July: 'We are making preliminary arrangements for another effort to run a large convoy through to Archangel in the first week of September.' In a follow-up message he added:

> In addition to my previous message. We are taking preliminary steps to run a convoy of 40 ships in the first week of September. I must, however, tell you outright that unless the air threat to German surface ships in the Barents Sea is so strong as to prevent them from operations against the convoy we shall have little chance, as the experience of PQ 17 convoy has shown, of getting so much as one-third of the ships safely through. As you certainly know, this situation was discussed with Maisky and I understand the latter has informed you that we think minimum air cover to be indispensable.

Stalin's reply was short and sweet:

I am grateful to you for agreeing to sail the next convoy with war materials to the USSR early in September. Although it will be very difficult for us to withdraw aircraft from the front, we shall take all possible steps to increase air cover for supply ships and convoy.

Treatment of British Service Personnel in North Russia

Visas, Mail and Reliefs

Up until July 1942 the Russians had not presented any particular difficulties over the issue of visas for the entry and exit of service personnel, while their mail had been delivered without any censorship or delay. The difficulties seemed to develop during the summer of 1942 when the convoy programme was disrupted, with the Russians apparently unable to recognize or accept the need for naval personnel to remain in North Russia when there were no convoys running. These personnel were regarded as unemployed, idle and a potentially negative influence on the native Russian population and attempts were made to limit their numbers and activities. It would also seem that the Russians never recognized or accepted the Royal Navy Conditions of Service that allowed for naval personnel to be relieved after nine to twelve months in post.[25]

In July 1942 the Russian authorities imposed a requirement for all British service personnel to be in possession of visas to enter and then later to leave the country. While in theory this might have appeared acceptable in principle when the arrangement had been agreed to by the British government, in practice, given the delays and time scales in granting the approvals involved, the process proved difficult, particularly for the conduct of operations at short notice as service personnel could not wait for weeks in Britain for the Russian authorities to issue visas. There were, however, also instances when the Admiralty apparently simply ignored the requirement.

Linked with the issue of visas was the question of reliefs. When service personnel were first sent to North Russia it had been agreed that their tour of duty should be up to twelve months, after which they would be relieved and return home. Although arrangements were made for those reliefs to be sent, they could not now travel to Russia as the authorities would not issue the necessary visas and this only served to further increase ill feeling among those personnel who became stranded in Russia.

PQ 17: Ongoing Recriminations

The recriminations over the fate of PQ 17 rumbled on. The First Sea Lord, in briefing the 1 August War Cabinet[26] on the circumstances leading up to and subsequent to the dispersal of PQ 17, claimed that the Admiralty possessed information on the night before the order to disperse was given indicating that the *Tirpitz*, having eluded waiting submarines, would, if she continued on her course, be in a position to attack the convoy early the following morning.[27] He then went on to explain that the convoy had been liable to three forms of attack: by air, U-boat and surface ships. If the convoy had remained concentrated, the most dangerous threat appeared, in the circumstances as then known to the Admiralty,[28] to be from surface ships, and instructions were therefore issued for the convoy to disperse. In view of the slow speed of the ships (8-10 knots) and the short time in which the convoy had to disperse, the Admiralty had signalled an order to the convoy to scatter. This gave the convoy the impression that it was about to be attacked at any moment. The senior officer of the escort considered the best way to deal with the surface forces was to add his destroyer strength to Admiral Hamilton's force and asked permission to do so. This decision had been approved by Admiral Hamilton,[29] who it was considered had acted correctly until he received the order from the Admiralty to retire to the westward. It would have been preferable had he then ordered the escort destroyers to return to the vicinity of the convoy. His failure to do so could hardly be regarded as more than an error of judgement.[30]

Press releases published the same day only referred to the successful defence of QP 11 but remained silent on the fate of PQ 17.

Press Reports

Saturday, 1 August 1942

Naval Engagements
Fighting in the Arctic
Navy Protects Convoy

London, July 30: The Admiralty has announced details of two recent naval engagements amid pack ice, snow storms and heavy seas on the convoy route to Murmansk.

The first was an attempt for two days by British and Soviet destroyers and British minesweepers to save the 10,000-ton cruiser *Edinburgh* after she had been attacked and disabled by U-boats and destroyers. The second was a gallant action in which four British destroyers fought off five separate attacks by superior enemy forces.

The Admiralty on July 5 announced the loss of the *Edinburgh*, which was at first struck by a torpedo on April 30, disabling her steering gear. She was again hit on May 2, and later sunk by our forces when unmanageable and it was impossible to move her to harbour. Our destroyers *Foresight* and *Forester* together with two Soviet destroyers went to her assistance on April 30. For the next 39 hours valiant efforts were made by towing and also the skilful use of her engines to get the cruiser to safety. U-boats gathered, waiting a chance to attack the crippled ship, but the destroyers' vigilance thwarted them.

On the afternoon of May 1, a Soviet destroyer and the British minesweepers *Harrier*, *Niger*, *Gossamer* and *Hussar* brought up a tug but it was unable to keep the cruiser on her course unaided.

The *Harrier* and the *Hussar* early on May 2 sighted three large enemy destroyers. The *Forester* and *Foresight* engaged them in snowstorms and freezing spray. The *Forester* was struck in the boiler room and stopped. The commander Lieutenant Commander G.P. Chuddar was killed as he was leaning down from the bridge encouraging his men.

The *Foresight* ran up between the *Forester* and the enemy, which vessels our fire still prevented from closing in on the *Edinburgh*. The enemy later discharged a torpedo salvo and the *Edinburgh*, swinging uncontrollably at the critical moment, was struck and became unmanageable. The *Hussar* put up a smokescreen, while the *Harrier* and the *Gossamer*, despite heavy seas, took off the crew. The *Forester*, which was still firing, hit one of the enemy three times.

The *Foresight* was then hit in the boiler room also, but maintained a brisk fire.

The engine room staff got the *Forester* under way, and screened the *Foresight* when the enemy reappeared. The *Foresight* hit one enemy vessel, and it exploded and disappeared. There was a big explosion in a second of the enemy vessels, which retired. Before the *Foresight* got under way the remainder of the *Edinburgh*'s crew was taken off and the cruiser was sunk. The *London Gazette* to-night announced that Commanders M. Richmond, R.C. Melbey and Reg Roper, also Lieutenant Commander J. Grant, have each been awarded the DSO. They commanded the destroyers *Bulldog*, *Eagle*, *Amazon* and *Beverley* respectively escorting the convoy to Russia.

A faster and heavier enemy force was sighted on May 9.[31] The convoy was then skirting a great patch of drift ice. The *Bulldog* led the attack, opening up at 10,000 yards. The enemy concentrated on the *Amazon*, which remained in line, though hit. The Germans were forced to retire. Four more attempts were made to break up the convoy within the next three hours. The British finally tried to engage at close range, but the enemy broke off in ten minutes, and disappeared. The convoy's behaviour was exemplary.

PQ 17: Proposed Press Statement

On 3 August the War Cabinet[32] was presented with a note[33] by the Lord Privy Seal containing a draft statement on the attack on the July convoy, originally prepared by the Admiralty for issue to the Press prior to Churchill deciding that no public statement should be made at that stage. The Lord Privy Seal invited the views of the War Cabinet on the extent to which this draft might form the basis of any statement it might be necessary to make to Parliament in Secret Session. After a short discussion of the draft, during which suggestions for amendment were proposed, the First Lord of the Admiralty was invited to prepare a revised draft in the light of these discussions and the decision taken at the meeting on 1 August for the War Cabinet to consider at their meeting on the following day.

Revised Draft Press Statement

The War Cabinet was presented with the revised draft statement on 4 August,[34] copies being handed round at the meeting.[35] The Cabinet was told it was now regarded unlikely that the matter would be raised in the debate on the adjournment. The revised draft statement was then approved for use in Secret Session in Parliament, if necessary, and along with the material for use in reply to possible supplementary questions, subject to the omission of paragraph 2 of the latter. The revised draft statement now read:

1. It is now possible to give some account of the recent convey to North Russia, which the enemy claimed to have practically annihilated.
2. The losses which were suffered in this convoy were serious, but they did not approximate to the exaggerated claims put forward by the enemy. The claims made by the enemy have, in fact, been of such a character that it is clear that the German High Command has no knowledge of the actual facts and has been endeavouring, by disseminating exaggerated accounts, to extract information which will enable the claims and reports of German pilots and U-boat commanders to be checked. It is intended to withhold information which would be of value to the enemy, such as the number of ships which have arrived in Russia and the actual losses sustained.
3. The difficulties of convoying supplies to North Russia have always been great. The lack of sea room owing to the ice conditions in the Barents Sea, the perpetual daylight at this time of the year and the existence of bases for strong enemy air and U-boat forces along the

flank of the convoy route have all combined to confront the Royal and Merchant Navies with a formidable task, which they have faced with great gallantry. On this occasion there was an added enemy threat of surface attack by heavy units which had moved to bases in Northern Norway.

4. Certain dispositions to counter the enemy threats were made. The House will readily understand that it is not in the country's interest to disclose, even in secret session, the operational details of these arrangements. It can, however, be said that special patrols by both Russian and British submarines formed a part of these dispositions.

5. In the event the passage of this convoy was normal until the convoy was well to the eastward of Bear Island. For some days the convoy had been constantly shadowed by aircraft, a number of U-boats had tried to attack, and there had been two attacks by torpedo-carrying aircraft. The losses suffered by the convoy during this period were not serious.

6. At this stage, as the result of aerial reconnaissance, the information at the disposal of the Admiralty led to the conclusion that an attack on the convoy by strong German surface forces was imminent. As the threat from surface forces was considered to be a greater menace than that due to U-boats or air attack, orders were given by the Admiralty for the convoy to disperse. Cruisers and destroyers of the escort at once formed a striking force with the object of attacking the enemy before he could reach the Merchant ships.

7. An enemy force, including the battleship *Tirpitz*, did, in fact, put to sea and steered a course to intercept the convoy. Soon afterwards, however, the *Tirpitz* was attacked by a Russian submarine, who claimed to have hit the battleship with two torpedoes. The Admiralty have no information as to damage suffered by the *Tirpitz*, but the enemy surface forces abandoned their attempt to intercept and destroy the ships of the convoy, and they returned to the shelter of the fiords. This decision on the part of these very powerful enemy forces may have been due to the dispersal of the convoy which had deprived him of a concentrated target or perhaps to the threat of the Allied dispositions which cannot be discussed.

8. The enemy decision to withdraw resulted in no contact being made between our surface forces and those of the enemy.

9. Unfortunately, the losses among the ships of the convoy due to air attack and U-boat attack increased after the convoy had scattered.

But as has already been stated, the eventual final losses, though serious, did not approximate to those claimed by the enemy.
10. It is now possible to state that the loss of life among the crews of the Merchant ships was happily not nearly as heavy as might have been expected.

This revised draft statement very much represented an attempt to appreciate the situation and justify the decisions taken with the benefit of hindsight. The reference to the striking force made no mention of its withdrawal, or the heavy cover force, the knowledge of whose continuing presence would undoubtedly have deterred the *Kriegsmarine* from putting to sea. There was, in the event, no publicity and no Parliamentary Debate until December 1946;[36] the matter remained wrapped in a cloak of secrecy. As the C-in-C Home Fleet would later observe:[37]

When the order to scatter the convoy was received, it had covered more than half its route with the loss of only three ships. Now its ships, spread over a wide area, were exposed without defence to the powerful enemy U-boat and air forces. The enemy took prompt advantage of this situation, operating both weapons to their full capacity. In spite of widespread searches by a few Coastal Command aircraft which had proceeded to North Russia after their patrols and by minesweepers and corvettes in these waters, a fortnight elapsed before the results of these attacks and the fates of the various ships of the convoy were fully known. Of the thirty-four ships remaining when the convoy was scattered, twenty-one, including the fleet oiler *Aldersdale* and one rescue ship, were sunk and thirteen, including one which was refloated after running aground in Nova Zemlya, eventually reached Archangel.

Chapter Five

Future Convoys' Competing Operational Priorities

Operation TORCH

The First Lord of the Admiralty submitted a memorandum dated 6 August to the War Cabinet[1] on the subject of convoys to North Russia in which he advised that the navy currently had in addition to its normal commitments three main priorities: Operation TORCH, the Malta convoys and the PQ convoys. It was impossible to undertake more than one of these concurrently and, in addition, a certain amount of time was required to transfer forces from one operation to another. It was also impossible to run a PQ convoy during August given the need to run a Malta convoy. It was still planned to run a PQ convoy early in September, but it was impossible to state how many if any further PQ convoys could be run during the remainder of 1942. If TORCH took place as early as hoped, it would not be possible to run another PQ convoy before that operation.

The uncertainty surrounding the date and requirements for TORCH and any additional Malta convoy made planning PQ convoys extremely difficult, particularly whether another PQ convoy could be run between TORCH and the end of the year. During the War Cabinet discussion on the memorandum the following afternoon,[2] the First Sea Lord reported that arrangements were still proceeding to run a convoy in September, but again this depended on the outcome of the next Malta convoy; should the escort suffer severe casualties it might not be possible to provide a sufficient escort for the convoy to North Russia.

The question of whether a further PQ convoy could be run a month later depended on the date fixed for Operation TORCH. If that operation took place as early as hoped it would not be possible to run another PQ convoy before TORCH took place. If, however, Operation TORCH took place a month later than the present target date, it might be possible to run another PQ convoy in October. After lengthy discussion the War Cabinet decided that the date for Operation TORCH must take priority over an October PQ convoy. An early decision was required by the United States' authorities, particularly as the Americans were already loading ships for the October PQ convoy. Churchill was invited to send a telegram to the president pressing for an early decision on this matter. The Deputy Prime Minister was invited to send a telegram to Churchill[3] (see telegram).

The War Cabinet was informed[4] on 11 August that Churchill, who was in Moscow, had asked for further PQ convoys to be run after the September convoy.[5] The War Cabinet and Defence Committee, after considering the matter, advised Churchill that it was quite impossible to carry out TORCH and a PQ convoy at the same time, whatever risk was taken elsewhere. Hence if TORCH was to take place on 7 October, a PQ convoy could not be run in October. Even allowing for very generous assistance from the Americans, the requirements for TORCH for destroyers and other escort craft were so great they could only be provided by ceasing to run the Sierra Leone and Gibraltar convoys and heavily cutting the escorts for coastal convoys with consequent loss of imports. There seemed considerable doubt, however, whether the Americans would be ready for TORCH by 7 October. At the time Eisenhower was indicating 5 November as the start date, in which case it might just be possible to run an October PQ convoy. Everyone was seized with the importance of carrying out TORCH at the earliest possible moment, and everything possible was being done to persuade the Americans to work to an early date in October, in which case an October PQ convoy would not be possible. It would be most unwise, therefore, to commit to an October convoy as the British would have to go back on their word if they found that it interfered with TORCH. PQ convoys after TORCH must depend on the length and subsequent requirements of TORCH operations, the measure of success of Operation PEDESTAL[6] and whether the latter would need to be repeated later in the year.

In reply to the Minister of War Transport's enquiry as to whether loading for PQ 19 should continue, the Deputy Prime Minister stated that in view of the uncertainty which still remained about the date of Operation TORCH, no final decision could yet be taken and it followed that loading for PQ 19 must continue for the present.

Plans for September Convoy

In order to run a September convoy on the previous basis (as regards force protection measures), a number of pre-conditions had to be met. The first was the need to replenish the stocks of stores and ammunition required to support the ongoing operations of the RN ships based in North Russia. Much of the ammunition reserves intended for North Russia had been lost in the merchant ships of PQ 17 and there was also a shortage of food. Four destroyers – the *Marne*, *Martin*, *Middleton* and *Blankney* – had therefore been sailed on 20 July to Archangel with ammunition and stores to replenish the escorts and merchant ships of QP 14.

The second pre-condition was the need to make arrangements to improve the level of air cover and striking power, particularly at the Russian end of the route. The German surface ships at Narvik continued to represent an ongoing threat that could only be dealt with by sending heavy bombers from Britain to attack them in harbour, and by stationing torpedo-bombers in North Russia to attack them if they sailed out into the Barents Sea to attack the convoys. The ability to mount such attacks depended on the Russians being able to provide a base where these bombers could land after carrying out their attack air strike and from which they could then be operated efficiently and effectively. Russian agreement was obtained and the American cruiser *Tuscaloosa* and three destroyers sailed from Greenock on 13 August with the men and equipment for No. 144 and 455 Squadrons (RAAF).

The Resumption of Convoys after Operation TORCH

Churchill was out of the country in Russia and the Middle East for most of August, and with the focus of attention on arrangements for Operation TORCH, it was not until late August that the subject of resumption of convoys to North Russia arose again. Churchill was most anxious that everything in his power should be done to send convoys to Stalin and on the 26th he wrote to the First Sea Lord:

1. It is true that no one can tell how far an enterprise like TORCH once begun, will carry us. Nevertheless we should now make plans to resume the PQ convoys late in October or the beginning of November. It may be that losses in TORCH, or great and hopeful developments there will force or induce us to concentrate all our efforts in the Mediterranean. But the results of battle explain themselves and we have to accept them.
2. Although I indicated in my conversations with Stalin, and it is upon the record, that TORCH would affect the PQs I think it would be a great mistake at this crisis to send him news which amounts to the fact he will get nothing more after the September convoy this year. We should therefore get the utmost help we can from the President, and push ahead with plans for the PQs until or unless we are made to give them up by main force. If not there will be overwhelming reason for not doing so.

September Convoy: German Assumptions

The same day at a conference of the German naval commander-in-chief with the Führer at *Wehrwolf* ('Hitler's Bunker'),[7] Admiral Raeder reported:

> Evidently Convoy PQ 18 did not sail. We can thus assume that our submarines and planes, which totally destroyed Convoy PQ 17, have forced the enemy to give up this route temporarily or even to fundamentally change his whole system of supply lines. Supplies to northern ports of Russia remain decisive for the whole conduct of the war waged by the Anglo-Saxons. They must preserve Russia's strength in order to keep German forces occupied. The enemy will most probably continue to ship supplies to northern Russia, and the *Seekriegsleitung* ['Maritime Warfare Command'] must therefore maintain submarines along the same routes. The greater part of the Fleet will also be stationed in northern Norway. The reason for this, besides making attacks on convoys possible, is the constant threat of an enemy invasion. Only by keeping the Fleet in Norwegian waters can we hope to meet this danger successfully. Besides, it is especially important in view of the whole Axis strategy that the German 'fleet in being' ties down the British Home Fleet, especially after the heavy Anglo-American losses in the Mediterranean and the Pacific.

Postponement of Convoy PQ 18

There was not in the event time for another convoy to be run to North Russia before the withdrawal of the Home Fleet units for Operation PEDESTAL. PQ 18 was therefore postponed until 2 September. The possibility of running the westbound convoy in the meantime was examined, but adequate submarine cover could not be provided.

Churchill later noted:

> It was not until September that another convoy set off for north Russia. By now the scheme of defence had been revised, and the convoy was accompanied by a close escort of sixteen destroyers, as well as the first of the new escort carriers, the *Avenger*, with twelve fighter aircraft. As before, strong support was provided by the fleet. This time, however, the German surface ships made no attempt to intervene, but left the task of attack to aircraft and U-boats. The result was a particularly fierce battle in the air, in which twenty-four enemy aircraft were destroyed out of about a hundred which came into the attack. Ten merchant ships were

lost in these actions, and two more by U-boats, but twenty-seven ships successfully fought their way through.

PQ 18 finally sailed from Iceland on 2 September and on the 7th Churchill again telegraphed Stalin:

> Convoy PQ 18 with forty ships has started. As we cannot send our Heavy ships within range of enemy shore-based aircraft we are providing a powerful destroyer striking force which would be used against enemy's surface ships should they attack us east of Bear Island. We are also including in convoy escort, to assist in protecting it against air attack, an auxiliary Aircraft Carrier just completed. Further, we are placing a strong line of submarine patrols between convoy and German bases. The risk of an attack by German surface ships still, however, remains serious. This danger can only be effectively warded off by providing in Barents Sea air striking forces of such strength Germans would not risk their Heavy ships any more than we would risk ours in that area. For reconnaissance we are providing eight Catalina flying boats and three Photographic Reconnaissance Unit Spitfires to operate from North Russia. To increase scale of air attack we have sent thirty-two torpedo-carrying aircraft which have suffered loss on the way, though we hope at least twenty-four would be available for operation. These with nineteen bombers, including torpedo-carrying aircraft, forty-two short-range and forty-three long-range fighters which we understand you are providing would almost certainly not be enough to act as a final deterrent. What is needed is more long-range bombers. We quite understand immense pressure put upon you on the main line of battle makes it difficult to supply any more Russian army long-range bombers. But we must stress great importance of this convoy in which we are using seventy-seven warships requiring to take in 15,000 tons of fuel during the operation. If you can transfer more long-range bombers to the North temporarily please do so. It is most needful for our common interests.

Stalin responded two days later:

> I received your message on September 7. I realise the importance of the safe arrival in the Soviet Union of PQ 18 convoy and the need for measures to protect it. Difficult though we find it at present to assign extra long-range bombers for the purpose, we have decided to do so. Orders have been given today to assign an additional force of long-range bombers for the purpose mentioned by you.

Churchill telegraphed Stalin again on 13 September: 'I am much obliged for the 48 long-range bombers, 10 Torpedo Bombers and 200 fighters, including 47 long-range fighters, which I now learn you are sending to help bring in PQ 18.'

The following day the War Cabinet learned that[8] 'Twelve ships of the convoy on its way to Russia have been reported as lost.'

President Roosevelt telegraphed Churchill on 15 September:[9] 'The news this morning about the PQ convoy is discouraging but they may not be able to hit it again and I presume we can wait for a few days to make a final determination.'

In a minute to the COS Committee on 16 September,[10] while PQ 18 was still en route to Archangel, Churchill stressed the importance of both maintaining contact with Russia and keeping the Russian forces resupplied as one of the three or four most important vital war objectives, the sacrifice and effort that must be made by the Allies, and the consequences of a weakening of the Russian military capability. He noted that President Roosevelt had already stated he regarded maintenance of the PQ convoys as an operation of equal importance with TORCH, although he was ready to skip one or perhaps two PQ convoys for the sake of TORCH. The alternatives Churchill had set out, recognizing Roosevelt's views, were to continue with the PQ convoys (perhaps missing one or two) in addition to TORCH and all that implied, throughout 1943 and 1944, recognizing that the scale of the convoys must be increased as the Russians had been solemnly promised larger quotas and would become more dependent on imported arms as their own territory was reduced by enemy invasion, or to clear the Germans out of the north of Norway by some form of Operation JUPITER. When balancing the potential losses in sending these convoys at least three times in every two months against the grievous consequences of telling the Russians they could be sent no more, he concluded that it might well be JUPITER, with all its cost and risk, that would be found not only necessary but cheapest in the long run. He recognized, however, that the fitting of Operation JUPITER into the war plans could only be considered in relation to TORCH, the outcome of which could not be forecast and if JUPITER and TORCH were put into action, there could be no ROUNDUP[11] until 1944, but TORCH by itself was no substitute for ROUNDUP. The prime minister reported that the chiefs of staff had examined the question very fully, but overall took a rather unfavourable view of the possibility of being able to provide the necessary forces and particularly the shipping for JUPITER in addition to TORCH.

Roosevelt sent his final reply two days later. The subject was the Persian supply route, but Roosevelt added: 'If the decision is against running further convoys I will of course do everything I can with Stalin.'

The Strategic Implications of PQ 18

Though the Admiralty could not possibly have been aware at the time, we now know that the success achieved in the successful passages of PQ 18 and QP 14 would mark a turning-point in this phase of the war in the Arctic. There would be no more large-scale deployments of Luftwaffe units in the far north until late 1944. Before the next convoy cycle, developments in the Mediterranean and North Africa would result in the transfer of the Ju 88 and He 111 heavy bomber and torpedo-bomber force from Norway. The increased pressure on the Luftwaffe resources brought about by the North African campaign therefore produced temporary relief for the convoys to North Russia and minimized losses of matériel vital to the Russian war effort. The ability and success of the escort carrier in anti-aircraft defence was also, as German records confirm, a key deterrent, although perhaps not one fully appreciated by the Admiralty at the time.

The War Cabinet received a report on 17 September from the Secretary of State for Foreign Affairs' report on the delivery of equipment and supplies under the first Moscow protocol between October 1941 and June 1942.[12] In summary this detailed the amounts of military and non-military supplies shipped to North Russia by various routes under the first protocol, and in describing the arrangements for shipments by sea by the northern route noted the following:

> Except during the month of April 1942, at least two convoys per month arrived regularly in North Russia up to the end of May, but during the early part of the period, although sailings were planned on a 10-day cycle, frequent complaints were received from the Soviet Embassy and the Trade Delegation regarding the late shipment of high-priority goods; during the winter difficulties imposed by the severe weather – particularly in connection with the movement of aircraft – often made it impossible to clear the whole of each monthly quota from loading ports by the end of the month. Although the point was made that the first convoy carrying Protocol supplies had not left this country until the 17th October, and that consequently some part of each month's supplies had to be carried forward into the early days of the succeeding month, the backlog (which was aggravated by the large numbers of lorries which at that time were being shipped in completely assembled form (see paragraph 28)) became acute. The matter was reported by the Chairman to the Prime Minister, who was in Washington at the time, and issued a Directive on the 4th January enjoining all Departments to ensure that January quotas were

shipped in full before the end of that month. Although this could not be literally fulfilled, an improvement resulted.

Meanwhile the consent of the Soviet authorities had been obtained for the use of Murmansk for the handling of supplies, but it nevertheless became apparent in March 1942, the increasing danger of attacks on convoys by enemy surface vessels, as well as by aircraft and submarines, made it necessary to limit the number of sailings in each month, and also the number of ships to be escorted in any convoy, to not more than 25. At the same time, as a result of a directive issued by the President in January, the United States authorities had begun to dispatch ships at an ever-increasing rate – e.g. 14 ships sailed from North America in February, 32 in March and 56 in April, although even larger numbers than these had been allocated.

On the 22nd April the Minister of War Transport drew the attention of the Executive to the congestion which was to be expected in Iceland as a result of the limitations mentioned and foreshadowed the arrangements (which were afterwards introduced) by which United States ships carrying low-priority cargos would be brought to United Kingdom ports for discharge and restowage in such a way as to provide the maximum quantity of high-priority cargo in the minimum number of ships. This arrangement was not introduced without difficulty, after the matter had been taken up with the United States Government on the highest level, and had also formed the subject of an exchange of telegrams between Premier Stalin and the Prime Minister. Although the Admiralty have been pressed to take more ships in each convoy, the increasing risks and the dangers of the passage, as well as the serious losses sustained by our escorting Naval vessels and by the supply ships, have deterred the Naval Staff from agreeing to increase the number of vessels escorted to more than 35.

Archangel was never able to use more than 9-11 berths and became unusable towards the end of December on account of ice conditions. The inability of the Soviet authorities to provide adequate ice-breaking facilities, and the damage by enemy action to the large icebreaker *Stalin* early in January made it impossible to reopen that port until June.

At Murmansk only eight ships at a time could be handled to begin with and labour conditions were unsatisfactory. Later, however, the position greatly improved as a result of successful Russian improvisation and, until the town was partly destroyed by repeated bombing attacks at the end of June, the port was in full operation and was not unduly congested. Although five vessels – three British, two American – were sunk in the harbour (two partly discharged and three after discharge), practically the whole volume of supplies delivered at the port was cleared without loss.

In the first fourteen convoys to North Russia, British shipping losses were remarkably low; only three merchant ships lost, one of which was sunk on the homeward voyage. In the last three convoys, however, we have unfortunately lost 13 vessels (one of them Dutch) out of the 27 carrying March, April and May quotas. In these convoys alone 250 fighter aircraft, 303 tanks, 88 anti-tank guns and a large quantity of ammunition, spares and other goods were sunk, besides 70 Canadian Valentines and 151 Bren carriers loaded on American ships.

In the face of most determined enemy attacks by surface, submarine and air forces, and in spite of extremely severe weather conditions during the winter months, our convoys, which have included a large number of vessels sailing from North America and their naval escorts have steadily fought their way through to North Russia with undaunted courage; even the exceptional hazards of these Arctic voyages have not deterred British and Allied merchant seamen from voluntarily engaging, time after time, in these perilous tasks. In all 218 ships had been escorted.

Between October 1941 and the end of June 1942, 17 convoys, comprising 100 merchant ships, carried British Protocol supplies to North Russia from the United Kingdom. They sailed at an average rate of 11 per month, but there had necessarily been wide variations in the intervals between sailings for operational reasons. The time taken between loading ports in the United Kingdom and the port of arrival in North Russia varied between 17 days and over 2 months.

The arrival of PQ 18 in North Russian ports on 21 September completed delivery of the Moscow protocol quota for June and part of the July quota under the second protocol. No more convoys would be scheduled to sail to North Russia before the end of the year. This left forty merchant ships – eleven British, twenty-eight American and one Russian – awaiting convoy at the end of September.

PQ 18 Publicity

The Foreign Secretary made two speeches in October 1942 on the subject of convoys to Russia. The first of these was published on 3 October:

Saturday, 3 October 1942

Arctic Convoy:
Supplies for Russia

Speaking in the House of Commons recently, the Foreign Secretary (Mr Anthony Eden) disclosed that a fleet of 75 warships of the Royal Navy of varying tonnage escorted the recent Anglo-American convoy to Russia. The convoy, he said, had safely delivered in Russia the largest total of munitions yet transported in a single voyage from the United Kingdom and the USA. The safe delivery of these goods, which included large numbers of aircraft, tanks, guns, ammunition and stores of all kinds, was a great feat of arms.

An Admiralty message states that the attack on the convoy from Norwegian bases commenced on Sept. 12th and continued without remission for four days. During the whole of this period enemy aircraft and U-boats made determined attempts to break through the convoy defences, at times as many as 60 bombers and torpedo-planes taking part in the attack. In all, more than 100 attacks were launched from the air and submarines menaced the convoy throughout. Some of the ships comprising the convoy were lost, and the destroyer *Somali* was torpedoed and eventually sank, but the great majority of the ships arrived safely and delivered their precious cargoes of munitions. The return journey was then made, the convoy of empty vessels being subjected to several attacks by U-boats, but not from the air.

During the passage of the two convoys, comprising British, American and Russian ships, 40 enemy planes were seen to crash and a large number were severely damaged. Two U-boats almost certainly were destroyed, and four probably seriously damaged. We lost four naval fighters, but three pilots were rescued. The RAF Coastal Command provided invaluable patrols and reconnaissances throughout the operation.

Chapter Six

September 1942 Convoy Suspension PQ 19 Independent Sailings

The conflict of priorities between the PQ convoys and TORCH was resolved when in the War Cabinet discussions on 21 September[1] on matters affecting future operations, Churchill reported that the Americans had confirmed the date for Operation TORCH as 8 November. If a further PQ convoy (PQ 19) was sent before TORCH that operation would have to be delayed until either 24 or 28 November according to whether or not the ships of PQ 18 were brought back from North Russia. Churchill considered that such a delay would be inviting disaster, particularly as rumours were already circulating regarding an impending operation; a good deal of rumour was, of course, inevitable when the size of the operation was taken into account. Furthermore the weather would worsen as the winter went on; three weeks had already been lost through the Americans having changed the plan of the operation.

PQ 19 was now no longer an option, but orders had already been given for the loading of ships for that convoy to proceed. It was suggested this might be interpreted by the enemy as preparation for an attack on Norway and thus serve a useful purpose by confusing the Germans as to Allied intentions.[2] Despite the uncertainty and conflicting priorities, Churchill stressed that he was unwilling to tell the Russians that the convoys to North Russia were to be suspended until this became absolutely necessary.

Ten days previously the United States' authorities had ordered 180 Airacobra aircraft in ships intended for PQ 19 to be unloaded for TORCH. The Russians had found out and had taken the news badly. The Russian ambassador had called on Churchill that afternoon to complain. Churchill told the ambassador something much worse than this was in store for him. It was evident from the ambassador's attitude that the Russians would be greatly upset when they heard of the decision to suspend the convoys. Churchill asked the First Sea Lord to investigate whether any possible means could be found to continue sailings to North Russia on a greatly reduced scale. The First Sea Lord agreed to do so, but reiterated that any ships going to North Russia had to be prepared to meet three forms of attack: surface ships, U-boats and aircraft.

Operations JUPITER and TORCH: Cancellation of PQ 19

In view of the very grim picture that suspension of the convoys would present to Russia, Churchill again argued that further consideration should be given to Operation JUPITER.[3] At his meeting with Premier Stalin in Moscow on 12 August, Churchill said he would consider carrying out the operation with two British divisions. Stalin said he would contribute three Russian divisions and took an optimistic view of the proposal. Churchill's minute of 16 September to the chiefs of staff committee was then read to the War Cabinet. Recognizing that this would come as extremely unwelcome news to Stalin, in an attempt to soften the blow Churchill once again raised the possibility of mounting an operation to drive the Germans out of Northern Norway: Operation JUPITER, which had been a pet project of his since May of that year.[4]

Churchill then reported on a long conference he had held that morning with the chiefs of staff, at which General Eisenhower, various United States officers and British Admirals Cunningham and Ramsay had been present. As a result of the meeting, three draft telegrams had been prepared. The first was to President Roosevelt dealing with the general position, including Operation JUPITER, the prospects of ROUNDUP[5] and of future PQ convoys; the second was to Premier Stalin relating to Operation JUPITER;[6] and the third was to Stalin stating that PQ convoys must be suspended until January 1943.

In the general discussion that followed the Cabinet agreed that carrying out Operation TORCH at the earliest possible date should take priority, notwithstanding its effect on other operations including the PQ convoys. It was agreed that the telegram to Premier Stalin should be dispatched as soon as possible, but not sent until President Roosevelt had been consulted on the content.

The War Cabinet then approved the dispatch of two telegrams from Churchill to President Roosevelt. The first related to Operation JUPITER, Operation ROUNDUP and the further running of PQ convoys to North Russia (No. 153). The second set out the detail of the telegrams Churchill wished to send to Premier Stalin at an early date (No. 154).

Churchill's telegram to President Roosevelt[7] of 22 September referring to his conference with the chiefs of staff and US officers noted that the final date for TORCH had now been confirmed and continued:

> 3. We now know PQ 18 carried 27 ships safely to Archangel and 13 are sunk. For PQ 19, 40 ships are already loaded but it is impossible to send this Convoy without throwing back the date of TORCH by three weeks. We all regard any delay in TORCH as inadmissible.

4. The time has therefore come to tell Stalin, 1st, there will be no PQ 19 and secondly we cannot run any more PQs till the end of the year, i.e. January. This is a formidable moment in Anglo-American-Soviet relations and you and I must be united in any statement made about convoys.
5. We are solemnly pledged to the supply of Russia and the most grave consequences might follow from failure to make good. For 1943 there may be two choices. 1st to run from January onwards Arctic convoys under the present conditions of danger, waste and effort, observing we used 77 warships for PQ 18 and think ourselves fortunate to have lost no more than one-third of the Merchant ships.
6. Secondly the operation called JUPITER. It is more than doubtful whether the developments of TORCH will leave shipping and escort resources sufficient for JUPITER unless you can help at any rate with the latter. We must, however, also know what importance Stalin would attach to the operation and what contribution he would make to it. See the account of my last conversation with him where I mentioned two divisions and he offered three. Our estimate here is larger numbers would be required, and I repeat the shipping problem is unsolved and is anyhow dependent on TORCH developments.
7. It seems to me simply to tell him now no more PQs till 1943 is a great danger, and I therefore wish to open staff conversations on JUPITER under all necessary reserves. See the telegram I propose to send him after consulting Mackenzie King, which, as you will see, leaves both British and Soviet governments free to decide when the results of the Joint Staff study is completed. Of course if you were able to take an interest in this it would be most helpful. As in a few days it will be necessary to unload and discharge PQ 19 I felt this new project necessary to break the blow.

[Paragraphs 8 to 13 referred in detail to Operations TORCH, ROUNDUP and BOLERO.]

14. To sum up, my persisting anxiety is Russia, and I do not see how we can reconcile it with our consciences or with our interests to have no more PQs till 1943, no offer to make joint plans for JUPITER, and no signs of a spring, summer or even autumn offensive in Europe; I should be most grateful for your counsel on all this. We wish urgently to send the telegram (of which copy follows separately) to Stalin and hope you will back it up as strongly and as soon as you can.

This was immediately followed by the second telegram[8] setting out the text of the message Churchill intended to send to Stalin, which read:

1. As I told you in Moscow, we are convinced the most effective contribution we and the United States can make in 1942 to the defeat of Germany is to launch TORCH at the earliest possible date.
2. The date which has finally been fixed with the President is early in November.
3. The effect of TORCH must be either (a) to oblige the Germans to divert air and land forces to counter our move, or (b) to compel them to accept the position created by the success of TORCH, which would then create a further diversion of the threat of attack against Sicily and the South of Europe.
4. The considerable success of the last convoy was achieved only because no less than 77 warships were employed on the operation. Protection on anything like this scale will be impossible until the end of the year, when the naval escorts which we must now assemble for TORCH can again be made available in Northern Waters.
5. In the meanwhile we are trying to find means of sending you supplies on a reduced scale by the Northern route during the rest of 1942.
6. We intend to resume the full flow of supplies from January 1943.
7. In order to reduce losses of Merchant ships by enemy action and thus make the convoys in 1943 as effective as possible, we are anxious to examine with you the possibility of carrying out Operation JUPITER during this winter.
8. I therefore suggest to you I send to Moscow General McNaughton, Commander-in-Chief of the Canadian Army arriving in the early days of October, so he may discuss the matter fully with your staff. He has already made a preliminary examination of this question.

Ends 22.9.42.

Unlike the passage of PQ 17 that had resulted in serious losses of men, ships and matériel and had been characterized by a marked reluctance on the part of the War Cabinet to make any public announcement, the arrival of PQ 18 in Russia generated a positive outpouring of praise for those involved. The first official announcement of the outcome of PQ 18, published in *The Times* of London on Thursday, 24 September 1942, read as follows:

> Another important convoy, carrying large quantities of war material, has arrived in North Russian ports. Losses were suffered among ships in the

convoy, but despite heavy attacks by enemy aircraft and U-boats, the great majority of ships have arrived at their destinations.

The convoy consisted of British, American and Russian Merchant ships. It is not intended to assist the enemy by informing him of the extent of his lack of success against this convoy but it is possible to say that his claims on this occasion have been even more exaggerated than usual.

No ship of the escort of this convoy was lost.

President Roosevelt replied to Churchill on 26 September:[9]

I agree with you the realities of the situation require us to give up PQ 19. While I think this is a tough blow for the Russians, I nevertheless think the purposes for which the escorts are to be used both as to time and place make decision inevitable. PQ 19 would not, however, have sailed under any circumstances for another ten days and I feel very strongly we should not notify the Russians until time arrives and we know with finality the convoy will not go. I can see nothing to be gained by notifying Stalin sooner than is necessary, and indeed much to be lost. Furthermore I believe within ten days we could come to a final conclusion regarding the Air Force in Trans-Caucasia regarding which Stalin should be notified at the same time.

For security reasons I think it would be unwise to unload any of the ships at Iceland. While it is true we are short of shipping we probably do not need these particular ships for TORCH and I had think we had better make the sacrifice of letting the ships remain in Iceland rather than giving the enemy the information we are not running the next convoy. I believe TORCH should not be delayed a single day. We are going to put everything into the enterprise and I have high hopes for it.

Churchill responded to Roosevelt two days later:[10] 'Earliest date PQ 19 could have sailed is October 2 – i.e. five days from date of your message of September 27. However, if you think well, we can keep as if it really was sailing, till 7th or even later. Bulk of the ships are in Scottish ports.'

On the same day, the 28th, Churchill wrote to both the Service Chiefs of Staff Committee and the First Sea Lord on the matter. He told the COS Committee:

The price to be paid in cutting down Russian supplies is heavy, and the moment when PQ 19 is cancelled is by no means the best for notifying the Russians. The question therefore is one of timing, and the answer depends upon the view taken of the German advance into the Caucasus. By the middle of October it should be possible to see more clearly over the whole scene, and I suggest we wait until then before addressing the Russians and the Americans on the subject of trans-Persian tonnages.

At the same time the First Sea Lord was asked to

> Consider in what way the ships of PQ 19 could best be used to make the enemy believe it was intended to run another convoy as it would be a great advantage to us, and indeed a help to TORCH, if the Germans are induced to keep their submarines, aircraft and surface ships in the north this winter, doing nothing. Everything should therefore be done to favour the idea of an October convoy.

In the meantime Stalin remained unaware of the proposed suspension of the convoys, almost ten days having elapsed before Roosevelt's reply to Churchill's telegram of 22 September arrived on 5 October.[11] In this the president said:

> I have gone carefully over your proposed message to Stalin of September 22.
> So far as PQ 19 is concerned, I feel most strongly that we should not tell Stalin that the convoy will not sail. After talking with Admiral King, I would urge that a different technique be employed, in which evasion and dispersion are the guiding factors. Thus let PQ 19 sail in successive groups, comprising the fastest ships now loaded and loading for Russia. These groups would comprise two or three ships each, supported by two or three escorts, and sail at twenty-four-hour intervals. They might have to go without the full naval covering support that would protect the convoy from the *Tirpitz* or heavy cruisers, but that must simply be a risk that we have to take. We know that so far as air attack is concerned the weather would in all probability not be against us every day and that the longer nights will be of help.
> I believe we would stand a good chance of getting as high a proportion of the ships through as we did with PQ 18. Under any circumstances I think it is better that we take this risk than endanger our whole relations with Russia at this time. I know that you and Pound will give this proposal of mine every consideration. I should tell you that our Ambassador (Admiral Standley) has asked to come home to deliver in person a very important message, and I have some fears as to what that message might be.

The message went on to discuss Operation VELVET[12] and ended: 'Please let me know when you send your message to Stalin, and I will immediately send him a similar message, but I am certain both our messages should be so phrased as to leave a good taste in his mouth.'

Churchill notified Roosevelt of Stalin's reply the same day:[13]

> I have just received the Telegram immediately following (passed in Churchill's telegram No. 158) from Stalin. It seems to me that in addition to VELVET we ought to make a desperate effort to meet him as far as possible and include the promise in our impending telegram about PQ 19. This is becoming urgent now as much unloading has to be done and assembly of PQ ships complicates somewhat TORCH. Should be most grateful to hear from you at earliest.

(Telegram No. 158 repeated the text of Stalin's message as quoted above read: 'Following is text of Telegram to Stalin referred to in my No. 157.')

Independent Sailings: Operation FB

Churchill read out to the War Cabinet[14] on 6 October the telegram[15] received from Roosevelt the previous day. Following a preliminary discussion it was agreed to reconvene later that day to consider the matter further. The War Cabinet met again at 10.30 pm[16] to consider the draft reply prepared by Churchill and the chiefs of staff. The draft read as follows:

> Your 189. There is no possibility of letting PQ 19 sail in successive groups with reduced escorts as you suggest. I append a note by the Admiralty on this subject. Neither can the fact that the convoy is not sailing be concealed from the Russians any longer. Maisky is already aware of the position, though not officially informed, and I expect he has let Stalin know the general prospect. We are preparing ten ships to sail individually during the October dark. They are all British ships for which the crews will have to volunteer, the dangers being terrible and their sole hope if sunk far from help being Arctic clothing and such heating arrangements as can be placed in the lifeboats. Absolutely nothing else is possible unless you are able to help by providing some American ships for independent sailing after November 9, should experience have proved that the chances are sufficiently good.

2. I believe that the blunt truth is best with Stalin but that there has been advantage in the delay of a fortnight in telling him, which you proposed. I feel strongly he should be told now.

Paragraphs 3 and 4 went on to discuss VELVET and concluded:

5. If therefore we offer VELVET as now defined, plus increased aircraft deliveries and the individual ships on the PQ route I trust this will be sufficient to bridge the gap before TORCH opens.

W.S.C. 7.10.42.

The Admiralty note read:

1. Arrangements already made to sail about 10 ships from Iceland (C) during dark period 28th October to 8th November. These would sail singly at about 200-mile intervals with occasional larger gaps and rely on evasion and dispersion.
2. We had already considered sailing small groups with weak escort but in our view there is no halfway between independent sailings and fighting through with full escorting forces.
3. Our reasons are:
   (a) Possibilities of evasion are slight as German air reconnaissance for North Russian convoys is very intensive and anything in the nature of a group of ships would be continually shadowed.
   (b) A group is more likely to draw attack by enemy surface vessels which are still waiting in their northern anchorages.
   (c) Anything short of full covering support invites disaster both to the group and naval forces.
   (d) To send a total of 40 ships in groups of 2 or 3 ships with 2 or 3 escorts would employ as many escorts as were required for PQ 18. TORCH is absorbing every available craft.
4. The voyage in anything but a full escorted convoy is so hazardous that it should only be undertaken by volunteers who clearly understand the risk. The chance of crews of stricken ships surviving when they take to their boats is remote.

The implications of the draft telegram to Roosevelt were discussed at length by the War Cabinet on 7 October.[17] The First Sea Lord reported that he had considered the suggestion merchant vessels sailing singly by the northern route to Russia should be escorted by submarines. These merchant vessels would travel at a speed of 9 knots if British or 10 knots if American. The only submarines able to keep pace were the large P-class, all of which were earmarked for TORCH. The only possible plan would be to sail the ships in pairs with one submarine to each pair. Three submarines would be required. On investigation, however, even this plan had little to recommend it. As soon as a pair of ships had been located by the enemy's air reconnaissance, the submarine would have to dive. With a submerged speed of 3 knots, it would rapidly fall behind and not be available to rescue the crews if the ships were bombed. Moreover, a P-class submarine could only take on board twenty-five to thirty men over and above the crew, whereas the minimum crew of each merchant ship would be fifty. When on the surface, the submarine would be exposed to the danger of being torpedoed by a U-boat. To make three submarines available would mean weakening the forces required to prevent the enemy reinforcing North Africa across the Mediterranean.

After a lengthy discussion the telegram approved by the War Cabinet was dispatched to the president on 7 October.[18] The section suggesting what should be said to Premier Stalin read as follows:

5. I was greatly relieved that so large a proportion of the last convoy reached Archangel safely. This success was achieved only because no less than 77 warships were employed on the operation. Naval protection will be impossible until the end of the year. As the necessary escorts are withdrawn from TORCH, they can again be made available in northern waters.
6. Nevertheless, we intend in the meanwhile to do our best to send you supplies by the Northern route by means of ships sailed independently instead of in escorted convoys. Arrangements have been made to sail about ten ships from Iceland during the moonless period 28th October-8th November. The ships will sail singly, at about 200-mile intervals, with occasional larger gaps, and rely on evasion and dispersion.
7. We hope to resume the flow of supplies in strongly escorted convoys from January 1943. It would of course greatly help both you and us if the Germans could be denied the use of airfields in Northern Norway. If your Staffs could make a good plan the President and I would at once examine the possibility of co-operating up to the limit of our ability. End.

W.S.C. 7.10

Roosevelt wrote again to Churchill on 7 October:[19]

In reply to your 159, I agree to the method of delivering supplies by the Northern Route until such time as they can be adequately protected by convoy. I will move at once to get American ships and crews to add to the ten which you are planning to sail. We may have better luck than we think with this.

Roosevelt suggested a number of amendments to Churchill's draft, and then continued:

I agree that this wire must go off at once and I can see no advantage in further interchange between you and me on the text.

I leave it to you to send the message. On my part I intend to follow it up with a message of my own which will support your case.

I think there is nothing more important than that Stalin feels we mean to support him without qualification and at great sacrifice.

Roosevelt. Released at 1705 PM, October 7, 1942.

The War Cabinet considered on 7 October the terms of a further draft telegram to President Roosevelt on supplies and military assistance to Russia.[20] These were amended in discussion and the War Cabinet authorized its despatch.[21]

The following day[22] the Cabinet, after considering President Roosevelt's reply, agreed on the content of the telegram to Premier Stalin and authorized its despatch. The section relating to the convoys now read:

5. I was greatly relieved that so large a proportion of the last convoy reached Archangel safely. This success was achieved only because no less than 77 warships were employed on the operation. Naval protection will be impossible until our impending operations are completed. As necessary escorts are withdrawn from TORCH they can again be made available in northern waters.
6. Nevertheless, we intend in the meanwhile to do our best to send you supplies by the northern route by means of ships sailed independently instead of in escorted convoys. Arrangements have been made to sail ships from Iceland during moonless period October 28th to November 8th. Ten of ours are preparing in addition to what Americans will do. The ships will sail singly at about 200-mile intervals with occasional larger gaps and rely on evasion and dispersion.
7. We hope to resume flow of supplies in strongly escorted convoys from January 1943.
8. It would, of course, greatly help both you and us if Germans could be denied the use of airfields in Northern Norway. If your Staffs could make a good plan, the President and I would at once examine the possibility of co-operating up to the limit of our ability.

The same day Churchill informed[23] Roosevelt:

1. I have despatched Telegram to Premier Stalin. Exact text is in my immediately following Telegram. All the suggestions contained in your No. one nine two have been adopted.
   a. You did not fill in the blank in paragraph four of my No. one six zero. I have therefore used the following words in my Telegram to Premier Stalin: 'President Roosevelt will cable separately about United States contribution.'

This telegram was immediately followed by a second[24] from Former Naval Person to President and marked personal, which read: 'Following is text referred to in Para one of my immediately preceding Telegram: Prime Minister to Premier Stalin.' (Text was as appears above.)

Some weeks had passed without a response to Churchill's message to Stalin of 8 October and so on the 24th Churchill cabled Roosevelt:

You have seen my message to Stalin which I sent you for your concurrence and dispatched on the eight October (our series message number one six seven). There is also the Telegram you sent him quoted in your number one nine three to me.

On the same day that I sent my long Telegram I sent a short one to him imparting a piece of secret news.[25] On the thirteenth October I received the somewhat cryptic answer thank you. Otherwise I have had no response.

We asked our Ambassador to which Telegram the thank you referred. Molotov's private secretary though repeatedly pressed has given an evasive answer. But Maisky has now indicated in response to an indirect inquiry he regards Stalin's reply as referring to the longer message. Have you had any answer to your message quoted in your one nine three?

In the War Cabinet on the 26th[26] the Secretary of State for Foreign Affairs reported that the Russian ambassador had approached him in a state of considerable excitement at a luncheon at the Persian Legation earlier in the day complaining as a result of instructions issued by the Ministry of War Transport, three American ships loaded for Russia now in Iceland were being sent back to this country to be unloaded and this would have a deplorable effect in view of the difficult situation between our two countries. The Foreign Secretary informed the ambassador that he knew nothing of the matter, but if the ships were American, it was presumably a matter for the American government. On investigation, it was established that the ships had been diverted by the US authorities who had been asked in future that they inform the USSR when they found it necessary to make these changes. This incident was only another example of the suspicious attitude the Russians were seen to be adopting towards Britain.

Roosevelt for his part was not particularly concerned about the lack of response from Stalin, replying to Churchill on the 28th: 'I am not unduly disturbed about our respective responses or lack of responses from Moscow.'

Merchant Ships Stranded in North Russia

When the convoy programme was suspended large numbers of Allied merchant ships had been waiting for many months in Russian ports to return to the west. With the imminent arrival of the almost total darkness and sub-zero temperatures of the Arctic winter, the decision was taken to bring back to the UK in November as many of those ships from PQ 16, PQ 17 and PQ 18 still in North Russian ports as were in a suitable condition to make the journey home safely. This was intended to be a comparatively small operation to bring about thirty of them back to the UK. The C-in-C Home Fleet requested that the convoy be limited to twenty merchant ships given the potential hazards, but the Admiralty overruled him, directing that thirty ships be included. This was QP 15.

When the convoy programme was suspended, eleven merchant ships had been loaded in British ports for PQ 19. Six of these, which had reached the Orkneys, were held there; of the remainder, five went on in the independent sailings (Operation FB). Three of these would be lost and only two arrive.

As it was impossible to run PQ 19 as a normal heavily-escorted convoy, it was now planned to sail thirteen ships independently from Reykjavik to North Russia and ten ships independently from Beyslushaya, North Russia[27] to Iceland at approximately 100-mile intervals, following up these sailings with Convoy QP 15 on about 11 November.

The first operation code-named Operation FB took place between 29 October and 14 November 1942. The sailings detected by the Germans resulted in increased air reconnaissance and U-boat patrols. Only five eastbound and three westbound merchant ships reached their destinations. As a result, the Admiralty and Ministry of War Transport did not feel justified in repeating the experiment.

Chapter Seven

Treatment of British Service Personnel in North Russia

Mail for British Service Personnel in North Russia

In September 1942 difficulties began to arise over the delivery and distribution to British ships of mail from the UK. Up until then British service personnel serving ashore had been receiving their mail as normal. Now the Russian civil authorities insisted on censoring all private correspondence unless the mailbags had been properly sealed and had received a visa from the Soviet Embassy in London; a very time-consuming process and one that proved a particular source of annoyance to the intended recipients serving in an otherwise isolated location with no other means of communication with home.

Control of Personnel Movements

The difficulties over visas and mail were exacerbated in November 1942 when the Russians introduced additional regulations that made it almost as difficult for naval staff involved in convoy operations to leave the country as it was to enter. These involved completing a four-page declaration form, producing five photographs of passport size, giving fourteen days' notice of intention to leave so that the matter could be referred to Moscow, reporting in person to the police in Murmansk for scrutiny of documents and finally, having obtained an exit visa, embarking only in the presence of a representative of the NKVD.[1]

Although these regulations had been present in the background in milder form for some months, they were now enforced without notice just as a group of service personnel was about to depart and had the potential to be highly disruptive to planned personnel exchanges, especially at short notice. The fact that the trip to Murmansk from Polyarny under winter conditions might involve an absence of three or four days made the situation more inconvenient. In addition to the entry and exit visas, requirements were also introduced for a registration card with which all personnel had to be provided, and various local passes, all of which had to bear the holder's photograph. This was measure was regarded by the British naval authorities in North Russia as exhibiting an excessive degree of control (and presumably reflecting a degree of suspicion) over personnel whose primary role was to assist the Russians and which was regarded as out of all proportion to the way in which the Russians in the United Kingdom were being treated.

Restrictions on Personnel Numbers

It had by now become evident that the Russians increasingly resented what they regarded as a continued unnecessary presence of large numbers of British servicemen in their country, particularly during the times when there were no convoys running. They seemed unable to comprehend the reasons why these personnel had remained; essentially to maintain the operational capability to run the convoys and operate the related communications facilities. They had begun to restrict the movement of British personnel from ship to shore and even from ship to ship, obstruct the landing of stores, interrupt and censor personal mail and generally to make life as difficult and inconvenient as possible. The difficulties in establishing hospital facilities and in particular the refusal to allow a hospital unit at Archangel to treat convoy casualties had already seriously strained Anglo-Soviet relationships, while word of the Russian authorities' intransigence had quickly spread throughout the British Merchant Navy.

Churchill had written previously to Molotov, the Russian Foreign Minister,[2] on 27 September following the refusal to allow the establishment ashore of a British naval hospital:

> The Foreign Secretary tells me that he has sent you a message about the British Military Hospital at Vaenga being ordered to close and go home. I should be glad if you would look into this matter personally yourself. Terrible cases of mutilation through frostbite are now arriving back here, and I have to consider constantly the morale of the Merchant seamen, who have hitherto gone so willingly to man the Merchant ships to Russia. The British Hospital Unit was sent simply to help, and implied no reflection on Russian arrangements under the pressure of air bombardments, etc. It is hard on men in hospital not to have nurses who speak their own language. At any rate, I hope you will give me some sound reason, which I can give should the matter be raised in Parliament, as it very likely will be.

Now on 2 October he finally received the following somewhat dismissive response; the only reply Churchill received from Molotov on the subject:

In my letter to Mr Eden, I asked him to acquaint you, Mr Prime Minister, with the content of my reply on the question of the British medical personnel in Archangel and Vaenga (Murmansk). I think that if you glance at the Memorandum of the Soviet Foreign Office of August 27, and my letter of September 12 addressed to the British ambassador you will have the full information on the matter and will be in a position to draw the necessary conclusions as to the real state of affairs, particularly in regard to certain irregularities in the actions of the respective British naval authorities.

These negotiations on hospital facilities that began on 25 September continued until 2 October, when the Russian government finally granted permission for a certain number of British medical collaborators to work in Soviet hospitals, but refused to allow a separate British service medical establishment to be set up on shore. Then on 5 October the SBNO Archangel reported that the C-in-C Soviet Northern Fleet had informed him official permission had now been granted for the establishment of a Royal Naval Auxiliary Hospital ashore at Vaenga Bay.[3]

Four days later, the SBNO was informed that an opportunity might occur in the near future for the transport of a limited amount of stores and personnel to North Russia and asked if any were required for the medical unit. Additional medical staff and stores were then sent out later in October to Murmansk for the Vaenga Hospital under Operation EZ, carried out by the cruiser *Argonaut* with the destroyers *Intrepid* and *Obdurate*. The principal objective of the operation was the evacuation of about 38 officers and 207 other ranks of the Royal Air Force who had formed the crews and ground staff of the two squadrons of Hampdens and three PRU Spitfire aircraft sent out in July 1942 in Operation EU. The opportunity was taken to include personnel and stores for North Russia and return personnel to the UK. Those sent out were Commodore Meek (relief for Rear Admiral Boddam-Whetham), the medical officers and ratings for the hospital unit at Vaenga and a few reliefs for time-expired officers and men out there. Those returning, apart from the RAF personnel, were mainly from Archangel and included Rear Admiral Boddam-Whetham (commodore of Convoy PQ 18),[4] survivors of PQ 17 and PQ 18, and various service personnel from Moscow and North Russia; a total of 75 officers and 341 men. All efforts to establish the independent RN hospital at Archangel were unsuccessful.

Churchill did not hear again from Stalin himself until his reply of 3 October handed to him by Mr Maisky on 5 October in which Stalin first requested additional supplies of fighter aircraft and then continued:

2. Supply ships with munitions have reached Archangel and are being unloaded. This is a great help. However, in view of the shortage of tonnage we could forgo for a while certain kinds of aid and thereby reduce the demand for shipping, provided the aid in the shape of fighter aircraft is increased.

NB: Another slightly different version of the text of this message is quoted in Churchill's *History of the Second World War*.[5]

Debate on the King's Speech

On 11 November in the debate in the House of Commons on the King's Address to Parliament[6] Churchill, commenting on the calls by the Russians for the opening of a Second Front in Europe and noting the pressures the Allies were under in other theatres of the war summarized the strength of the German forces in Norway and the efforts that had been made to send supplies to North Russia. He reported:

> The main part of the German fleet has been for some months tied to the Northern fjords. There are about 350 of their best aircraft gathered up in the Far North to impede our convoys to Russia. Here is another front we have found it very costly to maintain. Let me tell you about that. Of the 19 convoys we have sent to Russia, everyone has been an important fleet operation, because the enemy's main fleet was close at hand. The latest one required the use of 77 ships of war, apart altogether from the supply ships. The Foreign Secretary if he is well enough – my right hon. friend has a temporary indisposition to-day – or if not, the Undersecretary of State for Foreign Affairs, will recount in some detail later on in the Debate the immense output of munitions which we have sent to Russia during a period when we ourselves were being vehemently reproached, and naturally reproached, for the comparative ill-equipment of our own troops. Indeed I think that the effort and achievement of this country, industrial, naval and military, during the year 1942 should be a source of pride and thanksgiving, not only to all in these islands, but to our Allies both in the East and in the West.

Deterioration in Anglo-Soviet Relations

The Secretary of State for Foreign Affairs submitted a further report to the War Cabinet on 13 November[7] on supplies to Russia in which he noted:

In the past two months I have had occasion to bring before the War Cabinet more than one sign of deterioration in the state of Anglo-Soviet relations. Our present failure to maintain the flow of supplies has contributed to the difficulty of keeping on good terms with Russia.

This failure has arisen from decisions in the strategic sphere which have had an inevitable repercussion on the flow of supplies to the USSR. As this paper will show, the decision to discontinue convoys to North Russia until January 1943 will result in our having to hold up the despatch to Russia of the bulk of our commitments, as well as United States commitments, under the Second Protocol which would normally have gone by this route for the months of July to December, i.e. the first six months of the period covered by this agreement. I need not emphasise how serious a loss this represents to the Soviet Union at the present time and how difficult it may prove for us to catch up on these arrears when convoys are resumed.

I feel, therefore, that my colleagues ought to be aware of the details of the situation in regard to supplies, which I have described above. As the difficulties result from transportation rather than supply limitations, my review of the situation will be mainly concerned with shipping and transport problems.

5. The Tripartite Agreement concluded at Washington on the 6th October, 1942 (W.P. (42) 438) gave binding force to an offer which had been made to the Soviet Government on behalf of the United States and United Kingdom Governments on the 29th May. This offer said (in effect) that within the limits imposed from time to time by the shortage of ships, by the necessity for providing naval escorts for convoys by the Northern route, and by the undeveloped inland transportation in the Persian Gulf area, the United States and ourselves would supply the shipping necessary to lift that part of the export programme, comprising 3,300,000 short tons to the Northern ports and 1,100,000 short tons to the Persian Gulf ports during the year ending the 30th June, 1943. This programme includes, of course, not only the major military items – aircraft, tanks, Bren carriers and M/T vehicles – but the large tonnage of munitions, raw materials, electrical and industrial plant and machinery, medical supplies, food-stuffs, oil products, and so forth, which we and the Americans have agreed to make available.

By the Northern route the last escorted convoy of 40 merchant ships (PQ 18) completed delivery of the Moscow Protocol June quota and carried a part of the July quota under the Second Protocol. It reached North Russian ports on the 21st September. No further escorted convoys are at present scheduled to sail by this route before the end of the year.

The effect of this state of affairs is that there were 40 merchant ships – 11 British, 28 American and 1 Russian – awaiting convoy at the end of September. Thirteen of these have sailed independently and three have arrived in North Russia. Of the remainder, five are believed to be sunk, two have been brought back and are safe, and three are still on passage. I understand that the Admiralty and the Minister of War Transport do not, in the light of this result, feel justified in repeating the experiment.

The 11 British ships carry materials which count against the remainder of July, the whole of August, and a small part of the September monthly quota from the United Kingdom.

Most of the September quota, and the whole of the October, November and December commitments are in theory piling up awaiting a shipping opportunity. If the Admiralty's present intentions of sailing a convoy of not more than 30 merchant ships about the first week in January are carried through, there will be room in the convoy for very few new ships to carry the four months' quotas of major military items and between 20,000 and 30,000 tons of non-military goods (electrical equipment, machine tools, cordite, &c.) which will have accumulated by the end of the year. There may, however, be shipping space on some of the American ships which require dry docking before they sail, to be found by discharging low-priority cargoes and restowing with aircraft, lorries and tanks.

Apart from this accumulation, no less than 25 American ships, which have failed to find places in the PQ convoys, have had to be discharged in this country by arrangements agreed between the American and Soviet authorities. Although some of the priority items on these ships have been restowed and shipped to Russia, the prospect of on-carrying the rest of the cargo is so remote that most of it will have been taken into consumption by the United States Army Authorities or handed over to British Government Departments.

This being the position on the Northern route, it is not surprising that the Soviet Ambassador has been pressing me to find some other means of despatching material of the highest priority to his country. The Air Ministry are examining the question whether, by fitting long-range tanks, they can manage to fly some of the 520 Hurricanes which are due to be despatched from the United Kingdom before the end of the year direct to a North Russian aerodrome 1,060 miles from the Shetlands. Unfortunately, it has not yet been possible to find shipping space for any of these aircraft on vessels bound for the Persian Gulf via the Cape, although 150 Spitfires which the Prime Minister offered to M. Stalin in October are due to be despatched by that route by the end of November.

Continuing Treatment of British Service Personnel in North Russia

The visa war with the NKVD reached a crucial stage by the end of 1942 as more and more replacements were required for British personnel serving in the Soviet Union. Several outstanding visas for incoming British replacements had by now been refused.

The Head of the Naval Section of the Military Mission in Moscow, Rear Admiral Miles, urged the adoption of strong measures at the highest level because he felt that unless all the necessary personnel were obtained, it would not be possible to continue running the convoys. He wrote on 4 January to the Director of Naval Intelligence: 'We shall not get anything through unless we are prepared to take a really strong line with a threat of say the stoppage of convoys or the withdrawal of our and their Missions.'

The Naval Mission took little comfort from an assurance that the visa problem would be raised with the Soviet government, with Miles stating he was 'very glad to hear this matter is being taken up by the Foreign Office, but I don't expect much from it if they continue to negotiate in their usual spineless way.'[8]

Chapter Eight

November 1942: Resumption of Convoys

In a memorandum to the War Cabinet dated 13 November[1] the Foreign Secretary had explained that owing to the discontinuance of the convoy sailings, most of the September quota and the whole of the October, November and December commitments were in theory piling up awaiting a shipping opportunity. The following day Churchill, clearly still determined to make progress, wrote to the First Sea Lord:[2]

> I am most anxious to run a Russian Convoy (late) in December. For this purpose the United States is to be asked to make available for our needs at least 25 destroyers, which they can easily save from the massive escorts which they are using for the big troop convoys for TORCH. Such a request might well be coupled with our meeting their wishes in regard to the (loan) of aircraft carriers. If we had another 25 destroyers ... to our hands, we would be much easier.

The typescript is then annotated in Churchill's handwriting: 'Let me have a note on this.'

At the Defence Committee (Operations) Meeting on 16 November[3] Churchill stated that he had undertaken in a telegram to Premier Stalin[4] to make every effort to resume convoys to North Russia by January 1943 and hoped that this would be achieved. The First Sea Lord reported that it was now hoped to sail a convoy of about thirty ships from Iceland on 20 December.[5] With Archangel closed by ice, the North Russian ports could not handle a larger convoy. It seemed doubtful, however, whether it would be possible to sail further convoys early in 1943 and at the same time find escorts for Operation BRIMSTONE.[6] The Cabinet noted the proposal to sail a convoy to North Russia in late December. The First Sea Lord would provide Churchill with details regarding the sailing of this convoy, and material for a telegram to the president on the provision of destroyers.

While awaiting the advice of the First Sea Lord, Churchill wrote to Roosevelt on 18 November:

From: Prime. Am. Embassy, London
To: The President of the United States
Former Naval Person to President Roosevelt
No. 196, November 18th, 1942

I know your earnestness about sending another convoy to North Russia as soon as possible. We can have thirty-one ships ready to sail from Iceland on two two December.

As *Tirpitz*, *Hipper* and two small enemy cruisers are stationed in Norway, it is essential to have with the convoy, in addition to their close escort, a striking force of sixteen destroyers to deal with the German Surface Forces.

We can provide the close escort for convoy but, owing to TORCH commitments and the casualties to destroyers in that operation we can only provide seventeen out of the twenty-nine destroyers required for a screen for the battle fleet and cruisers and the destroyer striking force mentioned above. I am reluctant to risk sending this convoy unless we give it adequate protection. It is hoped therefore that you would be prepared to send twelve long-endurance destroyers to assist in passing the convoy in.

It would be desirable for your destroyers to arrive at Scapa by seventh December in order to give time for them to get accustomed to working with our fleet.

Roosevelt Rejects Churchill's Request

Roosevelt's reply the following day, based on advice and a draft provided by Admiral King, read as follows:

PRESIDENT TO PRIME MINISTER
Replying to your message No. 196 of November 18 I am in complete agreement that every effort should be made to send another convoy to Russia at the earliest possible date. It is noted that you can make available escort vessels for the close escort and some for the covering and striking forces but you feel that twelve additional destroyers are necessary for adequate protection.

You are familiar with the necessity of our radical reduction of escort forces even to retaining in the Atlantic destroyers urgently required in the Pacific in order to provide escort vessels for TORCH.

The movement of essential follow-up convoys from America to Africa is contingent upon availability of escort vessels and the TORCH operation must be adequately supported, destroyer losses and damage to destroyers in recent naval operations in the Pacific have been so serious as to necessitate an immediate return of the destroyers borrowed from the Pacific for TORCH. This will leave in the Atlantic only minimum requirements for follow-up convoys to Africa and makes it impossible for us to provide the destroyers for the Russian convoy suggested in your message Number 196. I wish I could send you a more favorable answer.

Further Correspondence with Stalin

The Defence Committee (Operations) had discussed at their meeting on 23 November[7] a further draft telegram from Churchill to Premier Stalin on future convoys. There was some confusion in the Cabinet as to Churchill's intentions when he had said that the PQ convoys, once resumed, must on no account be discontinued as this would not be possible if operations against Sicily or Sardinia required naval forces of a magnitude comparable to TORCH. It would not be possible to find the escorts for a PQ convoy at the same time as offensive operations in the Central Mediterranean. Churchill explained that what he had intended to convey to the First Sea Lord was nothing that should prevent the resumption of the PQ convoys. It would certainly be desirable after they had been resumed that they should be continued without interruption. If, however, their interruption was essential on account of offensive operations that would draw forces from the Russian front, the situation would be changed, and Premier Stalin would understand.

The committee approved the draft telegram to Premier Stalin as amended in discussion and agreed that nothing should stand in the way of resumption of the PQ convoys at the end of the year. Thereafter the policy should be to continue the sailing of PQ convoys, but this should not be interpreted as precluding their temporary discontinuation if this was necessitated on account of larger offensive operations that would favourably affect the situation on the Russian front.

The North Atlantic Convoy Situation: Shortage of Escorts

Roosevelt's response of 19 November was not the reply Churchill was hoping for. Three days later he received the First Sea Lord's advice on the situation. In the minute dated 22 November, which was long and not entirely encouraging, the First Sea Lord reported that the situation in the North Atlantic was such that it could not be allowed to continue as at present. The Minister of War Transport had represented that if our convoys continue to be knocked about in the Atlantic as at present, there were signs that the merchant seamen might refuse to sail.

In order to deal with the North Atlantic situation, approval had been given for the provision of very long-range aircraft, but these would not be fully operative for some considerable time and in any case the First Sea Lord did not feel that air protection could be relied on entirely to deal with this dangerous situation in the Central Atlantic as there were so many days on which aircraft might not be able to fly. It was essential, therefore, that the escort situation be improved. Owing to TORCH, it was quite impossible at the present time to strengthen all the escorts and the situation must be dealt with as best possible by using reinforcing groups.

Certain proposals had been put to the Canadians and Americans for temporarily augmenting the escorts over the western portion of the mid-ocean voyage. These they had agreed to, although it seriously weakened their escorts on the run west of Newfoundland and would have to be cancelled if the U-boats moved again in strength to that area.

Two reinforcing groups were required in order to deal with the western half of the dangerous area. The Royal Navy could just scrape together one of these groups from ships returning from TORCH, and the First Sea Lord was explaining to the Americans the urgency of the requirement and asking them to release a group of British ships working on the convoy route between Guantanamo and New York.

With regard to the PQ convoys, one could be run on 22 December by reducing the destroyer striking force from sixteen vessels to seven, but this might necessitate 6in gun-armed cruisers going right through with the convoy. The First Sea Lord did not favour the substitution of cruisers for destroyers, but as the Americans had refused to help out there was no alternative.

The First Sea Lord reminded Churchill that under previous arrangements the Russians had been told that the Allies would try to run three convoys every two months. A cycle of this nature would now be out of the question, and at best it would only be possible to run a convoy every thirty-three days. This would put a severe strain on the destroyers of the Home Fleet and it was not known for how long they would be able to sustain it. It was doubtful, however, whether the Russians could accept a convoy of thirty ships more often than once every thirty-three days as they only had twelve unloading berths and each ship took ten to twelve days to unload. It also seemed very doubtful whether their railways would be able to cope with even one convoy of thirty ships every thirty-three days.

The point was also made that the question of PQ convoys was intimately connected with Operation BRIMSTONE and other future operations. It was quite clear that unless the Americans provided a large part of the naval forces for BRIMSTONE etc., it would be necessary for the PQ convoys to cease while BRIMSTONE was carried out, over a period of two to three months or even longer. Even with American help it would not be possible to launch BRIMSTONE until the follow-up period of TORCH completed in February, and impossible simultaneously to meet the follow-up of BRIMSTONE and maintenance of TORCH. On the basis of this advice Churchill would finally get his convoy, although it would sail with a significantly smaller naval escort than PQ 18.

At this time there arose a significant difference of opinion between the C-in-C Home Fleet and the Admiralty over the mid-winter policy for sailing and protection of the convoys to North Russia.[8] In the opinion of the C-in-C, the lack of daylight between late November and mid-January made air reconnaissance in the Arctic virtually impossible. Provided a convoy was of such a size that it could be handled and kept together, it stood an excellent chance of evading both U-boat and surface attack, and even of completing the passage without the enemy knowing of its existence. A large convoy, on the other hand, was likely to fail to keep in company and to split, as did QP 15, into a large number of small groups covering a vast area with each group unaware of the others' position or composition. Such small groups would be more liable to detection by U-boats than a single concentrated convoy and present the enemy surface forces with an ideal opportunity for an offensive sweep. The convoy cover forces were always handicapped by having to identify a radar contact before they were free to attack; the enemy did not need to do so. The splitting of the convoy into a large number of scattered units would greatly add to this handicap.

The C-in-C Home Fleet argued that it was obviously advantageous to run as many merchant ships as possible through to North Russia during this short dark period rather than defer the commitments until air reconnaissance could start again. Though it would be impossible to provide strong surface escort for a large number of small convoys, the chances of evasion were, in his opinion, so good that the risk of interception by superior surface forces should be accepted. He requested that about six merchant ships, escorted by three trawlers, should be held ready in Iceland to sail shortly before the arrival of QP 15 if the U-boats were drawn out of position by that convoy, but the Admiralty did not agree. They proposed instead to wait until 22 December and then sail a convoy of thirty-one ships with an escort of what the C-in-C described as of summer dimensions. The experience of QP 15 confirmed his opinion that a convoy that size could not be handled effectively; the Admiralty proposal, moreover, would waste the first half of the dark period.

Correspondence with Stalin on Future Convoys

The Defence Committee (Operations) discussed at their meeting on 23 November[9] a further draft telegram from Churchill to Premier Stalin on future convoys. There was some confusion in the Cabinet as to Churchill's intentions when he had said the PQ convoys, once resumed, must on no account be discontinued as this would not be possible if operations against Sicily or Sardinia required naval forces of a magnitude comparable to TORCH. It would not be possible to find the escorts for a PQ convoy at the same time as offensive operations in the Central Mediterranean. Churchill explained that what he had intended to convey to the First Sea Lord was that nothing should prevent the resumption of the PQ convoys. It would certainly be desirable that once they had been resumed, they should be continued without interruption. If, however, their interruption was essential on account of offensive operations that would draw forces off the Russian front, the situation would be changed and Premier Stalin would understand.

The committee approved the draft telegram to Premier Stalin as amended in discussion and agreed that nothing should stand in the way of resumption of the PQ convoys at the end of the year. Thereafter the policy should be to continue the sailing of PQ convoys, but this should not be interpreted as precluding their temporary discontinuation if this was necessitated on account of larger offensive operations that would favourably affect the situation on the Russian Front.

So on 24 November Churchill replied to Premier Stalin and, after thanking him for his message of 14 November, wrote:

> Although the President is unable with great regret to lend me the twelve American destroyers for which I asked, I have now succeeded in making arrangements to sail a convoy of over thirty ships from Iceland on December 22nd. The Admiralty will concert operations with your officers as before. The Germans have moved the bulk of their aircraft from North Norway to South Europe as a result of TORCH. On the other hand, German surface forces in Norway are still on guard. The Admiralty are pleased so far with the progress of the QP convoy, which has been helped by bad weather and is now under the protection of our cruisers which have been sent out to meet it.

The C-in-C Home Fleet therefore signalled the Admiralty on 25 November his intention to limit the convoy in size and asked for the assembly of the first ten merchant ships to be hastened. This small convoy was to be escorted by four destroyers from the Home Fleet and any minesweepers and trawlers that could be made available.[10] The Admiralty, however, insisted in their reply of 26 November that it was essential to provide a covering force strong enough to deal with the scale of attack they expected, and considered that the only alternatives were either to sail thirty ships in company or in three groups so close together that one force could cover all three. After further discussion, including a visit to London by his chief of staff, the C-in-C Home Fleet was directed to sail the convoy in two groups of sixteen ships, each escorted by seven destroyers and some smaller craft; and the Home Fleet, reinforced by two 6in-gunned cruisers, was to provide cruiser cover in the Barents Sea.

The large numbers of U-boats that usually surrounded and accompanied these 7-knot convoys were regarded as a serious menace to covering cruisers so far from base. The experience of the past year, and especially the loss of the *Edinburgh*, had underlined this risk. After balancing this against the risk of surface attack, the C-in-C's intention had been for the 6in-gunned cruisers, if they became available, to provide cover as far as 25° east, then return to Iceland. The Admiralty, however, was insistent that the cruisers should cover the convoys right through to the Kola Inlet. This insistence, the C-in-C Home Fleet later conceded, was in the event fully justified, otherwise the cruiser force would probably not have been present at the action on New Year's Eve [when the *Scharnhorst* was sunk].

Stalin replied on the following day, 29 November:[11]

> Thank you for your message, which I received on November 25. I fully share your view it is highly important to promote our personal relations.
>
> I express gratitude for the steps you are taking to send another large convoy to Archangel. I realise at the moment this is particularly difficult for you, especially in view of the considerable operations by the British fleet in the Mediterranean.

Churchill read to the War Cabinet on the 30th[12] what he described as the very cordial reply received from Stalin dated two days previously (in reply to the telegram from himself dated 24 November), in which Stalin expressed gratitude for the decision to send a new big convoy to Archangel. The Cabinet also learned on the same day that twenty-six of the thirty ships in the latest convoy from Russia (QP 15) had reached the UK by the 30th and two further vessels might make port.[13]

Proposed Convoy Programme from January to March 1943

The subject of convoys to North Russia was discussed again in the War Cabinet[14] on 15 December, the day that the first convoy of the new cycle – JW 51A of fifteen merchant ships and a fleet oiler – sailed from Loch Ewe, when the Foreign Secretary sought guidance on future convoy arrangements to North Russia. He explained that the matter had been discussed at the Allied Supplies Executive the previous afternoon and arrangements had now been made for a December convoy (re-numbered JW 51) to sail in two parts.[15] This would clear the backlog of all but two of the American and British ships awaiting convoy in Iceland for several months.

It was proposed that the January convoy (re-numbered JW 52) should also sail in two parts. Arrangements had been completed for the first part of sixteen ships. The position with regard to the second part of the January convoy was that while there were substantial quantities of low-priority goods (foodstuffs, machine tools, etc.) available for loading, neither the War Office nor the Air Ministry could agree to make any substantial quantities of tanks and aircraft available without interfering with allocations earmarked for overseas theatres of operations. A similar position would arise with future convoys, assuming the continuance of a monthly cycle of sailings. For example, the War Cabinet was informed that over and above 250 Hurricanes were included in the first part of the January convoy, but all available Hurricanes were now required in the Middle East.

Reference was made to the request made to Churchill by Premier Stalin during August last to the effect that the Soviet government was more anxious to get lorries than tanks. The War Cabinet was informed that there was an acute shortage of lorries in this country; 4,000 had been offered from Canadian production but would have to be collected by ships sent from the UK to fetch them. It seemed that the best plan might be to send them in Soviet ships via Vladivostok.

The Minister of War Transport stated that the United States had recently transferred a number of ships to the Soviet flag, now employed between the west coast of America and Vladivostok. This action had naturally reduced the number of ships the United States was able to make available for North Russian convoys. The Russians were also using a number of their ships on this Pacific route. It looked as though in future the size of the convoys might have to be reduced from thirty to twenty ships. Even so, it would be very difficult to make suitable British ships available for regular monthly convoys to North Russia. (In the event only a maximum of ten could be spared each month.)

Churchill noted that Britain was under an obligation to send material to the Russians and wished to inform Stalin that arrangements were being made to send convoys in January (in two parts), February and March. Every endeavour must be made to fulfil British obligations and send high-priority supplies to the Russians. However, the British were under no obligation to supply Russia with 6-pounder tanks up to the full number provided in the protocol. If the United States was sending goods across the North Pacific, the British must reconcile themselves to smaller convoys going to North Russia. He asked the Secretary of State for Foreign Affairs to consider the matter with the Allied Supplies Executive (ASE) and submit a report for consideration by the War Cabinet, setting out what the British could send to Russia during January, February and March in fulfilment of their obligations and the implications of the course proposed.

Churchill reported to Stalin on 30 December:

3. The December PQ convoy has prospered so far beyond all expectations. I have now arranged to send a full convoy of thirty or more ships through in January, though whether they will go in one portion or in two is not yet settled by the Admiralty.

Results of Convoy Sailings between August 1941 and December 1942

The effect of the shipping losses during 1942 had been to convert each sailing on the Northern Route into a major fleet operation, with a strict limitation placed on the number of merchant ships that could be sailed each month. Between August 1941 and the end of 1942, twenty Russia-bound convoys with 320 merchant ships sailed. Of these, 243 ships arrived, 23 turned back and 52, along with 2 naval auxiliaries, were lost. Of the 240 merchant ships in the 13 westbound convoys, 214 arrived, 9 turned back and 17, including 1 naval auxiliary, were sunk. The losses were, however, much more serious than these figures indicate since most of them occurred in the short period between March and September 1942. In addition, the Royal Navy lost two cruisers, four destroyers and six other vessels on the route.

Progress of the Winter Convoy Cycle

The progress of JW 51A and JW 51B was discussed at the War Cabinet on the evening of 4 January 1943[16] when it was reported that the first half of the December convoy (JW 51A) to Russia had arrived safely, but the second (JW 51B) had been attacked by German surface forces with two merchant

November 1942: Resumption of Convoys   105

ships sunk. The destroyer escort of this convoy had fought a very gallant action until the arrival of the cruisers *Sheffield* and *Jamaica* which, in spite of inferior gun power, had driven off the enemy. One destroyer had been sunk and another damaged while the Germans had lost one destroyer. The First Lord of the Admiralty was invited to supply the Secretary of State for Foreign Affairs with the complete story of this action so he could communicate it privately to the Russian government.

More detail was supplied in the War Cabinet Weekly Resume No. 175, from 7.00 am on 31 December 1942 to 7.00 am on 7 January 1943[17] which reported:

A convoy from the United Kingdom[18] has arrived in North Russian ports. Enemy warships attempted unsuccessfully to intercept it.

On the morning of the 31st December, HM destroyer *Onslow* with four other destroyers, which were escorting a convoy to North Russia, engaged an enemy force of one cruiser and three destroyers north of Varanger Fiord. During the ensuing action HM destroyer *Achates* was sunk and HM destroyer *Onslow* was damaged, but in order to avoid repeated torpedo attacks, the enemy was compelled to retire under cover of smoke away from the convoy and towards the covering force consisting of HM cruisers *Sheffield* and *Jamaica* and two destroyers. The force shortly afterwards engaged an enemy ship, probably the pocket battleship *Lützow*, which was hit and forced to retire. Later they engaged a destroyer which was left in a sinking condition, and forced a cruiser, either *Nürnberg* or *Hipper* to retire at high speed to the south-westward. When it was established that the enemy had withdrawn, our covering forces returned to protect the convoy. Twelve of the fourteen Merchant ships in the convoy arrived safely on the 8th. Two Merchant ships with HM minesweeper *Bramble*, which had parted company with the convoy on the 29th, are as yet unaccounted for.[19]

Seventy-eight ratings and an unknown number of officers were rescued from *Achates*. Our cruisers suffered minor damage and *Onslow*, in which there were 41 casualties, reached harbour on the 1st.

A homeward-bound convoy from North Russia has reached home waters. Strong cover was provided by HM ships. This convoy was not sighted by the enemy.

Planned Convoy Programme from January to March 1943

Returning to the subject of future Russian convoys, the War Cabinet held a special conference on 5 January[20] to consider a minute of the 4th from the First Sea Lord[21] on the subject. The conclusions were as follows:

(i) A convoy of twenty ships (including two Oilers) should be run on 17 January (JW 52)
(ii) A convoy of twenty-eight to thirty ships should be run on 11 February (JW 53). This convoy would include at least 6 additional ships from America
(iii) A convoy of thirty ships should be run in the second week in March. The 10th being the earliest date. Twenty of these ships would be new arrivals from America.

The Minute from the First Sea Lord read:
PRIME MINISTER:
(NOTES):
Note 1. From now onwards convoys will not be divided into two parts.
Note 2. PQ Convoys are now called JW and homecoming QP Convoys are termed RA.
With reference to Item 3 of the Cabinet Minutes of 28 December, the present plan for the North Russia Convoys is as follows:

(a) To run JW 52 on 17 January consisting of 16 ships with a dark period (cruiser) escort and cover as for JW 51A and 51B.
(b) To run RA 52 back concurrently.
(c) To run RA 53 back on arrival of JW 52, thus avoiding having escorts immobilised at the Kola Inlet.
(d) It will then be necessary to gather our forces for a convoy with full destroyer escort cover.
(e) To run JW 53 consisting of 18 ships certain, possibly 24 if loaded in time, on 11th February protected by a destroyer striking force on the scale of used for PQ 18.

Note annotated at this point see postscript.

(f) A Fleet Carrier for the Home Fleet and an escort carrier for the convoy will probably be required and British air striking and reconnaissance forces should if possible be provided in North Russia.

2. After sailing JW 52 on 17 January, another 18 ships will be collected by 22 January but it is not possible to assemble sufficient escorts to take another convoy so soon after JW 52, and further this date is considered by Commander-in-Chief to be one which would require a daylight sail of escort; i.e. a destroyer striking force.

3. The Home Fleet can run JW 53 on 11 February with a destroyer striking force from its own resources assisted by the usual close support from the Western Approaches.

4. If it is necessary to run North Russian convoys without assistance from the USA the cycle must be at least 36 days, whereas if we get reinforcements the cycle can be reduced to 27 days. It may not be possible to run convoys over a 36-day cycle if:
   (i) We have further destroyer losses
   (ii) The size of the convoys is increased.
5. With the increased hours of daylight from February onwards cruiser cover east of Bear Island will no longer be practicable and we shall have to revert to a destroyer striking force to protect the convoy.
6. It remains to be seen whether a destroyer striking force will prove effective.

A.V.A. 4 January 1943

P.S. Since writing this, message received through Harriman that they hope to find six more ships, and enquiring if we could take them in JW 53. We have replied our present intention is to be able to take up to 30 ships in this convoy.

Undiplomatic Exchanges with Stalin

Churchill was reminded by the Foreign Office on 6 January 1943 of the telegram sent to Premier Stalin on 29 December 1942 in which he said: 'I have now arranged to send a full convoy of 30 or more ships through in January, though whether they will go in one portion or two is not yet settled by the Admiralty.' This telegram had been approved by the Defence Committee before its dispatch and Premier Stalin had acknowledged receipt. The conclusions of the conference held on the previous day, however, showed the number of ships to be sent in the January convoy was twenty and decisions had been taken about the size and approximate dates of the following two convoys. Churchill was then asked whether he wished to correct the figure for the January convoy or to give Premier Stalin information about the following convoys.

Matters were exacerbated when the Russians somehow got wind of the new convoy arrangements. The Russian ambassador M. Maisky became somewhat agitated, and told the Foreign Secretary on the 6th[22] that Churchill had promised Stalin convoys of thirty ships in January and February and now the January convoy was only to consist of fifteen! The Foreign Secretary had spoken to the First Lord of the Admiralty who said it was planned to send a convoy of fifteen in January and thirty on 10 February and did not see what more could be done, at any rate without the aid of some American destroyers. The Foreign Secretary thought that it might be found possible to send a further convoy of fifteen ships at the end of February, and failing that thought it might be as well if Churchill could send a personal message to Stalin explaining the position. The only undertaking to Stalin to be found about convoys was in the last paragraph of the telegram, which mentioned a convoy of thirty or more in January but said nothing about February or subsequent months.

Churchill replied to the Foreign Secretary and others on the 9th[23] in somewhat trenchant terms:

> Monsieur Maisky is not telling the truth when he says I promised Stalin convoys of thirty ships in January and February. The only promise I have made is contained in my Telegram of December 29th Paragraph 3, which was agreed to by the Admiralty. I now understand twenty ships only are to go on January 17th, and thirty on February 11. I think it a great pity the Admiralty could not take the whole thing as promised. On the other hand they have undertaken the February convoy.
>
> Maisky should be told I am getting to the end of my tether with these repeated Russian naggings, and it is not the slightest use trying to knock me about any more. Our escorts all over the world are so attenuated, losses out of all proportion are falling upon the British Mercantile Marine. Only this morning news has come in of six out of nine great tankers being sunk, full of oil and greatly needed, because we can only provide an escort of one destroyer and a few corvettes for this vital convoy. The Admiralty have definitely stated if the Americans do not lend us any more destroyers nothing can go after the February convoy until the 30th March, a thirty-six day cycle only being possible to us.

Shortfall in Merchant Shipping

The First Lord of the Admiralty took issue with one of Churchill's comments in his minute of the 9th, noting on the 12th that it was 'a great pity the Admiralty could not take the whole 30 ships promised for the convoy on January 17th.' In fact the Ministry of War Transport had been asked to have twenty-eight ships ready so they could be run either as one convoy on 17 January or in two halves, according to experience with the convoy that had just got through. The Ministry of War Transport was unable to get more than eighteen ships ready and consequently the convoy could consist of only twenty vessels (the eighteen ships plus two British oilers). This outcome was not due to any failure on the part of the Admiralty.

Two days later Churchill sent a further message to Stalin to clarify the situation, in which he said:

1. The December convoy has now been fought through successfully and you will have received details of the fine engagement fought by our light forces against heavy odds.
2. The Admiralty had intended to run the January convoy in two parts of fifteen ships each, the first part sailing about January 17th and the second part later in the month. Since it is clear from the experience of the last convoy the enemy means to dispute the passage of further convoys by surface forces it will be necessary immediately to increase our escorts beyond the scale originally contemplated for January. A still further increase will be necessary for later convoys owing to the increased hours of daylight.
3. We have, therefore, had to revise our arrangements. Instead of running the January convoy in two parts we will sail 19 ships (including two Oilers) instead of the 15 originally contemplated on January 17th. This will be followed on about February 11th by a full convoy of twenty-eight to thirty ships. Thereafter we will do our utmost to sail a convoy of thirty ships on about March 10th, but this is dependent on the Americans assisting us with escort vessels. If they cannot provide this assistance this convoy could not sail until March 19th at the earliest.

Stalin replied to Churchill on 16 January: 'Your message of January 11 has reached me. Thanks for the information.'

The Casablanca Conference: Implications for Convoys to North Russia

While the conditions of British service personnel in North Russia remained an ongoing source of concern for the Admiralty, wider strategic considerations would also now impact on the Anglo-Russian relationship and sustainment of the convoy programme, the most significant of these being the outcome of the Casablanca Conference. Prime Minister Churchill and President Roosevelt met in Casablanca, North Africa between 17 and 22 January 1943 to discuss the future strategic direction of the war. Stalin had been invited to attend, but declined to do so. The continued provision of military supplies to Russia was high on the agenda with particular emphasis on the plans for running convoys during the year. The conference identified the availability of Home Fleet resources as a constraint on the size and frequency of convoys so that only one thirty-ship convoy could be run every forty to forty-two days, reduced to twenty-eight days once fleet oilers were included. The US navy was requested to provide twelve additional destroyers to enable the cycle to be reduced to twenty-seven days, but it was recognized that even with these resources, if the

Germans employed their surface ships boldly and maintained the same level of air and U-boat attacks as in the previous summer, it remained within their power to stop the PQ convoys altogether.

The US pressed for the Russians to do more to attack the German bases in Northern Norway to reduce the risks as these targets were out of range of aircraft from the United Kingdom. In fact, the Russians had been requested in 1942 to assist with escorts and with air attack but, although they had provided limited assistance with the former, they always found some reason for not sending their surface ships out as far as Bear Island where the danger was greatest. In any event their promises of action could not be relied upon: they had made only limited attacks on German airfields and lacked the training and expertise to carry out attacks on German shipping. They were now manning the two British squadrons of Hampdens sent to North Russia in September 1942, but when the *Lützow* and *Hipper* put to sea, the Russians failed to take any action against them with these aircraft when asked to do so. The Germans now had seven airfields between Bodø and Petsamo, all well-defended, and the Russians three in the Murmansk-Archangel area. The possibility of conducting amphibious operations to capture these German airfields had been most exhaustively studied but found impracticable; experience in Malta had shown the bombing of airfields to be very unprofitable.

Although Operation TORCH had resulted in the strength of the German Air Force in Norway falling from 300 to 53 aircraft, the convoys remained exposed to air attack along the route for about ten days of the passage, giving the Germans time to reinforce their airfields in Northern Norway from elsewhere before the convoys passed out of the danger zone. There was also the problem of sustaining both the North Russian and Mediterranean convoy operations simultaneously. One problem was whether a thirty-ship convoy every forty days would be considered sufficient for Russia or if there would be pressure to increase the rate of deliveries. Timing was an issue; the worst three months were from February to mid-May when the daylight hours were increasing and the navigable channel was restricted by ice. Later in the year the ice retreated, so although the days were longer, the passage of convoys became less dangerous.

Churchill had informed Stalin that the PQ convoys might be stopped if the scale of German attack became too heavy. The conference recognized, however, that any suggestion of Allied intent to do so was likely to lead to heavy pressure to increase deliveries during the early part of the year when conditions were unfavourable. This meant either increasing the size of the convoys or reducing the cycle, while the dangers likely to be faced in 1943 were much greater than in the previous year. Churchill still regarded aid to Russia as a sound military dividend and pressed the US to reconsider whether sixteen destroyers could be made available to reduce the length of the convoy cycle to twenty-seven days. The USN was unable to do so; indeed the overall escort vessel situation was so tight that it would be necessary to suspend the Russian convoys from around 14 June to meet the needs of Operation HUSKY. Churchill pointed out that there was already a shortage of sixty-five escorts to protect the convoys in the Atlantic service and HUSKY would make this shortage more acute.

The First Sea Lord insisted that there was no substitute for destroyers in protecting convoys. At the present time sixteen destroyers and eight warships of other types were being utilized with the convoys running on a forty-day cycle. If this were to be reduced to twenty-seven days, it would be necessary to double this force in order to operate two convoys. President Roosevelt's advisor Mr Harry Hopkins asked whether the destroyers and escort vessels that were now with these convoys could not be released for use elsewhere if the convoys were eliminated entirely. The First Sea Lord advised that these would be released, except for those Home Fleet destroyers to be kept available to watch for a breakout of the German fleet into the Atlantic. Churchill nevertheless argued for the Russian convoys to continue throughout Operation HUSKY based on a forty-day cycle rather than attempt the twenty-seven-day cycle prior to HUSKY and suspend the convoys during HUSKY. He also said that no promises had ever been made to take supplies to Russia, only to making munitions available to the Russians at our ports.

General George C. Marshall, the US Army Chief of Staff, in referring to Mr Hopkins'[24] opinion of the Chief of Staff's attitude towards aid to Russia, noted that the current conferences had decided the first charge against the United Nations was the defeat of the submarine menace, with aid to Russia being the second. He added that continuation of the rate of losses suffered in the Murmansk convoys would hurt Russia as much as the US and the UK. Such losses made it impossible to attack on other fronts and thus eliminate the possibility of forcing the Germans to withdraw ground and air troops from the Russian Front. He said the losses in 1942 had come just at the time of the build-up for BOLERO, and the success of Operation HUSKY must not be put at risk. Churchill agreed that if the passage of convoys on the northern route became prohibitive in cost (rate of losses), they must be stopped. It would be right to bear in mind the possibility of continuing convoys through the HUSKY period, but to make no promises to Stalin because the Royal Navy could not support the convoys and simultaneously play its part in Operation HUSKY.

Churchill stated that the discussion should rest on the point that discontinuance of the convoys would depend upon the rate of losses suffered.

Stalin must be told to rely on a forty-day schedule and that the continuance of the convoys could not be guaranteed during Operation HUSKY. It should also be made clear to Stalin that the US and the UK were under no obligation to continue the convoys. It was agreed to defer a final decision on discontinuing the convoys until the first of May.

The Chief of the Imperial General Staff (never the most enthusiastic supporter of the Russian commitment) complained of the climate of Russian secrecy and suspicion:[25] 'One unsatisfactory feature of the whole business of supplying Russia,' he said, 'was their refusal to put their cards on the table. It might well be we were straining ourselves unduly and taking great risks when there was no real necessity to do so.'

Nevertheless, at the end of January 1943 there remained a strategic intent to run supply convoys to North Russia during 1943, subject to the overriding demands of Operation HUSKY.

Chapter Nine

Operation GRENADINE and Anglo-Russian Diplomatic Relations

Planning activity had continued on the assumption that the convoys to North Russia would continue to run during the spring and summer of 1943, up to the date of Operation HUSKY. It was, however, recognized that as the hours of daylight began to increase rapidly, the threat of surface, air and submarine attacks on convoys on the scale of those of the previous spring could reappear. In an attempt to counter this threat, the Admiralty and Air Ministry decided to send two squadrons of Hampden torpedo-bombers to North Russia as they had for PQ 18 to act as a torpedo strike force against enemy surface forces operating against JW and RA convoys. At the beginning of the negotiations on this planned deployment, it was explained to the Russians that the role of the force was as stated on 13 January, with the operational control arrangements the same as for Operation ORATOR[1] which appeared to have been satisfactory to the Russians at the time. The new operation was code-named GRENADINE.

The Russians at first agreed in principle and it was also proposed, subject to their agreement, to operate a reconnaissance force made up of Catalina and photo-reconnaissance aircraft from North Russia. An advance party of 12 officers, 12 NCOs and 110 airmen (with personal baggage only), would require passage in the escorts of JW 53.[2] The C-in-C Home Fleet was requested to inform the Admiralty when and where this party should report for embarkation. The main party of 20 officers, 33 NCOs and 382 airmen (with personal baggage only) would require passage in the escorts of JW 54 due to sail on 27 February.

Continuing Deterioration in Anglo-Russian Relations in the North Russian Ports

Meanwhile Anglo-Russian relations in the North Russian ports had become even more strained. On 14 February, the SBNO North Russia reported the introduction by the Russians of a local customs and passport procedure that was perceived as intended to humiliate the British and was considered a precursor of further humiliation to come, and also submitted a summary of other local procedures introduced by the Russian authorities. The SBNO requested an early signal stating the number of bags of ordinary mail and number of packages and weights of stores in the escorts of JW 53. Without this information he might have to return mail and stores to the UK. Official mail forwarded from the Admiralty to Scapa Flow was accompanied by visa waybills.

Errors and Misunderstandings

Not all the difficulties experienced by British service personnel in the North Russian ports were the result of Russian political, cultural or institutional differences. Although perceived by the chiefs of staff as a consequence of Russian intransigence, they arguably rather reflected degrees of error and misunderstandings in the way communications with the Russian authorities were managed.

The British viewed the Russians as difficult, uncooperative and obstructive, while the Russians for their part perceived the British as patronizing and prone to ignoring Russian sensitivities and procedures. There is evidence to suggest that the Royal Navy sought to operate in the North Russian ports as it did elsewhere around the world with less emphasis on consultation and compromise than expected by the Russians who regarded the behaviour of the Royal Navy as displaying a certain disregard for the host nation's own rules and regulations. All and any attempts by the Russians to impose regulations were perceived as negative and intended to humiliate. There is also evidence that the Royal Navy did not fully disclose the wider nature of its activities conducted from the North Russian ports; e.g. intelligence-gathering, which did nothing to counter Russian suspicions. All this was accompanied by an atmosphere of mutual paranoia.

In a number of cases the disagreements arose over incidents that owed more to cock-up than conspiracy. A typical example surrounds the confiscation of the Meaconing radio monitoring equipment (see below), which had been incorrectly consigned to the Russians, recovered by the British, and then confiscated by the Russians until the situation was resolved. There were also, as the Russians later made clear and the British admitted, deliberate attempts to bypass Russian procedures and regulations regarding mail and visas.

The Confiscation of Radio Monitoring Equipment

The SBNO reported that Russian customs officers had entered the Meaconing[3] Station on 20 February without contacting him and sealed up the transmitter pending receipt of the documentation that gave permission for it to be landed. Tests of the equipment had reached an advanced stage and it had been hoped to have the equipment in operation for the next convoy, but this would not now be achieved. The SBNO assumed that the Russians must have known such documents never existed and there had never been a requirement for any. There had, in fact, been a degree of administrative cock-up in the arrangements for dispatch of the equipment from the UK as we shall see later.

Russian Opposition to GRENADINE

The advance party for Operation GRENADINE was already on the way when, also on 20 February, the Soviet Naval Staff raised questions about the role and operational control of the GRENADINE force with the British Military Mission in Moscow. The Soviet Admiralty now stated that they could not accept an RAF force in North Russia that was not under Soviet operational control and that selected its own target objectives. The Russians claimed they had understood that operational control and selection of targets would be their responsibility, but had now been told operational control would be independently exercised by the RAF without their involvement.

The British Military Mission in Moscow was prepared to accept that this might either be a genuine misunderstanding or an attempt to evade an agreement now unattractive to the Russians, but it appeared almost certain to those RAF officers on the spot that if selection of targets was left to the Russians, the Hampdens would not be used exclusively against German surface forces as intended. They considered the Russians most unlikely to relinquish operational control, but on the question of role would probably be prepared to compromise if the OC Force was allowed discretion to accept Soviet-selected and suitable targets during non-convoy periods. The mission therefore requested further clarification of the role of the force and the system of operational control.[4]

The Air Ministry response to the mission two days later (on the 22nd)[5] made it clear that the role of the force was to protect Allied convoys en route to and from North Russia, with operational control exercised by Coastal Command through the local RAF commander who would coordinate his operations with those of the British surface forces. The force was neither organized nor supplied with materials or personnel for operations outside its designated role. It was certainly not intended to employ it during the non-convoy periods except in special circumstances. The whole object of the force was to ensure the safe arrival of ships carrying urgently required materials to Russia and accordingly its targets were likely to be limited to German surface craft and U-boats. The RAF also considered that they had far more experience than the Russians in operations of this kind and for this reason were unwilling to place the force under Russian operational control. Nevertheless, they were prepared to coordinate its activities with any operations that the Russians might consider as long as this could be done without prejudice to the main role of the force.

The head of the mission, Admiral Miles, later that day signalled the SBNO:

Owing to misunderstanding, which Russians allege has arisen over role and operational control of proposed RAF torpedo force, following ruling has now been obtained from Chiefs of Staff.

a. Role: to protect Allied convoys on route to and from Russia.
b. Operational control by Coastal Command through local RAF commander who has to coordinate his operations with those of British surface forces.

This ruling communicated to-day to Soviet Admiralty. In reply Russians said they would not accept any force for operation in Russia which was not under their operational control and they therefore refuse proposed fighter aircraft torpedo-bombers thus reversing their previous decision.

Latest Russian decision has been signalled to Chiefs of Staff and the next step rests with them. In the meanwhile RAF personnel and stores due to arrive in JW 53 must not be disembarked.

On the same day (the 22nd), the Soviet ambassador in London handed the Foreign Secretary a memorandum setting out the Russians' objections to the numbers of British service personnel deployed in North Russia, the context of which continued to enforce the current restrictions on the conditions for issue of visas.

The mission's reply to London on the following day[6] reported that the situation had been explained to the Russian Admiralty, whose DCNS[7] stated they could not accept any principle of non-Soviet control of any forces operating in Russia and therefore must refuse to accept the GRENADINE Force. When asked to explain the change in stance from Operation ORATOR, the DCNS stated he was only interested in organization and control of the proposed force. If the force was under Russian operational control the allotted tasks would be the protection of Allied convoys to and from Russia and attacks on German sea communications. The view from the mission was that the Russian decision would have to be regarded as final unless the argument for

Operation GRENADINE and Anglo-Russian Diplomatic Relations 117

operational control was conceded or if the Russians were told that the convoys would be stopped on the grounds that the Russian Air Force alone could not provide adequate protection. Further instructions were requested as the advance party and stores were due to arrive in the Kola Inlet in two days' time.

The exchange of telegrams between the chiefs of staff and No. 30 Military Mission Moscow on the role and operational control of the Hampden squadrons destined for North Russia was discussed in detail by the chiefs of staff at the Defence Committee (Operations) Meeting[8] on the evening of the 23rd[9] at which the First Lord of the Admiralty quoted various examples of the lack of cooperation and obstruction encountered from Russian officials over matters connected with the running of the Russian convoys (see also above). The committee then invited the Foreign Secretary to make representations to the Russian ambassador on the lines suggested by the Chief of the Air Staff and to instruct HM Ambassador in Moscow to make similar representations to Premier Stalin; the chiefs of staff would also submit a note to the Foreign Secretary quoting recent examples of Russian obstruction and lack of cooperation. There was also real concern that the Russians could not be relied on to deploy the planes against the German surface forces when required to do so, as when the Admiralty had called on them in January to attack the *Lützow* and the *Scheer* with the bombers remaining from the PQ 18 Force, the Russians had failed to respond. The Russian authorities in Murmansk had now closed down the special radio equipment used for interfering with enemy signals giving the position of Allied convoys (the Meaconing sets), and also insisted that two of the four wireless transmitters at Polyarny and three wireless transmitters at Archangel be closed down. All these actions were judged prejudicial to the safety and operational control of the convoys.

The chiefs of staff now made it clear that they were not prepared to tolerate these actions, which were perceived as 'another example of the unjustifiable suspicion, lack of co-operation and intolerable interference on the part of the Russians.'[10] The First Sea Lord and his colleagues were 'firmly in agreement the time had come for strong representations to the Russians about their general lack of co-operation and mistrust of or interference with actions taken for the sole purpose of assisting them.' The chiefs of staff had been exasperated with the Russians many times before, but this time the Cabinet supported them.

On the following day, 24 February, the Murmansk Customs Authority informed the SBNO that the trailer containing the Meacon equipment had arrived at Archangel marked DOLININ.[11] It had therefore appeared to be a legitimate aid shipment and been dealt with according to the regulations governing import of such goods consigned to the Russians. Before reaching its destination, however, it had somehow been handed over to the British mission.

As the British were unable to produce an import licence, the transmitter was to remain sealed until the position was clarified. The fact that the trailer was clearly marked DOLININ and not SBNO should have given the SBNO a clue that something was amiss.

The SBNO reported on the 24th that he had, at the request of the Russian chief of staff, now given orders that no transmission of any kind should take place from the Meaconing installation. He had been informed this order was to remain in force until permission had been received from the Russian War Office to commence operating. He was then to inform the local Russian naval staff.

The Ongoing GRENADINE Debate

The Soviet ambassador weighed into the debate on 24 February when he wrote to the Secretary of State for Foreign Affairs about the proposal to send a number of RAF squadrons to North Russia for the protection of convoys. Referring to their conversation of 15 February when the Foreign Secretary had asked him to assist in reaching agreement on Operation GRENADINE, M. Maisky reported that he had consulted Moscow and been told there were problems accommodating the number of personnel involved. The Soviet government therefore proposed cancellation of the operation but, recognizing that aerial protection of convoys was a matter of great importance, would take its own measures to secure the required protection. In order to facilitate this, the Russian government suggested that all the aeroplanes it was intended to send be transferred there without the personnel so these machines could be used by Soviet fliers as there was no shortage of their personnel.

The Secretary of State for Foreign Affairs circulated the note from M. Maisky to Cabinet members on the 24th. The note read:

SECRET.
24th February 1943.
My dear Foreign Secretary,

In our conversation of the 15th February you asked me to assist in getting a satisfactory settlement of the proposal to send to the North of the Soviet Union a certain British Aircraft Unit. Following your request I telegraphed to Moscow and have now received a reply. The Soviet Government once more carefully considered and investigated the possibilities of accommodating the number of personnel which the Air Ministry desires to send there. As a result of this second investigation the Soviet Government has come to the conclusion housing space at

Winston Churchill at his desk in the Cabinet Room at No. 10 Downing Street. (*IWM MH 26392*)

Roosevelt and Churchill on board HMS *Prince of Wales* at Argentia, August 1941. (*US Navy Historical Center, NH 67209*)

Stalin, Roosevelt and Churchill on the portico of the Russian Embassy during the Tehran Conference, 28 November to 1 December 1943. (*Library of Congress*)

Treaty of Alliance and Mutual Assistance between Britain and Soviet Russia signed at the Foreign Office on 26 May 1942 by M. Molotov on behalf of the Soviet Union and Mr Eden. (*IWM CH 5722*)

British Foreign Secretary Anthony Eden. (*IWM HU 49409*)

M. Molotov stepping out onto the terrace of No. 10 Downing Street with Mr Churchill and M. Maisky, the Soviet Ambassador, following behind, May 1942. (*IWM CH 5707*)

Churchill, Stalin and Harriman at the Moscow Conference, August 1942. (*National Museum of the U.S. Navy 24293784752*)

Dudley Pound and Winston Churchill aboard RMS *Queen Mary* in the United States, May 1943. (*IWM A 16717*)

Mr Harry Hopkins, President Roosevelt's special emissary. (*Library of Congress*)

HMS *Prince of Wales* at Placentia Bay, Newfoundland, August 1941. (*NH 67194A*)

Churchill in the uniform of the RAF with his Chiefs of Staff at the Anfa Villa, Casablanca, January 1943. Minister of Transport Lord Leathers can be seen standing, fourth from the right. (*IWM A 14132*)

President Roosevelt and Prime Minister Churchill at the Casablanca Conference. (*National Museum of the U.S. Navy, 80-G-38559*)

President Roosevelt signs the Lend-Lease Bill, March 1941. (*Library of Congress*)

USS *McDougal* (DD-358) alongside HMS *Prince of Wales* (53) in Placentia Bay, Newfoundland in August 1941. (*NH 67195*)

Winston Churchill, BBC broadcast. (*IWM H 41843*)

The Soviet Foreign Secretary V. Molotov. (*Dutch National Archives, The Hague*)

Lord Beaverbrook, Minister of Production. (*Dutch National Archives via Wikimedia Commons*)

British Ambassador to Moscow Sir Archibald Clark Kerr (fourth from left) shaking hands with General George C. Marshall, Chief of Staff, USA at the Tehran Conference. (*National Museum of the U.S. Navy, 24377421686*)

Prime Minister Churchill and President Roosevelt at the Casablanca Conference (*NARA*)

A.V. Alexander, First Lord of the Admiralty. (*IWM HU 59482*)

Admiral Ernest King, Commander-in-Chief (COMINCH) United States Fleet and Chief of Naval Operations (CNO). (*US Navy History and Heritage Command*)

Sir Stafford Cripps, British Ambassador in Moscow, 31 May 1940–January 1942. (*Dutch National Archives, The Hague*)

Soviet Ambassador to London Ivor Maisky. (*Mil.ru*)

Admiral of the Fleet Sir Andrew Browne Cunningham, October 1943-May 1946. (*Dutch National Archives via Wikimedia Commons*)

President Truman and Prime Minister Churchill meet for the first time. (*IWM BU 8944*)

Admiral Sir Dudley Pound, First Sea Lord June 1939 to September 1943.

British Chiefs of Staff in the garden of No. 10 Downing Street. Seated, left to right: Air Chief Marshal Sir Charles Portal; Field Marshal Sir Alan Brooke; the Rt Hon Winston Churchill; Admiral Sir Andrew Cunningham. Standing, left to right: the Secretary to the Chiefs of Staffs Committee, Major General L.C. Hollis; and the Chief of Staff to the Minister of Defence, General Sir Hastings Ismay. (*IWM TR 2842*)

Rear Admiral Douglas Fisher on HMS *Duke of York*, 1942. (*IWM A 12142*)

C-in-C Home Fleet Sir Bruce Fraser, May 1943–June 1944. (*IWM A 16489*)

Sir Henry Moore, First Sea Lord and Chief of the Naval Staff, 14 June 1944–24 November 1945. (*IWM A 25908*)

King George VI and Admiral Tovey.

A *Führer* conference. (*KBismarck.com*)

German Grand Admiral Erich Raeder. (*Bundesarchiv*)

German Grand Admiral Karl Dönitz. (*Bundesarchiv*)

SS *Waziristan*, the first merchant ship sunk en route to North Russia.

A Luftwaffe Heinkel He 111 KG26 armed with torpedoes, Norway 1942. (*asisbiz.com*)

HMS *Sheffield* under way. (*IWM FL 1938*)

An RAF Hampden bomber.

The battleship *Tirpitz* in Altafjord. (*NH 71390*)

KMS *Scharnhorst*. (*asisbiz.com*)

Damage sustained by HMS *Onslow* during the Battle of the Barents Sea. (*AD 14340*)

HMS *Edinburgh* at Scapa Flow. (*IWM A 6159*)

HMS *Trinidad* at Hvalfjördur, Iceland, 1942. (*IWM A 7683*)

HMS *Matabele*, the first Royal Navy warship lost on a convoy to North Russia. (*IWM A 6459*)

SS *El Almirante* – the first American ship to sail to North Russia. (*US Department of Transportation, Maritime Administration*)

HMT *Empress of Australia*. (*IWM A 37049*)

Hurricanes of 151 Squadron RAF at Vaenga, Murmansk, September 1941. (*IWM CR 38*)

Winston Churchill with British and Soviet representatives including Anthony Eden and Vyacheslav Molotov in London following the signing of the Anglo-Soviet Treaty on 26 May 1942. (*IWM CH 5712*)

Agreement between His Majesty's Government in the United Kingdom and the Government of the Union of Soviet Socialist Republics providing for Joint Action in the War against Germany, signed in Moscow on 12 July 1941 by Soviet Foreign Secretary V. Molotov and British Ambassador Sir Stafford Cripps.

the points mentioned is so limited it would be difficult to accommodate there the number of people which the Air Ministry wished, and even to house the number at first indicated to me by Sir Archibald Sinclair. The housing conditions of late have not improved, but, on the contrary, have worsened as a result of enemy action.

In these circumstances the Soviet Government believes it would perhaps be more prudent to cancel altogether the sending of the Air Force Unit in question to the North of the USSR. As, however, aerial protection of convoys is a matter of great importance the Soviet Government will take its own measures to secure the required protection.

This task would be greatly facilitated if the British Government would consent to send to the North of the USSR all the aeroplanes which it was intended should be transferred there, but without the personnel, so these machines can be used by Soviet fliers, as we have now no shortage of personnel.

If this suggestion is agreeable to the British Government the Soviet Government would be very grateful if it could be carried into effect.

Yours sincerely,
J. MAISKY.

The Soviet ambassador's note was discussed by the War Cabinet the following day.[12] In summarizing the situation, the Secretary of State for Foreign Affairs observed that the Russians had accepted the original plan, which involved sending 400 to 500 RAF personnel to operate these squadrons. Subsequently the Air Ministry had decided that larger numbers would be required, and it was at this point the Russians had raised difficulties. He had then explained the position fully to M. Maisky, who had previously promised to do what he could to help but had suggested, in view of the difficulties of finding accommodation for the personnel, that the proposal to send the RAF squadrons should be abandoned, the air protection of convoys should be undertaken by the Soviet Air Force and the aircraft should be handed over to the Soviet government to operate themselves in North Russia.

The Secretary of State advised that he intended to see M. Maisky again and tell him firmly His Majesty's government could not entertain this proposal. He would explain the difficulties of operating this air protection of convoys and show, because of the technical problems, the need for close cooperation with the British naval authorities etc. as it would be quite impossible for the Russians to operate these aircraft on their own. He would give a full statement of all the losses incurred up to date in the convoys and emphasize, as British ships and the lives of British sailors were at stake, that Britain must retain responsibility for their protection. He would end by pressing his request for the grant of the necessary facilities for sending these squadrons to North Russia and would say, if these were withheld, that the whole question of continuing the convoys would have to be reviewed.

There would be no opportunity of ascertaining in advance how far the United States government would support these representations, but he would explain to the US Chargé d'Affaires the line he was proposing to take. The War Cabinet then invited the Secretary of State for Foreign Affairs to make strong representations to the Soviet ambassador on the lines he had indicated.

The Foreign Secretary also briefed the British ambassador in Moscow on 26 February. The telegram[13] read:

> In the Soviet Ambassador's communication of 24th February he informed me the Soviet Government now suggest the agreed proposal for the dispatch of British squadrons to North Russia to provide Air protection for convoys should be cancelled and the Soviet Government should itself provide the required Air protection. The Soviet Government suggests the British aircraft involved should be transferred. The Soviet Government further suggests the British aircraft involved should be transferred to North Russia without the British personnel. This suggestion is based upon a lack of accommodation for the personnel.
>
> The Air protection of convoys depends upon a complicated procedure and requires considerable training and experience. A complete understanding between the naval and air forces involved is essential. The Soviet air personnel have no experience of British procedure concerning enemy sighting reports, communication procedures. Direct communication between aircraft and naval escorts is of course an essential part of the convoy escort procedures. Apart from the language difficulties it would take many months for British and Soviet personnel to attain a satisfactory standard of mutual co-operation in their immediate... of operation. For these reasons the suggestion the Soviet forces could provide the necessary protection or the Soviet authorities should exercise operational control of the British air squadrons sent to North Russia is clearly impractical.
>
> In these circumstances the additional Air protection, which is essential for the safety of the convoys, must be provided by British aircraft under British operational control if it is to be of any real use. The Soviet Ambassador has also intimated the number of British Personnel proposed to be sent is in the Soviet Government's view excessive. His Majesty's Government cannot agree the efficient protection of the convoys should

Operation GRENADINE and Anglo-Russian Diplomatic Relations

be impeded by attempts to operate the squadrons with fewer men than experience has proved essential. It is true a smaller number was sent to North Russia last year but this force was only designed to cover a single convoy. The present proposal is to cover a period of five to six months.

His Majesty's Government finds it impossible to believe the Soviet Authorities are unable to provide accommodation for 760 officers and men in all. They feel confident on consideration of the arguments, which in their view are unanswerable, the Soviet government will withdraw their proposals and give their final agreement to the British proposals for the operation of the British air squadrons in North Russia under British operational command as originally agreed.

In addition his Majesty's Government must draw attention to the fact that the Soviet authorities are taking certain measures which must seriously jeopardise the safe passage of the convoys.

For example, the Soviet authorities have sealed up, and prevented the operation of, the Meaconing Set, the purpose of which is to interfere with the signals of the enemy aircraft shadowing the convoy, and thus prevent the attacking force reaching them. The Soviet authorities have done this on the grounds that certain permits for the introduction of the set into the Soviet Union have not been obtained. The set has been under trial for a considerable period and it is particularly important that it should be used for the current convoy. It is at this moment that the Soviet authorities on purely technical grounds choose to prevent the use of the set in the joint Anglo-Soviet interests. His Majesty's Government requests that this set should be immediately released for use in order that it may be available for the convoy which should be reaching North Russia within a few days.

A still more serious interference with arrangements for operation of the convoy is, however, the Soviet order that two out of four W/T transmitters at Polyarny and up to three transmitters at Archangel are to be closed down on the technical ground that no official permission for their operation has been obtained from Moscow. The facts are that these sets have been in use many months and that the Soviet civil authorities have been fully informed in regard to their installation. The loss of the W/T transmitters would involve:

(a) A most serious loss in intelligence derived from enemy wireless. A large amount of enemy W/T traffic is intercepted at Polyarny both by British and Soviet stations and retransmitted to the British Naval Authorities in the United Kingdom. This will either have to

cease or be greatly diminished. Moreover direction-finding bearings will be received if at all too late to have any value for immediate operational purposes.
(b) Various difficulties in maintaining routine communications between the British Naval authorities in the United Kingdom and North Russia and between British warships protecting convoys and the British Naval authorities in North Russia. This would have a crippling effect on the whole of our communications connected with the routing and protection of the convoys.
(c) A reduction in the number of transmitters requested by the Soviet authorities would also most seriously interfere with communication with the British Ministry of War Transport on the subject of the administration of the convoys.

It is therefore essential that the full number of transmitters at present at Polyarny and Archangel should be allowed to continue in use. His Majesty's Government requests that immediate instructions to this effect may be given to the Soviet authorities concerned.

Additional transmitters are now on passage to North Russia for communication between the bases from which the Royal Air Force aircraft will operate and between the bases and the aircraft themselves. These additional transmitters will be essential for the operation of the squadrons and it is requested that no impediment be put in the way of their installation and operation.

The Soviet Government have, moreover, in recent weeks introduced a series of vexatious formalities in connection with the landing and examination of British Government stores and official mail intended for the use of the British Naval and Ministry of War Transport personnel at North Russian ports, and members of other British Missions in the USSR. Similar vexatious formalities restricting the day-to-day movements from ship to shore and vice versa of British personnel have also been introduced. These formalities seriously interfere with the speedy and efficient execution by the British personnel in question of the work assigned to them in the organisation of the convoy system. Such restrictions would not be imposed in the case of Soviet stores or personnel landing in the United Kingdom. Moreover, additional difficulties have been created by the action of the Soviet authorities in restricting the issue of Soviet visas to personnel whom the British authorities consider to be essential in North Russia for the efficient execution of the duties which have to be performed in connection with the operation of the convoy system.

His Majesty's Government, who are responsible for the running and escorting of the convoys carrying supplies to North Russia for the Soviet Forces, consider it essential that their proposals in regard to the operation of British Air Squadrons in North Russia should be accepted by the Soviet Government in their entirety and that no further difficulties should be created by the Soviet authorities concerned in respect of the other matters mentioned.

Continuing Restrictions on British Service Personnel in North Russia

The realities from a British perspective of these Russian obstructions were well detailed in the SBNO North Russia's Monthly Report dated 26 February in which he complained of the continued refusal of the Russians to grant visas for certain personnel and to allow the hospital unit to be set up in Archangel. The delays in obtaining visas coupled with the delay in providing reliefs for ratings sent home was resulting in a shortage of interpreters, signalmen and W/T operators, with those remaining in Archangel having to work double shifts. To make matters worse, the restrictions were only being applied to Royal Navy personnel as Royal Air Force personnel were allowed free movement with no passports, visas or other restrictions.[14] Ironically this applied in particular to the RAF officers and men who had recently arrived at Grasnaya as an advance party to the 500 RAF officers and men being sent out in connection with the Hampden and Catalina squadrons (GRENADINE). It was unclear why the Royal Navy was being treated in one way and the Royal Air Force another, particularly when the RN party was working shorthanded.[15]

The SBNO also forwarded the translation of a letter dated 21 February from the Chief of Staff, Northern Fleet, which contained further allegations relating to non-compliance with local procedures. The SBNO regarded these allegations as mostly untrue and in other cases explainable, while it was only in the last few days that the full force of the customs regulations had been notified. Although these regulations might conceivably have been in existence before this, they were certainly never brought to his notice and included restrictions on ships and boats proceeding alongside British merchant ships in the Kola Inlet. These incidents formed a pattern from which it was evident that a change of policy towards the British had been initiated – it was thought dictated from a high level – in which the local Russian naval commander-in-chief and his chief of staff had played little if any part. All of this again highlights the deficiencies in communication and consultation.

Another report from the SBNO on 28 February cited further instances of the difficulties being experienced with Russian customs and the handling of mail. The outgoing personnel draft had been searched by customs and their luggage turned inside out with particular interest shown in carefully packed items. Private letters had been examined page by page. The export of all English as well as Russian money had been forbidden. Although incoming official mail had been cleared satisfactorily, private mail was being held on board HM ships for safe custody. As a special concession to avoid it going to Moscow, the Russians had said they would allow it to be dealt with in the local Post Office; i.e. letters opened and examined. Although this was possibly reasonable under other circumstances, the SBNO did not intend to allow the Russians to get their hands on it in view of their general attitude. So far as outgoing mail was concerned a representative of the NKVD Murmansk would probably visa official mail, but there was no prospect of clearing private mail except through Russian hands, which the SBNO did not intend doing.

GRENADINE Again

The GRENADINE affair was next discussed in the War Cabinet on Monday, 1 March[16] when the Secretary of State for Foreign Affairs confirmed that, following the decision on 25 February, strong representations had been made to the Russian ambassador the next day regarding the objections raised by the Russian authorities. The ambassador in Moscow had also been instructed to make similar representations to the Soviet government, but to date there had been no response. The First Lord of the Admiralty added that to make matters worse the Russian authorities had now confiscated the radio equipment essential for operational purposes connected with convoy protection.[17] The following day the SBNO reported that the advance party of the air personnel intended to operate the torpedo strike force in North Russia for the protection of JW and RA convoys had been refused permission to land from JW 53 by the Russian authorities and was to return in cruisers to the UK (the *Cumberland* and *Norfolk* sailed on 2 March).

On the 4th the British ambassador informed[18] the Foreign Office that M. Molotov had given him his answer that night which adhered to the Soviet standpoint regarding dispatch of the British air squadrons. The Soviet government had, however, issued instructions to re-examine the question of the Meaconing sets in a way that suggested this difficulty could be resolved provided the working of the equipment was coordinated with the Soviet naval authorities, but there appeared to be room for agreement about the wireless transmitter. On the question of vexatious formalities, the Soviet response sought more detailed information, which the ambassador would endeavour to supply. As to the mail, after grumbling about breaches of regulations, the

Soviets insisted that the regulations should be observed but suggested that mutual concessions might be made.

On the same day the Assistant Chief of the Naval Staff (Home) (ACNS (H)) saw the head of the Soviet Military Mission in London and reported the outcome of their discussion to the Head of the Military Mission in Moscow and the SBNO by signal the following day. The message read:

> During a visit from Admiral Kharlamov[19] yesterday A.C.N.S. (H) explained the situation concerning the North Russian convoys stating it as representing his personal view. Admiral Kharlamov was told the difficulties placed in the way of our running the convoys were intolerable, and would, unless removed, lead to sabotaging the convoys. He took this very seriously and asked for details when the various items from the Hospital Unit to GRENADINE were outlined to him. It was made clear to the Admiral the mere removal of the particular restrictions was not enough but there must be a change of atmosphere to one of real cooperation and confidence in North Russia. He was asked to make it clear to the Russian authorities concerned not only were the restrictions quite unacceptable but all our needs were perfectly normal operational requirements for the security of the convoys and agreed to do what he could to help.

Also on 4 March, the head of mission informed the Air Ministry that the Soviet government's formal reply to the British memorandum on GRENADINE had now been received and passed by signal from the embassy to the Foreign Office. The reply, of considerable length, repeated the refusal to accept the GRENADINE Force, the principal points made being lack of accommodation in North Russia for GRENADINE personnel and the Soviet claim to have ample experience in convoy protection. The reply also claimed a sufficient force for convoy protection would be provided by the Russians, which would be improved if the GRENADINE aircraft were handed over without crews and went on to claim that it would be difficult to arrange cooperation between British-manned torpedo-bombers and Russian fighters.

The British ambassador in Moscow forwarded the translation of the extremely lengthy Russian response of 4 March to the British memorandum of 26 February to the Foreign Office the following day:

> The Soviet Government having acquainted themselves with the memorandum of the British Government of February 26th 1943, and having carefully studied the questions raised therein, consider it necessary to make the following communication.

2. The Soviet Government have already informed the British Government owing to the exceptionally great difficulties in finding accommodation for British airmen in Murmansk area, the bombing of which is still continuing, they consider it inexpedient to send a British air force into this area, the more so since the Soviet Government are prepared to ensure the air protection of the convoys by the air force at their disposal. The Soviet Government consider it necessary to re-affirm this statement without entering into polemics on the subject in a tome, which would be out of accord with our common interests.

As regards the statement made in the British memorandum about the necessity of ensuring complete co-ordination between Naval and air forces participating in the operation, this problem has been successfully solved up to now and it suggests can be adequately ensured in future. It cannot be denied the Soviet Air Force possesses great experience in operations for the protection of British naval convoys, and all the appropriate technical questions, (method of presenting reports on discovery of the enemy, communications, etc.) can be satisfied by the appropriate Soviet military authorities jointly with British representatives. Moreover this British Air Force is intended to operate from Soviet territory and to carry out flights primarily within the Soviet Zone. Consequently this group of British aircraft would, in the first place, have found it necessary to co-ordinate its operations particularly with the Soviet system of anti-aircraft defence and with any Soviet ships and submarines which might happen to be within its sphere of operations. It is obvious also operations of this air group would to a certain extent have required cover from the Soviet fighter aircraft with which it would have been necessary to co-operate, and with which the operations of the British aircraft would have had to be co-ordinated as closely as possible; this problem can certainly be more successfully solved if all the aircraft are manned by Soviet aviators. Naturally, if the British government should find it possible to place at the disposal of the Soviet naval command, which at present has no shortage of aviators, aircraft for this purpose without British flying personnel, the question of defending convoys would be settled still more successfully.

The Soviet Government cannot agree with the statement made in the memorandum to the effect the Soviet authorities are adopting certain measures which must create a serious threat to the safe passage of convoys. On the contrary, the Soviet authorities have adopted and are adopting all possible measures to facilitate the safe passage of convoys into the Northern ports of the USSR.

As regards the sealing of the Meaconing set, it has been established this set, which arrived at the beginning of last summer and has not since been used, was imported into the USSR in violation of Soviet customs rules, in accordance with which the Chief of Murmansk customs drew up an appropriate regulation on February 11th last, which was officially brought to the attention of the British representatives. A warning must be given the Soviet authorities are unable to overlook cases in which the appropriate customs regulations are violated. Nevertheless, being prepared to meet the wireless wishes of the British Government halfway and in order to successfully protect convoys, the Soviet Government have issued instructions this position should be re-examined and the representatives of the British naval authorities should be granted permission to use the Meaconing set on condition its work is co-ordinated with the Soviet naval authorities in the North.

As regards British wireless transmissions in Soviet northern ports the following has been established:

In response to an entreaty of representative of British Naval Mission, Commander Courtney, permission was given by the Soviet Naval Authorities on March 7 1942 to establish 8 British wireless transmitters at Murmansk, Polyarny and Archangel. At the same time, precise limits were set for the capacity of each transmitter. However, since that time, the British Naval Mission has, without obtaining the agreement of the Soviet authorities, increased the capacity of their radio transmitters and, in certain cases, has in fact increased the stipulated capacity several times. In this connection the People's Commissariat of Naval Intelligence instructed the appropriate Authorities on February 22nd last to request the representatives of the British Naval Mission in the north to reduce the capacity of the naval wireless transmitters; i.e. to bring them into line with the stipulated capacity but they have not yet issued any order to close down these wireless transmitters. At the same time, it was pointed out should the British representatives consider it necessary to increase the capacity of their wireless transmitters, it would be necessary for them to apply to the Soviet Naval command for the necessary permission. The Soviet Government consider it necessary to inform the British government the orders of the Soviet Naval authorities on this question result from regulations operating in the Soviet Union, by which not a single foreign broadcasting station may be opened on the territory of the USSR without special permission from the appropriate authorities.

The Soviet Government have taken into consideration the request of the British Government and have given instructions to the effect the desire of the British Naval mission for some increase in capacity of the registered British wireless transmitters which are necessary for operating system of convoys should as far as possible be taken into account by the Soviet naval authorities.

3. As regards certain vexatious formalities referred to in the memorandum concerning the procedure for going on shore, checking British Government stores, mails, etc., it is not clear to the Soviet Government which formalities are referred to. If any concrete facts are communicated on these subjects which confirm the existence of any restrictive formalities, the Soviet Government are prepared to issue instructions for their repeal or possibly for their alteration within the limits of the current regulations. Inasmuch as the British Memorandum also mentions formalities relating to check of official and ordinary mail arriving at and leaving the northern ports, the Soviet Government would like to draw the attention of the British government to the following cases of violations committed by British personnel in this matter. In August 1942 twenty-two packages of mail were brought into the USSR on British ship *Bramble*; on August 26th, twenty-three packages of mail on ship *L-50*; and on November 18th seventy packages of mail, all without the necessary permission of the Soviet authorities. All these are violations of Soviet regulations and were notified at the time to the British Embassy and in individual cases in order to meet the request of the Embassy halfway, exceptions were made in the form of free admission of British mail arriving without documents. On these questions the Peoples' Commissariat for Foreign Affairs sent several letters to the British Embassy, August 31, September 7th, December 8th and 19th last. Therefore the Soviet government are entitled to expect the British Government will give the necessary instruction to the appropriate British authorities to observe the existing regulations of the USSR on this subject and not to violate them.

The Soviet government considers the practice of collaboration and joint work between the Soviet and British military authorities separate and reciprocal concessions, exceptions, etc. are undesirable and avoidable for both parties whether this relates to primary questions, the receipt or despatch of mails, customs regulations and so on. However, the Soviet Government consider in this matter each government should act on the principle of its citizens, including the representatives of the military authorities, respecting and strictly observing the current regulations and procedure in the other country.

Churchill's Reaction

Churchill appears to have been less than impressed by the Russian response, and in fact was at first moved to suspend the convoy programme altogether as on receipt of the official Soviet response he penned on 5 March a draft riposte to Stalin. Circulated to the chiefs of staff and others for comment, this read as follows:

> FROM PRIME TO PRESIDENT STALIN
> 1. I frankly do not understand at all the reasons in which lie the decisions of the Soviet Government about the arrangements for the Arctic convoys; however, it is my duty as an ally to try to meet your wishes to the best of our abilities and without casting away imprudently His Majesty's ships and resources. I therefore propose for your consideration the following.
> 2. We cannot of course send the convoy of 34 ships prepared for March 25, as there will be no satisfactory air arrangements to cover its arrival at your end and there is no use in having the convoy scattered and sunk. Final orders to this effect will have to be given by 7 March. Meanwhile a number of ships are already moving to their unloading ports.
> 3. I propose that the Soviet Government should undertake the task of importing by the Northern Route the articles agreed in the Protocol. The Protocol expressly relieves us of any responsibility other than delivery of the goods at British or American ports, but Icelandic ports could certainly be included. We shall hold the goods therefore at your disposal as soon as you fetch them and leave to you the task of bringing them safely in, which I earnestly trust you will be able to accomplish.
> 4. Although our shipping stringency is of the most acute order, we will turn over to the Russian flag ten British ships, to be manned by Soviet crews at any port you wish in Great Britain, the United States or Iceland. I daresay the United States will do the same, but for them I cannot speak.
> 5. The Royal Navy will offer protection against the German Fleet to any convoy you may send in all the region west of Iceland, provided the necessary arrangements are made between the Naval Officers concerned.
> 6. We will hand over to you all our plant, Meaconing sets and Hudson aircraft at present in Russia, and recall all personnel immediately.
> 7. I regret very much that we are not able to get this March convoy through to you as it will not be possible to resume after we become involved in HUSKY, even if you should desire it.

8. I am studying very carefully all means of increasing the flow of supplies through the Persian Gulf and should the Mediterranean be opened this summer this route should become much shorter. With regard to Red Cross Supplies to Russia for which £21/2 millions have been subscribed by the British nation, some of these will be sent in the flotilla of destroyers which will go to fetch back our personnel and efforts will be made to send the rest in by the south.
9. Your Excellency will realise that these grave changes in our arrangements and intercourse will hardly escape Parliamentary discussion and that we shall have to give in Public Session our account of the reasons why the present changes have had to be made.

W.S.C. 5.3.

GRENADINE Misunderstandings, Excuses and Blame

The chiefs of staff considered Churchill's draft telegram to Stalin at their meeting on the morning of the 5th. Sir Orme Sargent and Mr Warner of the Foreign Office were present and expressed agreement with the recommendations made by the chiefs of staff, who advised Churchill that any message to Premier Stalin relating to the undertaking should come jointly from Churchill and the president since the United States and Great Britain had a joint undertaking to send supplies to Russia. The minute went on:

3. It was never intended that the March convoy should have air protection, since the weather in northern waters is unsuitable at that time for air operations. It is therefore thought that our case would be stronger and more logical if we were to allow the March convoy to proceed as originally arranged and to reserve our threats for all subsequent convoys.
4. If you decide to accept the above recommendation, the convoy will have to leave not later than 25th March. If it is delayed beyond that date, it will be impossible to get the escorts back in time for the convoy which is to leave early in May, and if the convoy does not leave in early May, it will not be able to sail at all since it will run into HUSKY. Consequently if the March convoy is to sail, orders to that effect must be given at once.
5. In this connection, the Chiefs of Staff were informed that instructions were given to the Minister of Transport some days ago that loading of the March convoy was to cease, and that the cessation of loading had

become known to the Russians in this country who had immediately run around to the Admiralty and the Foreign Office to ask the reason. If you should now desire loading to be recommenced, it is important that the Russians should not be given the impression that this reversal of orders is due to any weakness on our part. The explanation that might be furnished is that the latest Telegram from our ambassador in Moscow shows a tendency on the part of the Russians to be more accommodating in the matter of the Meaconing Set, and it had therefore been decided to continue loading in the hope this essential adjunct to the convoy will be permitted to function effectively.

6. The Chiefs of Staff invite attention to the following points of detail in your draft Telegram:
   (a) Reference Paragraph 2, Line 1: The March convoy consists of 30, not 34 ships.
   (b) Reference Paragraph 3: It is not quite correct to say that the Protocol expressly relieves us of any responsibility other than the delivery of goods at British or American ports ...

The above represents the position on the Protocol of October 1st 1941; but in the Second Protocol, which covers the period July 1942 to June 1943, we and the United States have jointly undertaken to supply the shipping necessary to lift that part of this programme for which USSR ships cannot be made available.

   (c) Reference Paragraph 5, Line 2: There are now no Hudson aircraft in North Russia.
   (d) Reference Paragraph 6, Line 1: The first echelon of personnel for the Hampden squadrons did not disembark owing to Russian intransigence, and are already on the way back. An advance air party of four officers are the only personnel we have in Russia at the moment working in connection with the convoys. In addition there are certain signals personnel there working for No. 30 Mission.
   (e) Reference Paragraph 7: I can find no trace of Premier Stalin having been told that there will be no convoys to North Russia while HUSKY is in progress. Mr Orme Sargent doubted whether this Telegram provided a suitable occasion to break this news to him.

7. Neither the Chiefs of Staff nor Sir Orme Sargent have yet had an opportunity of seeing this minute. I am fairly sure, however, that

it represents their agreed view in all essentials, and in view of the urgency of the matter, I thought it best to submit it to you at once. Any amendments desired by the Chiefs of Staff will be notified at once.
8. I have sent a copy of the Minute to the Foreign Secretary.
Signed ISMAY 5 MARCH 1943

General Ismay copied Churchill's telegram and the chiefs of staff initial advice to the Minister of War Transport. In the covering minute he wrote:

As a result of a Telegram from our Ambassador in Moscow saying that the Russians were refusing to have our two squadrons of Hamdens [sic] stationed in North Russia, Churchill drafted a Telegram to Stalin (ANNEX I) for consideration by the Chiefs Of Staff in consultation with the Foreign Office.

2. My Minute to Churchill (ANNEX II) shows the conclusions reached.
3. Churchill has telephoned me that he was not aware that air protection had not been contemplated for the March convoy, and therefore that he would almost certainly[20] give the orders for this convoy to sail as arranged.
4. I have telephoned Sir Cyril Hurcomb[21] the full story, and asked him to pass it on to you.
5. This letter is in confirmation, and leaves by special messenger.

H.L. Ismay 5 March 1943

By now it had become clear that there had been something of a misunderstanding over the timing of GRENADINE and the line being proposed by Churchill seemed something of an overreaction.

Churchill, in a personal minute of 6 March to the COS Committee, Foreign Office and Ministry of War Transport, demanded to know:

1. Who was it who moved the Foreign Office on the basis the March convoy could not sail without air protection? The Chiefs of Staff approved the memorandum was sent to the Russians. When was it realised by the Chiefs of Staff the air squadrons were not needed in any case for the March convoy but only for sailing in May? I certainly wish I had known this before and we ought to have known it.
2. In these circumstances, now known for the first time, the March convoy should go of course as 30 ships. There is no need to offer any

Operation GRENADINE and Anglo-Russian Diplomatic Relations 133

explanation to the Russians. I have so instructed the Minister of War Transport over the telephone. But this should be officially confirmed.
3. Meanwhile there is plenty of time to redraft the message to Premier Stalin and arrange it with the United States. My draft Telegram, which was written under the misapprehension referred to in Para 1, is to be cancelled and returned.
4. What are the proposals in any case for convoys after the one for May 2? What is the position the Chiefs of Staff adopt about the safety of sending the May 2 convoy without the Hampden aircraft?

W.S.C. 5/3/43

The chiefs of staff submitted a further minute to Churchill on 6 March in response to his questions of the 5th, which read:

1. The general position is briefly as follows:
   (i) The object of stationing British aircraft in North Russia is to protect our convoys from attack by German surface ships in waters where they cannot be afforded full protection by our own surface ships.
   (ii) It would have been desirable to have our own aircraft in place in time to protect the March convoy but it was realised it was likely weather conditions would prevent their flying in North Russia; and even if they did manage to get there it was unlikely weather conditions would probably prohibit or at least drastically limit their employment in protection of the convoy.
   (iii) The position in regard to the end May convoy is very different owing to the change in weather and climate. The Naval and Air staffs have always considered it would be very wrong to forgo the insurance provided by British aircraft in North Russia if it can be possibly avoided. They adhere to this view.
   (iv) Consequently all arrangements were made on the basis the early May convoy would be the first, in order of time, to be given British air protection.
2. With reference to the specific questions in Para 1 of your minute:
   (i) The Foreign Office was not asked to move on the basis the March convoy would not sail without air protection. None of the Service Departments were notified until yesterday orders had been given to unload the ships; and it was not until your draft

Telegram was received the Services were aware of any intention to stop the March convoy.

(ii) The Memorandum to which you refer dealt only with the general principles which govern air protection for convoys, no dates are mentioned. This Memorandum was never referred to the Chiefs of Staff as such, but the Chief of the Air Staff was present at the Cabinet Meeting at which it was approved.

(iii) The First Sea Lord and Chief of Air Staff have never contemplated the provision of air cover for the March convoy, but when they were considering your draft Telegram at the Meeting yesterday, they found it necessary to inquire further into all the details of the arrangements in order to confirm air protection could not in fact be made available.

3. Reference your paragraph 2, your decision has been promulgated to all concerned.
4. Reference your paragraph 3, it is submitted arrangements as regards future convoys, i.e. from early May onwards, should be concerted with the United States as soon as possible.
5. With reference to your paragraph 4, the Chiefs of Staff think it would be wrong to allow the May convoy to sail without taking out every possible insurance for its safety. They recommend if the Russian Authorities refuse to withdraw their objections to the presence of British Air Squadrons, they should be warned it may be necessary to stop the May convoy depending on the strength of the enemy surface forces in Northern Waters at the time. It is one thing to take a risk when it is unavoidable, but it is quite unnecessary to accept a risk that is wholly unnecessary.
6. Orders have been issued that the March convoy is to sail, but there are certain questions of detail requiring urgent decision. Lord Leathers has stated he must have an answer today to the two following questions:
   (i) Are the ships now lying at Murmansk, which contain the stores for GRENADINE to be off-loaded, or are they to return to this country with the stores still on board?

Two days later Churchill declared: 'Off loaded. We must hope for a favourable outcome.' Initialled W.S.C. 7/3.

A further note sent by the Chiefs of Staff Secretariat to the Ministry of War Transport's Private Secretary on 7 March confirmed:

In confirmation of my telephone message about Russian convoys, Churchill has approved the Recommendations in paragraphs 7 and 8 of General Ismay's Minute to Churchill dated 6th March (a copy of which was sent to you last night); i.e. that:

(i) The stores for GRENADINE in the ships at Murmansk are to be unloaded,

(ii) The stores and material for GRENADINE now in ships ready to proceed in the next convoy are <u>not</u> to be unloaded and the ships can move to their ports of departure.

Churchill wrote again to the Foreign Secretary on 7 March[22] about GRENADINE. In his minute copied to the chiefs of staff committee for action as required he said:

> I was ill during the early part of this business[23] but I certainly sustained the impression from you and other sources the Chiefs of Staff took the gravest view about the March convoy sailing without the protection of Hampden squadrons. It now appears they could never have got there in time. Thus we were all under a misapprehension. Perhaps you will comment on the statements made in Para 2. No final decision to stop the March convoy was taken but Lord Leathers was directed by me to convey this impression to the Russians with a view to procuring from them a more satisfactory answer on the points at issue. This was a bluff, affecting for a week or so only four or five ships, which probably should not have been persisted in, certainly not without consulting the Cabinet and the United States.
>
> We must hope for the best. The stores for GRENADINE should be unloaded at Murmansk and the ships loaded with material for GRENADINE should not be unloaded but proceed at once to their points of departure.
>
> About the May convoy, the Chiefs of the Staff will have to make up their minds whether the absence of the additional insurance of the Hampden aircraft would be sufficient reason for the very great step of stopping the convoy. I must also know within a week or so what plans are proposed for subsequent convoys. Until we know what are the Admiralty proposals we cannot take any decision either on the merits or as to how the news if adverse should be broken to the Russian government.

The Secretary of State for Foreign Affairs[24] informed the War Cabinet on 8 March that no solution had yet been reached on the difficulties the Russian authorities were making about the proposal to send RAF squadrons to North Russia but approval had, however, now been granted for the operation of the radio equipment that had previously been confiscated.

The Russian Problem

The chiefs of staff discussed the Russian problems at their meeting on 9 March.[25] The first topic under Item 9 was the response to the minute from Churchill on the Soviet memorandum handed to the British ambassador in Moscow. The minute read:

> GENERAL ISMAY
> WHAT do C.O.S. Committee say?
> (Intd.) W.S.C.
> 7/3

It was suggested that the naval and air staffs examine this telegram, and that Rear Admiral Brind and Air Vice Marshal Bottomley in consultation should be asked to prepare a draft reply to Churchill's enquiry. The committee therefore invited ACNS (H) and ACAS (Ops) to examine the Soviet memorandum and prepare a draft commentary on it for submission to Churchill.

The second topic raised under Item 11 was Operation GRENADINE. The committee had before them a minute from Churchill to the Secretary of State for Foreign Affairs, in Paragraph 3 of which Churchill asked whether the chiefs of staff considered the absence of the Hampden aircraft would be sufficient reason for stopping the May convoy to Russia.

Sir Dudley Pound said that naval opinion considered dispatch of the convoy would depend primarily on the disposition of the German naval forces at the time. If these should be concentrated in great strength with the object of intercepting the convoy, even the presence of the Hampden squadrons in North Russia would not provide protection on the scale required and the convoy should not be dispatched. He considered it right, however, to continue in the meantime with preparations for sailing the convoy.

In these circumstances it was generally agreed that although the acceptance of the Hampdens by the Russians would not guarantee the sailing of the convoy, the additional insurance provided by their presence in North Russia would be sufficiently important to justify taking a strong line with the Russians and insisting that they should accept the squadrons on British terms before agreement to dispatch of the convoy. It was pointed out that cancellation of the convoy would not result in a decrease in total war effort, as the escorts and

Operation GRENADINE and Anglo-Russian Diplomatic Relations   137

materials released were urgently required elsewhere for use against the enemy. The committee then invited Lieutenant General Ismay to circulate for their consideration a draft reply to Churchill, prepared in light of the discussion.

Some Relaxation of Russian Restrictions

The SBNO reported on 10 March that the local authorities in North Russia had now released incoming mail with no formality other than counting the bags; an action he understood to have been taken on instructions from the Head of Customs in Murmansk.

The Future of the May Convoy

Copies of a draft minute to Churchill, prepared in light of the discussion at the previous day's meeting of the committee, were discussed by the chiefs of staff on 10 March.[26] The committee approved the minute with two slight additions and instructed the secretary to submit it to Churchill.

The chiefs of staff reply read as follows:

The May Convoy
1. All preparations should go forward on the basis the May convoy <u>will</u> run. These preparations should include the despatch of the Hampden squadrons to North Russia in time for them to operate in protection of the convoy. This they regard as an indispensable measure of insurance.

   Their reason is these squadrons represent the only means of providing protection for the convoy, once it is east of Bear Island, against strong German naval forces. The mere fact of their presence in North Russia may well deter the German surface ships from proceeding to sea. It is true if there are no strong German naval forces in Northern Norway at the time the convoy runs, the despatch of the British squadrons will prove to have been unnecessary. It is also true if the German forces in Northern Norway are reinforced, and particularly if really strong forces are moved to the vicinity of North Cape, it may be decided the risk of loss is too prohibitive to allow the convoy to run, irrespective of whether the Hampden squadrons are or are not in North Russia. But neither of these possibilities would justify us in neglecting an indispensable measure of insurance.

2. In the light of the above appreciation of the military aspect, the Chiefs of Staff are disposed to think we should tell the Russians we will not run the May convoy, unless they permit us to despatch aircraft to

North Russia as originally proposed by us and now refused by them. They realise, however, this is a political issue, which it is not for them to decide.

Convoys Subsequent to May:
3. Owing to the requirements of HUSKY it will not be possible to run any convoys subsequent to May. This was generally recognised at CASABLANCA and is recorded in the minutes of the Conference.

Recriminations over GRENADINE

Meanwhile the recriminations within the government over the handling of GRENADINE continued. A note from the Secretary of the Chiefs of Staff Committee dated 11 March[27] circulated a copy of a minute from the Foreign Secretary to Churchill which Churchill had annotated 'C.O.S. to see.' This read:

PRIME MINISTER
In your Minute M133/3 of the 7th March you invited me to comment on Paragraph 2 of General Ismay's minute to you of the 6th March about Operation GRENADINE.

I confirm I was not asked to take up the matter on the basis the March convoy should not sail without air protection.

The Defence Committee invited me on 23rd February to take up with the Soviet government the general question of obstruction and lack of cooperation on the part of the Soviet authorities in North Russia including their objection to the number of personnel suggested for Operation GRENADINE and the demand for operational control of our squadrons.

On the 24th February I received a letter from the Soviet Ambassador suggesting we should send no personnel at all but only the aircraft to be operated by Soviet personnel. This was considered by the Cabinet on the 26th February and it was decided the Russian proposal was quite impractical and we must make it clear to the Soviet Government we could not put up with this cumulative process of obstructiveness in connection with convoy protection. I proposed, and it was agreed, in order to show how seriously we viewed the matter we should say in default of the Soviet Government's agreement, we should be forced to review the whole question of continuing the convoys. I confirm I had not understood the squadrons were not needed for the March convoy.

The Memorandum, which I have handed to the Soviet Ambassador and telegraphed to Sir A. Clark-Kerr[28] for presentation to the Soviet Government (which Monsieur Maisky said would be helpful) was prepared by the Foreign Office in consultation with officials of the Admiralty and Air Ministry and the First Lord and Air Staff concurred in it. Though I made certain changes to the final draft these did not affect the substance which remained as agreed with Service Departments concerned. I made no specific reference to the March convoy either in the Memo or when in handing it to Monsieur Maisky. I told him if the Soviet Government felt unable to meet us we should have no alternative but to re-examine the whole question of the dispatch of future convoys.
A.E. 10 MARCH 1943

America enters the Debate

The Americans entered the debate the same day when Averell Harriman, the president's special representative, wrote to Churchill:

It is important for us to know at the earliest moment your decisions regarding future North Russian convoys. Leathers has informed me that the March convoy will proceed. I understand, however, that no decision has yet been reached regarding the next convoy scheduled to leave about May 1st and that the following convoy which had been expected to sail in June will probably not be dispatched.

We are now beginning to load ships in the United States for the May 1st convoy. If this convoy is not dispatched and if no further convoys are dispatched in the near future we will be embarrassed not only by waste of shipping, but because we will be forced to discharge these cargoes either in the United States or Great Britain. You will know the additional political difficulties with the Russians in discharging cargoes that they rightly or wrongly believe have become their property.

A definite decision regarding the June convoy is desirable in order that the War Shipping Administration may be relieved of its obligation to reserve for this purpose ships which otherwise could be scheduled for military use or as assistance to British imports for April loading.

Further Debate on the May Convoy

The ACNS (N) and ACAS (Ops) submitted their detailed report[29] to the Chiefs of Staff Committee[30] on 12 March commenting on detail of the Russian reply of 4 March. They considered that no further argument was necessary regarding the Meaconing set and the W/T transmitters; the reply could simply state the requirements and request that they be met as soon as possible. Regarding the various formalities,[31] some progress was being made, but there was no guarantee that difficulties would be fully resolved and they recommended that the reply take a firm line. While the need to conform to essential Russian requirements was appreciated, it was also expected of officers and men serving in North Russia to assist the passage of cargos and be given freedom to carry out their duties without being subject to humiliating restrictions.[32] Finally it was suggested that the reply concerning GRENADINE should not refer to the question of accommodation, which the Russians were now using as the excuse for not accepting the force, but make the point that it could not be agreed the Soviet Air Force had direct experience of cooperating with British surface forces since operations were not so far developed as to enable them to gain such experience. British Air Forces, having satisfactory experience of operating in North Russia, expected no difficulty in coordinating this operation with those of Soviet Air Forces. Any possible misunderstanding concerning the meaning of operational control should be clarified. The requirement was for the primary task of the British squadrons to be recognized as the security of the convoys. The senior British RAF officer should therefore, in conjunction with the SBNO, decide the target and time of attack. This might be argued to be tactical control, which it was agreed could be exercised within the general strategic direction of the Russian command.

Chapter Ten

March 1943 Convoy Suspension

On 13 March, Churchill told the COS Committee[1] that all preparations were to be made on the basis that the May convoy would run. He had sent an important military telegram to Premier Stalin[2] and preferred to wait a few days for his reply before entering upon this new and thorny topic which he was nevertheless prepared to do, but he was not satisfied that there was no possibility of running convoys after May on account of HUSKY. This was, he said, a most grave matter, and the Admiralty should make an intense effort to overcome the shortages and difficulties. Moreover, he was prepared to address the president again on the subject of some additional destroyers. The case for persuading the Russians to accept the Hampden squadrons would be greatly strengthened if they were to cover several convoys and not merely one. If it was found necessary to abandon all hope of resuming convoys before HUSKY he could then, in breaking the news to M. Stalin, suggest that the Hampden squadrons should cover the May convoy only and the machines would remain in Russia, with their 730 personnel coming back with the returning escort.

The Concentration of German Heavy Ships in Northern Norway

This problem of how to resolve the Operation GRENADINE impasse was, however, quickly overshadowed and overtaken by events. On 11 March, the *Tirpitz* moved from Trondheim to Altenfjord[3] north of Narvik to be joined by the *Lützow*, the *Scharnhorst*, a cruiser and eight destroyers. This now represented the most powerful concentration of German surface ships so far seen in Northern Norway and a resurrection of the threat of early 1942. The Admiralty were convinced that Admiral Dönitz, who had superseded Grand Admiral Raeder after his resignation as commander-in-chief of the *Kriegsmarine* in January, would be prepared to use these German vessels offensively. If he did so, convoys with escorts even on the scale of the previous spring and summer would be powerless. Only the battle fleet could offer protection in the Barents Sea, but the Admiralty had always opposed sending the fleet east of Bear Island in the past and now in March 1943 had additional reasons for resisting this. Dönitz's U-boat campaign in the Atlantic had reached its peak, the losses of Allied merchant shipping were more than double those of January, and the earlier fears of a German break-out into the North Atlantic were also now revived. Although we now know of the political, strategic and logistic constraints to which the German heavy ships in particular were subject and the limitations these placed in turn on their operational capabilities, the threat from the fleet-in-being continued to strongly influence Admiralty decision-making. Thus in the afternoon of 13 March the C-in-C Home Fleet signalled to the Admiralty: 'JW 54 and RA 54. I do not, repetition, not, consider it is a justifiable operation to run these convoys whilst enemy Heavy ships are concentrated as at present.'

When the Chiefs of Staff Committee met[4] to consider the minute by Churchill setting out the action to be taken with regard to the running of the May and subsequent convoys to Russia, the First Sea Lord, referring to his statement to the meeting of the committee on 13 March announced that the *Tirpitz*, *Scharnhorst* and *Lützow* had now been definitely located in North Norway. It had always been appreciated and accepted at Casablanca that if the Germans employed their surface ships boldly and kept up the same amount of air and U-boat pressure as in the previous year, it was within their power to stop the Russian convoys. After consultation with the C-in-C Home Fleet, he had come to the conclusion that that situation had now been reached. There was ice to the south of Bear Island, restricting the convoy route to a channel 200 miles wide and within easy reach of enemy aircraft based in Norway where the Germans now had a force estimated at thirty-nine Ju 87s, thirty long-range bombers and eighteen He 115s. In the face of this and the submarines that would be available, he could not justify the use of the Home Fleet in the Barents Sea as protection for the convoy against German surface units. Moreover, destroyers had insufficient endurance to reach Murmansk, which meant for the latter part of the voyage there would be no destroyer protection.

Even if the *Tirpitz* was removed elsewhere, the remaining surface units still constituted a stronger enemy force than had ever before been stationed in those waters and he felt that sending a convoy without battleship cover the whole way to Murmansk could not in these circumstances be justified. It would be impossible to spare an aircraft carrier to accompany the convoy; a factor that added strength to the argument for the dispatch of the Hampden squadrons to North Russia. If the battleship should be damaged by, for instance, submarine attack, enemy surface forces might seize the opportunity to attack her as she made her way home and the Hampdens would be the only insurance against such an attack. If, in present circumstances, an attempt was made to run convoys with only cruiser and destroyer escorts and the German fleet was to attack and sink a considerable number of these, participation in Operation HUSKY would be virtually impossible.

The First Sea Lord undertook to discuss with the First Lord of the Admiralty how to present the situation to Churchill as the Admiralty had not yet decided how far the preparations for the dispatch of the March convoy should proceed, wishing the enemy to believe for as long as possible that the convoy would sail. Referring to Churchill's instruction in paragraph 1 of his minute, he suggested that Mr Harriman should be informed that preparations for the May convoy should proceed. The First Sea Lord suggested that no action should be taken before he had consulted the First Lord. The committee agreed that the Admiralty would prepare a reply to Churchill's minute dealing with each of the points raised and invited Lieutenant General Ismay to delay informing Mr Harriman until after the First Sea Lord had consulted the First Lord of the Admiralty.

Some Relaxation in Constraints on British Service Personnel in North Russia

Meantime the head of the Military Mission in Moscow reported on 15 March that M. Molotov had agreed some relaxation in the constraints on personnel movements and mail. British boats might now be used (for personnel transfers between ships), though they would have to use a special quay. As regards mail, preliminary notification of number of packages and total weight was no longer necessary and examination of private mail would be made locally in northern ports, but there was NO RELAXATION ON OTHER POINTS.

Cancellation of the May Convoy and Suspension of the Convoy Programme during Preparations for the Invasion of Sicily

The chiefs of staff advised Churchill on 16 March that the First Sea Lord had informed them at their morning meeting that he proposed to submit a memorandum to Churchill recommending that the May Russian convoy (JW 54) should not be run owing to the concentration of German naval forces at Narvik. Pending a decision on the First Lord's memorandum, it was not possible to answer the question which Mr Harriman had addressed to Churchill in his letter of 10 March.

The War Cabinet Defence Committee (Operations)[5] met that night to discuss the Russian convoys. Churchill, referring to the minute[6] he had received that afternoon from the First Lord of the Admiralty proposing cancellation of the March convoy to Russia owing to the concentration of German surface units in North Norway, expressed surprise at this sudden change of plan, which was all the more unexpected since, within the last two or three days, he had been expressly invited by the chiefs of staff to inform Mr Harriman[7] that not only the March but also the May convoy would be sailing. The First Sea Lord said it had been impossible to make a definite recommendation until it was certain that the German ships were in fact concentrating. The *Tirpitz* had not been docked for twelve months and it seemed likely to the naval staff that when she left Trondheim, she would turn south to the Baltic.

Churchill recalled the conditions under which Convoy PQ 17 had suffered heavy losses when it was dispersed as a result of the threat of enemy surface units, yet it was due to submarine and air action that the heavy losses had been suffered as the surface vessels had withdrawn. Might not the same thing happen again? The First Lord of the Admiralty in reply recognized the very fact that the dispersal of the convoy and the subsequent withdrawal of the escorts had obviated the necessity for action by German surface vessels.[8] The attack had been left to their submarines and aircraft, with dire results.

Reverting again to the March convoy, Churchill suggested that if sailed it would provide a chance to bring about an action with the enemy fleet by making use of it as bait. The First Sea Lord, however, took the view that the German ships were extremely unlikely to accept battle with the Home Fleet unless its warships had been damaged by other forms of attack. Also the Home Fleet, if ordered to escort the convoy, would have to spend some six days in the most dangerous waters, with U-boats and aircraft concentrated against it from bases within easy range while the destroyers would have to return for refuelling, leaving the battleships without anti-submarine escort.[9]

Churchill again argued that use might still be made of the convoy as bait to draw out the enemy fleet and provide a chance to attack it even if the convoy proceeded only to a point this side of Bear Island and suggested that an aircraft carrier be made available in order to permit air attacks to be made on the German ships on their way to Altenfjord.[10] It was, however, impossible at the time to provide one with sufficient endurance for the purpose. Churchill accepted that it would be unjustifiable to risk the convoy, but continued to press for it to be run as a decoy to tease the enemy and entice them into the open and suggested that the convoy sail as arranged on 27 March and steam north for four or five days. The First Sea Lord said it would be possible for it to proceed for about six days, after which, unless the situation had changed and the enemy concentration been broken up, it should turn back to Iceland.[11]

Churchill argued that there was no certainty the German concentration would attack the convoys as the enemy could not know that it was intended to send one.[12] He suggested the enemy's purpose in making these dispositions might be altogether different from that envisaged. However, the First Lord of the Admiralty continued to argue that the location of the enemy forces was strategically correct for threatening the convoys. Moreover, the harbour at Narvik was better than at Trondheim and there was evidence that reconnaissance aircraft were looking for evidence of the sailing of a convoy.

Churchill then suggested that the Russians be informed the convoy was being started, but warned at the same time that it was not proposed to risk the battle fleet in the Barents Sea for the sake of one convoy. The First Sea Lord pointed out that twenty-three convoys had been run through to Russia in circumstances which, in his opinion, had never justified their sailing. He could not, given the present state of the U-boat war, afford to send the Home Fleet away to escort the convoy and risk the chance of the enemy breaking out into the Atlantic where they might create havoc among Allied convoys. The committee then went through the minute from the First Lord of the Admiralty paragraph by paragraph, with the following points made in discussion:

It had been estimated some thirty long-range bombers could be operating within twenty-four hours in North Norway with a further thirty in action forty-eight hours later. With regard to the thirty-nine dive-bombers, although the Ju 87 had a theoretical range of action of 200 miles it had never been known to operate further than 120 miles from its base. It was unlikely these aircraft would be used against the convoy.

The phrase into the Barents Sea was misleading; at the present moment the limit beyond which British surface units did not proceed, owing to danger from air attack, was a line running about 10^0 E. This line fell about 150 miles west of Bear Island.

Churchill enquired what percentage of the whole requirement was represented by the ten escorts who were lacking. On being informed there should have been ninety destroyers, he said the difference between eighty and ninety was an acceptable tolerance in an operation; it was impossible to calculate with exactitude the point beyond which any reduction would mean danger, but above which we could count on safety.

Mr Alexander said, until a few weeks ago, the shortage in escorts had not been ten, but forty. Since then we had made every possible rearrangement and economy and, as a result, had cut down the deficit. Mr Attlee said, by our actions in the past in running convoys to Russia, we had accepted enormous risks and had proved our staunchness as an ally.

Churchill again stated he was not in favour of putting a battle fleet into the Barents Sea. He thought it best to sail the convoy on the date proposed and endeavour by manoeuvres to entice the enemy into an action this side of Bear Island. We should also endeavour by submarine and mine-laying to play a game with the enemy and to use the convoy for a bait. Depending on the situation at the time, the convoy might make an attempt to reach its destination or, if the menace still existed, might be turned back to Iceland (C). A few days later, after refuelling, these ships might start off again. This would have the effect of keeping the enemy continuously on the alert, and it was quite possible they might make a mistake and allow themselves to be lured into action against our own fleet. He would be prepared to telegraph on these lines to Premier Stalin pointing out that, unless the enemy forces could be enticed out, the convoy could not be sent to Russia, as we were not prepared to endanger the Home Fleet for the sake of a convoy. If the convoy failed the first time, we could turn it back to Iceland (C) for refuelling from which it could make further attempts to get to Russia.

The First Sea Lord reminded Churchill Premier Stalin had been made fully aware of the conditions under which we would not be prepared to operate the convoys and read out an extract from the Telegram[13] Churchill sent to Premier Stalin on 17 July 1942.

Churchill said this reversal of policy must be reported to the Americans, since two-thirds of the ships in the March convoy were American. The First Sea Lord said there had been general agreement[14] with the Americans at Casablanca, the passage of convoys on the northern route if prohibitive in cost, must be stopped. In reply to a question by Churchill he confirmed, if the present convoy was forced to return to Iceland (C), and then set out again, there would be insufficient time left to run the May convoy before HUSKY.

Churchill then called for the air force to take energetic measures to deal with these enemy ships – a successful attack would be worth comparatively heavy losses in aircraft – and asked whether American day bombers could reach Narvik. It was explained this could only be achieved if they continued their flight to land at Murmansk. As accurate weather reports, either over the target or at the landing field in Murmansk, were not available this should risk the loss of aircraft with little likelihood of achieving any result.

The Committee agreed a Telegram be despatched to Premier Stalin in the sense of the above, and copied to Mr Eden in Washington with a request he present it personally to President Roosevelt. Mr Harriman should be apprised informally of the above conclusions, but official intimation must await the President's reaction to the Telegram to be sent to him.

Meantime the Admiralty and Commander-in-Chief, Home Fleet should devise the best possible plans for bringing the enemy fleet to action, and for damaging it by submarine or mine. It should be their objective to mystify and mislead the enemy as to our intentions. The Defence Committee agreed this approach.

Churchill then informed the War Cabinet on 18 March[15] of the Defence Committee decision to cancel JW 54 unless the enemy fleet concentration in North Norway could be enticed out. It was therefore proposed that the convoy should sail, but if this failed to entice the enemy into an action this side of Bear Island it should return to Iceland for refuelling. This decision was reinforced by the severe losses incurred in the Atlantic, about twenty merchant ships having been sunk in the previous two days. Naval resources were stretched to the utmost, and the strength of the escorts of Atlantic convoys inadequate to meet the enemy's concentration of U-boats.

Churchill then read out the telegram he intended to send to Roosevelt, setting out the lines on which he proposed the decision reached in regard to convoys to North Russia be communicated to Premier Stalin. He added that it would in any event have been necessary after the convoy proposed for May to discontinue convoys to North Russia until August owing to the extent of the naval forces required for HUSKY. He thought the balance of advantage lay in stopping convoys to North Russia for the time being, grievous as this would be to Premier Stalin, but would prefer not to make this communication for two or three days when there might be favourable news from the North African front.

Discussion then ensued on the position described by Churchill. The War Cabinet was in agreement that the advantage would lie in discontinuing convoys to North Russia for the present and concentrating all available escort forces on protecting the Atlantic convoys. They agreed, subject to President Roosevelt's assent, that Churchill should send a communication on the lines proposed to Premier Stalin in four or five days' time.

This was a painful decision. It not only meant the cancellation of just one convoy, but also the cessation of all supplies to Russia via the Northern Route until September as the invasion of Sicily planned for early summer 1943 (Operation HUSKY) had prior claim on all available naval escorts. There could also not have been a worse time to break the news to Stalin, as on 15 March the Soviet Army, exhausted by its victorious advance from Stalingrad, had lost Kharkov again to the Wehrmacht.

Churchill notified President Roosevelt on 18 March:

The German naval concentration at Narvik now comprises *Tirpitz*, *Scharnhorst*, *Lützow*, 6 cruisers and eight destroyers with U-boats and air forces also available. Admiral Doenitz has taken command. The move of *Tirpitz* to the north became apparent on Sunday last.

2. It is, in the opinion of the Defence Committee, impossible to run the March convoy [JW 54] due to sail 27th while this concentration is maintained. A German move through the leads to Alten Fiord under close air cover cannot be prevented. The convoy and its escorts would have to go south of Bear Island under air and U-boat attack. The principal units of the Home Battle Fleet would have to be sent into the Barents Sea as an escort, remaining 5 to 6 days exposed to U-boat and air attacks. This would of course open the Atlantic and enable the Germans to pass further Heavy ships, or if they chose, to come with their whole fleet across our main lines of communication with disastrous consequences to our convoys. We cannot therefore send the Battle Fleet into the Barents Sea and without it the convoy could easily be destroyed by German surface ships. I send you in my communication immediately following the Minutes of the First Sea Lord on which the Defence committee reached its conclusion.

3. However, as the German concentrations at Narvik may disperse, it is not proposed to unload convoy JW 54. It may therefore start under the protection of the Home Fleet as a blind, being called back to Iceland if the enemy keeps his station. Should an opportunity arise in April or May a renewed attempt to pass this convoy through will be made; meantime, two ships which have already started to load in United States ports for the May convoy (JW 55) should continue to load in order to avoid a premature disclosure to Russians at your ports the convoy possibly will not sail.

4. This news will be a heavy blow to Stalin and his Government, coming as it does in the mood revealed in paragraph one of his Telegrams to me, which I have repeated to you in my Telegram to Mr Eden; it will certainly excite their grievous resentment. I propose therefore to allow Operation PUGULIST[16] to develop before informing Stalin. This will also give time for me to receive your views and advise. We have not yet broken it to him convoys will have to be suspended altogether during Operation HUSKY, and I feel it will be right and wise to place the picture before him as a whole, dark though it may be. What do you think?

5. Sinkings in the North Atlantic of 17 ships in convoys HX229 and SC 122 are a final proof our escorts are evidently too thin. The strain upon the British Navy is becoming intolerable. If instead of carrying out blind proposed in paragraph 3 above it were definitely decided now not to run any more convoys to Russia until after HUSKY, this would release one escort carrier, several ocean-going escort vessels and six other escort vessels for immediate service and enable us to form support groups in the Atlantic, which are vital, and to bridge the April-May gap before our reinforcements, particularly of air power, come into play. My mind therefore is turning to a blunt and complete cessation until after HUSKY. Here again I should be most grateful for your advice.

Churchill also sent Roosevelt a copy of the report submitted by the Admiralty to the Defence Committee (Operations). All now depended on what President Roosevelt thought.

The Foreign Secretary reported to Churchill on 19 March that he had seen the president that morning and handed him Churchill's message about the Russian convoys.[17] The president had agreed that in the light of enemy dispositions it was right to postpone the March convoy; however, he was doubtful whether it would be wise now to decide on no further convoy until after Sicily, noting that if enemy concentrations were to disperse for whatever reason within the next few weeks the Allies might still be in a position to run a convoy. He would think the matter over further and send Churchill a personal message very shortly. The president's formal reply of the following day[18] read as follows:

Your message of March 18.
In the face of known German Naval and air force concentration on the route of the March convoy (JW 54) there appears to be no military justification for despatch at scheduled time.

In consideration however of possible political implications it is in my view advisable to inform Stalin only in view of known German preparations for its destruction and in view of the impossibility of providing at the present time adequate protection in the restricted waters, it is necessary to postpone its despatch.

I am in agreement with you to not unload convoy (JW 54), and as a deception, to start it under protection of the Fleet if you consider such a move desirable with the intention of directing the convoy to Iceland.

In another 3 or 4 weeks it may of course be necessary to break the news to Stalin that convoys to Russia must be interrupted until August or September in order to provide for the HUSKY effort, but it seems to me a delay in giving him the bad news would be the wiser course. Incidentally none of us can be positive about the situation in 4 or 5 months' time. Will you send me a copy of your proposed reply to Stalin?

The chiefs of staffs discussed Churchill's instruction in the telegram on the morning of 20 March and subsequently sought his guidance on certain points before submitting a draft telegram to Premier Stalin for his consideration. These points were as follows:

The President had agreed to postpone the March convoy. The Chiefs of Staff assumed this meant the cargo ships should remain loaded, but the escort vessels might be dispersed forthwith to anti-U-boat work. They pointed out if this latter was not done, it would be the worst of both worlds; i.e. we should incur Premier Stalin's displeasure without being able to use the escort vessels as support groups during the next month when we would be at our weakest in the Atlantic.

At the same time, the Chiefs of Staff thought Churchill should know the implications of dispersing the escorts and using them as support groups in the Atlantic convoys was it might, in the worst case, be as much as eighteen days before they could be collected again to take the convoy to Russia. Thus, by way of example, if information were received that the German naval concentration had dispersed to the Baltic on 1 April, it might be 19 April before the Russian convoy could sail.

The First Sea Lord also wished to make it clear if the convoy did not start by 7 May at the latest, it could not start at all owing to the demands of HUSKY. Working backwards this meant unless the German Naval concentration was dispersed by 19 April there could be no convoy before HUSKY.

It was impossible to say when another Atlantic convoy might be attacked as heavily as HX 299 and SC 122 and the First Sea Lord asked for Churchill's immediate approval to disperse the escorts for JW 54 to form the support groups.

Finally, the Chiefs of Staff suggested Churchill might prefer to postpone the despatch of a telegram to Premier Stalin until he had received the further telegram from President Roosevelt mentioned in paragraph 1 of the Foreign Secretary's telegram at Flag A and news of PUGILIST.

Churchill annotated the note against Paragraph 6 above: 'Approved. I have told 1SL verbally to use the escorts; and yes against Paragraphs 6a and 6b.'

The War Cabinet was informed on 22 March[20] that the enemy had effected a strong fleet concentration in Northern Norway, making it an unacceptable risk to send convoys to North Russia unless they were escorted into the Barents Sea by capital ships of the Home Fleet. As the Defence Committee had, however, always considered it an unacceptable risk to send capital ships of the Home Fleet into the Barents Sea, the decision had therefore been reached that the sailing of the March convoy to Russia would have to be postponed.

The question had then arisen whether if the sailing of the March convoy was postponed, the escort vessels to have accompanied the convoy should be used to combat the U-boat menace in the North Atlantic. Authority had now been given for this to be done and as a result it had been possible to immediately establish support groups that would be available to help the convoys fight their way through the U-boat concentration in the North Atlantic.

Churchill had consulted President Roosevelt, who agreed to postponement of the sailing of the March convoy. This decision would, of course, now have to be conveyed to Premier Stalin, but this had not yet been done. In the meantime the March convoy was being kept loaded and loading was also proceeding in the United States of two US vessels that had been earmarked to form part of the May convoy.

Churchill added that as it had been necessary to postpone the sailing of the March convoy he had thought it right to use the escort vessels that would have accompanied the convoy to help combat the serious situation in the North Atlantic, although it might take from fourteen to eighteen days to reconstitute the escorts required for the North Russian convoys when circumstances permitted the sailing of these to be resumed. The War Cabinet took note, with approval, of the action taken.

Three days later Churchill telegraphed Roosevelt again[21] through the Foreign Secretary, who was still in Washington. He told the president:

> The cargo ships of JW 54 are to be kept loaded, but we have decided to give up the idea of running the convoy even as a bait or as a blind. To do this would have been to get the worst of both worlds; i.e. Stalin's displeasure and no relief in the Battle of the Atlantic. The escort vessels have therefore been dispersed to form support groups in the Atlantic, it being understood if threat of German naval concentration were to disappear they would reassemble as quickly as possible to escort the Russian convoy. This reassembly might in the worst case take as much as eighteen days. Thus by way of example if we learned in April that

German naval concentration had dispersed to the Baltic it might be April 19th before the convoy could start. Further, on the basis of a HUSKY assault on about June 24th, the convoy must start by May 7th if it is to start at all.

The President proposes in his 263 of March 20th it would be wiser to postpone breaking the news to Stalin the convoys to Russia must be interrupted until August or September. I must admit my own instinct has always been to tell him the whole truth at once, only waiting till PUGILIST perhaps gives us some credit. The Foreign Office[22] has deployed the following arguments in support of my view:

To withhold information for three or four weeks will surely be much more dislocating to Russian plans for the use of the material they expect on convoys than if Stalin is told at once. The delay will therefore be likely to annoy Stalin. It will also look very inefficient if we are not able to foresee interruption in convoys caused by HUSKY until the last moment. How shall we explain to the Soviet Government our decision not to press for their acceptance of GRENADINE if we do not tell Stalin there will be for several months no more convoys to protect? Unless we do so our acquiescence in Russian refusal to accept air squadrons will look like a climb down since we told the Russians additional air protection was so essential during the summer, and if it was not available, we would have to consider with the Americans the whole question of despatch of future convoys. There seems no reason why Stalin should take the decision to suspend convoys better later on. A frank and immediate declaration of our inability will come as a shock to him but successive evasions and postponements will inspire him with suspicions of our intentions and of our honesty.

On the whole therefore I think we might just as well be hanged for a sheep as a lamb. Pray put this view to the President. My immediately following Telegram gives text of a message I should send to Stalin if he agrees. If he does not agree, paragraph 3 and paragraph 4 would be omitted from Telegram in question. I should be grateful for early reply but I should not in any event send my Telegram to Stalin until we know more about PUGILIST.

Before informing Stalin, Churchill telegraphed Roosevelt again on 25 March:[23]

I have sent you through Eden a draft of the proposed Telegram breaking the news to Joe, and I hope you will discuss with Eden whether it is not better to let him know the worst. My instinct is to tell him the whole truth as soon as PUGILIST takes a favourable turn. I am still confident of success. Patton's Corps has made a fine advance.

Roosevelt replied to Churchill three days later:[24]

> Referring to your proposed message to Stalin delivered by Mr Eden, I agree with you. I have after serious consideration further concluded it is not justified in wasting valuable tonnage by keeping the present Russian convoy (JW 54) loaded, and it is advisable to give Stalin the bad news now.

Roosevelt deleted all references in Churchill's draft to any possibility of a resumption of convoys before September. The only consolation the president could offer Stalin was a promise to increase the shipments being sent to Vladivostok. The amended message now read:

1. The Germans have concentrated at Narvik a powerful Battle Fleet consisting of the *Tirpitz, Scharnhorst, Lützow*, one 6-inch cruiser and eight destroyers. Thus the danger to the Russian convoys I described in my message to you of July 17th of last year has been revived in an even more menacing form. I told you then we did not think it right to risk our Home Fleet in the Barents Sea, where it could be brought under the attack of German shore-based aircraft and U-boats without adequate protection against either, and I explained if one or two of our most modern battleships were to be lost or even seriously damaged while the *Tirpitz* and other large units of the German Battle Fleet remained in action, the whole command of the Atlantic would be jeopardised with dire consequences to our common cause.
2. President Roosevelt and I have, therefore, decided with the greatest reluctance it is impossible to provide adequate protection for the next Russian convoy[25] and without such protection there is not the slightest chance of any of the ships reaching you in the face of the known German preparations for their destruction. Orders have, therefore, been issued that the sailing of the March convoy is to be postponed. (The cargo ships will, however, remain loaded so if German naval concentration should shortly disperse, the convoy could start for North Russia as soon as the necessary escort vessels could be again collected.)
3. It is a great disappointment to President Roosevelt and myself it should be necessary to postpone the March convoy. Had it not been for the German concentration, it had been our firm intention to send you a convoy of thirty ships each in March and again in early May

(and it is still our intention at least one of the convoys should be sent if position of German Heavy ships is such that the convoy has a reasonable chance of getting through). At the same time we feel it only right to let you know at once it will not be possible to continue convoys by the northern route after early May, since from that time onwards every single escort vessel will be required to support our offensive operations in the Mediterranean, leaving only a minimum to safeguard our lifelines in the Atlantic. In the latter we have had grievous and almost unprecedented losses during the last three weeks. Assuming HUSKY goes well we should hope to resume convoys in early September, provided the disposition of German main units permits and the situation in the North Atlantic is such as to enable us to provide the necessary escorts and covering force.

4. We are doing our utmost to increase the flow of supplies by the southern route. The monthly figure has been more than doubled in the last six months. We have reason to hope the increase will be progressive and the figures for August will reach 240,000 tons. If this is achieved, the month's delivery will have increased eightfold in twelve months. Furthermore, the United States will materially increase shipments via Vladivostok. This will in some way offset both your disappointment and ours at the interruption to the northern convoys.

In the War Cabinet meeting on 29 March[26] Churchill reported that he had sent a telegram to the Foreign Secretary in Washington on the 25th, in which he asked him to raise with the president the question of whether it would not be better to tell Premier Stalin at once that after May it would be necessary to postpone convoys to Russia by the Northern Route until August or September. (The president had been in favour of withholding this information for the present.) He had also sent to Mr Eden, for communication to the president, the draft of the telegram he proposed to send to Premier Stalin. The president had agreed that it was advisable to give Premier Stalin the bad news now and thought we should not be justified in keeping loaded the ships in the March convoy to North Russia. He had accordingly approved the terms of Churchill's telegram to Premier Stalin, subject to certain amendments. Churchill read to the War Cabinet the proposed message as amended.

The First Lord of the Admiralty thought Churchill ought to know, based on the latest information, the statement in Paragraph 1 of the draft telegram to Premier Stalin as to the German naval concentration at Narvik was no longer accurate. It was now known that most of these ships had left Narvik Fjord, but two or three days might elapse before it could be ascertained where they had gone, although the First Sea Lord felt confident it would be found they had gone to Altenfjord.[27] Churchill said the Allied Supplies Executive should now decide whether the ships of the March convoy should be unloaded. He thought, however, that the unloading might be postponed for a few days in view of the uncertainty as to the whereabouts of the German battle fleet.

The War Cabinet approved the terms of the draft telegram Churchill proposed to send, in his name and that of the president, to Premier Stalin, subject to such amendments as might be found necessary in the light of the latest available information on the location of the German battle fleet, and invited the Allied Supplies Executive to decide whether the ships in the March convoy should be unloaded.

The telegram, as approved and amended by Roosevelt, was sent to Stalin on 30 March in the format finally agreed:

> The Germans have concentrated at Narvik a powerful battle fleet consisting of the *Tirpitz*, *Scharnhorst*, *Lützow*, one 6-inch cruiser and eight destroyers. Thus the danger to the Russian convoys which I described in my message to you of July 17th of last year has been revived in an even more menacing form.
>
> I told you then that we did not think it right to risk our Home Fleet in the Barents Sea, where it could be brought under the attack of German shore-based aircraft and U-boats without adequate protection against either, and I explained that if one or two of our most modern battleships were to be lost or even seriously damaged while the *Tirpitz* and other large units of the German battle fleet remained in action, the whole command of the Atlantic would be jeopardised with dire consequences to our common cause.
>
> 2. President Roosevelt and I have, therefore, decided with the greatest reluctance that it is impossible to provide adequate protection for the next Russian convoy and that without such protection there is not the slightest chance of any of the ships reaching you in the face of the known German preparations for their destruction. Orders have, therefore, been issued that the sailing of the March convoy is to be postponed.
> 3. It is a great disappointment to President Roosevelt and myself that it should be necessary to postpone the March convoy.
>
>   Had it not been for the German concentration, it had been our firm intention to send you a convoy of thirty ships each in March and again in early May. At the same time we feel it only right to let you know at

once that it will not be possible to continue convoys by the northern route after early May, since from that time onwards every single escort vessel will be required to support our offensive operations in the Mediterranean, leaving only a minimum to safeguard our lifelines in the Atlantic. In the latter we have had grievous and almost unprecedented losses during the last three weeks. Assuming that HUSKY goes well we should hope to resume convoys in early September, provided that the disposition of German main units permits and that the situation in the North Atlantic is such as to enable us to provide the necessary escorts and covering force.

4. We are doing our utmost to increase the flow of supplies by the southern route. The monthly figure has been more than doubled in the last six months. We have reason to hope that the increase will be progressive and that the figures for August will reach 240,000 tons. If this is achieved, the month's delivery will have increased eightfold in twelve months. Furthermore, the United States will materially increase shipments via Vladivostok. This will in some way offset both your disappointment and ours at the interruption to the northern convoys.

March 30th, 1943

Churchill telegraphed Roosevelt on the same day to confirm its dispatch and suggested that Roosevelt send Stalin a supportive message. The Permanent Secretary to the Foreign Office advised Churchill that the Soviet Ambassador had been requested to call on the Foreign Secretary that evening to be handed a copy of Churchill's message to Stalin. Monsieur Maisky said this (news) was most unfortunate and would come as a great blow. He referred to the fact that a convoy of thirty ships was at present already loaded. Could these not be sent round the Cape by the Southern Route? The Foreign Secretary said he would report this enquiry of his, but he (Maisky) would of course understand that this would involve the escort and the ships being unavailable for any other purpose for about six months. Monsieur Maisky did not seem very impressed by this argument and said, on the other hand, Russia was to be deprived of these further supplies until next September. The Permanent Secretary had to remind him that the ships in question were required in the summer for operations that were designed to assist Russia as far as possible, but of course the Russian views on the nature of a Second Front did not coincide with ours. Monsieur Maisky then said he had today received from Monsieur Stalin a message he was instructed to give to Churchill and asked whether arrangements could be made for Churchill to receive him at any time

March 1943 Convoy Suspension

tomorrow when he could deliver this message and also speak to Churchill on the subject of convoys.

The Minister of Production also wrote to Churchill the following day about the future convoys to North Russia. He reported:

> It seems clear not more than one convoy can be run to North Russia before end of May. The March convoy JW 54 of 27 ships remains loaded in case the convoy can be sailed.
>
> 2. The Allied Supplies Executive agreed I should report to you their view that instructions should now be issued to stop the loading arrangements for the May convoy (JW 55). This convoy is due to start loading tomorrow.
> 3. If you approve this proposal the necessary detailed instructions should be given by the Minister of War Transport, to whom I am copying this minute.

Churchill approved the proposal to keep the March convoy loaded for the present since, if Tunis was retaken in April, the convoy might, in May, go through the Mediterranean to Persia. He continued: 'This is quicker than Maisky's suggestion of sending it round the Cape.' He went on to suggest the Minister 'invite M. Maisky to come with his Admiral to his Committee tomorrow or Friday and go into any suggestions he may have. Pray speak to me about this.'

Stalin's Reaction to the Suspension

Stalin was quick to respond on the same day and Churchill promptly forwarded the reply to President Roosevelt in his telegram T.442/3, noting:

> I have just received the following message from Stalin, which I consider is a very natural and stout-hearted response. I read the last sentence as meaning only the Soviet armies will be worse off and suffer more. The answer makes me the more determined to back this man with every conceivable means. If you like to send him some message it could only do good.

Stalin's reply read:

I have received your message of March 30 advising me you and Mr Roosevelt are compelled by necessity to postpone despatch of the convoys to the USSR till September.

I understand this unexpected action as a catastrophic diminution of supplies of arms and military raw materials and munitions to the USSR on the part of Great Britain and the USA, as transport via Pacific is limited by the tonnage and is not reliable, and the southern route has a small transit capacity. In view of this both just mentioned routes means those two routes cannot compensate for the discontinuation of transport by the northern route.

You realise of course the circumstance cannot fail to affect the position of the Soviet troops.

The convoy cycle was now suspended, but the repercussions over the fate of PQ 17 were never very far out of sight, surfacing again on 30 March following a debate in the House of Lords on the U-boat menace, details of which appeared in the press. The reports read:

LONDON MARCH 30 1943
34 SHIPS LOST OUT OF 38
CONVOY DISASTER RECALLED
LONDON, March 30:
Following Lord Winter's (formerly Commander R.T.H. Fletcher, a Labour MP) disclosure in the House of Lords, in a debate on the U-boat menace, that in one Arctic convoy to Russia 34 ships were lost out of 38. The *Daily Express*'s naval correspondent says that Lord Winter was apparently referring to the war's worst Allied convoy disaster last July, when the enemy claimed the annihilation of an entire convoy carrying 250,000 tons of aircraft, tanks, munitions and food.

Official German reports claimed that 10 Merchant ships were destroyed by bombers and nine by U-boats off Spitsbergen and that the others were destroyed in a pursuit battle in the Barents Sea.

What happened was that, after an incessant air attack which inflicted severe losses, the convoy evaded a German battle squadron, including the battleship *Tirpitz*, but was again attacked by bombers near Archangel. Then U-boats finished off stragglers, only four ships completing the voyage.

CHURCHILL ON NAZI CLAIM

Mr Churchill, in reply to a question whether he was aware of a recent German claim that 30 ships totalling 200,000 tons had been sunk in a recent U-boat attack against a convoy in the Atlantic, said: 'The enemy would greatly like to know how far adrift he is from the truth. I refuse to clarify the enemy's knowledge.

I may state, however, that the United Nations have afloat to-day substantially larger fleets than at the worst moment of the U-boat war and that the improvement is continuing.'

HOUSE OF LORDS DEBATE

Lord Hankey, for many years Secretary of the Committee of Imperial Defence and Secretary of the Imperial War Cabinet in the last war, spoke in the debate in the House of Lords on the U-boat menace.

'We have had our ups and downs', he said, 'but broadly speaking, at the end of each year we have been worse off than at the beginning of the year.'

'I fear we have not looked ahead enough in the past year, and that the enemy will continue to be one lap ahead. I am afraid that escort ships cannot affect the position in 1943. The only way we can affect the position is with planes.'

Lord Hankey said that shipping losses in December, January and February were reported to be lower, but during March there have been some very uncomfortable stories and the Germans have some very large claims. I know these are exaggerated, but they are rather confirmed by an official's statement from America.

Lord Hankey advocated the appointment of a whole-time Minister to deal with anti-submarine warfare.

ADMIRALTY PRIORITY

Lord Bruntisfield, Parliamentary Secretary to the Admiralty, replying for the Government, said that, for the purpose of combating the U-boat menace, there was the highest priority for the Admiralty. The number of long-range heavy aircraft for the use of the Navy was steadily increasing, but the mere provision of aircraft was by no means the whole story. The aircraft had to be equipped with anti-submarine devices, crews trained for special work, and bases constructed.

Turning to the suggestion of a fixed aerodrome in the Atlantic, Lord Bruntisfield said that, however attractive the scheme might appear, difficulties made it impracticable.

Commenting on the proposal that there should be a supreme command of submarine warfare, Lord Bruntisfield said it was difficult to see how such a command could operate effectively, as U-boat warfare was only one part of the task of keeping sea communications open. There was no question of making such an appointment as a Super-Commander-in-Chief or appointing a special Minister to deal with the anti-U-boat campaign. The Admiralty organisation had been adapted by continual improvements to deal with the war as a whole. It would be impossible to disentangle U-boat warfare and its control from the general organisation, and he would not recommend any attempt to do so.

Churchill read out Stalin's reply to the War Cabinet[28] on 5 April, which he thought, in the circumstances, courageous and not unsatisfactory, and indicated to the War Cabinet the lines on which he proposed to reply. He went on to note that the Minister of Production (in the absence of the Foreign Secretary) had at his request presided over a meeting on 1 April, attended by M. Maisky and other Russian representatives, Mr Harriman and the Minister of War Transport, to consider the situation that had arisen out of the decision to postpone the sailings of convoys by the North Russian route and to examine the possibilities of other supply routes. The Minister of Production said at this meeting that the US and British governments expressed their intent to continue shipping supplies to Russia to the full capacity of all available routes. He had informed M. Maisky it was hoped that the rate of clearance by the Persian Gulf route would increase from the present monthly rate of 80,000 tons to 240,000 tons in August next and further invited M. Maisky to indicate, within the limits of the port capacity available, the categories of supplies the USSR most wished to receive. The War Cabinet took note.

Churchill replied to Stalin on the following day:[29]

> I acknowledge the force of all you say in your Telegram about the convoys. I assure you I shall do my utmost to make any improvement which is possible. I am deeply conscious of the giant burden borne by the Russian armies and of their unequalled contribution to the common cause.

This was, Churchill conceded, a 'bleak' answer, but he was relieved. In fact, as Lord Cadogan later recorded in his diary, Churchill was 'delighted with it'. Fortunately relations with the Kremlin were about to enter an unusually congenial phase, which had perhaps influenced Stalin's response.

Effects of Suspension on the Protocol

However, if the immediate political ramifications of cancelling the convoys were not serious, the effects on the fulfilment of the protocol were. Thirty-four merchant ships had been loaded to sail for North Russia in March and there was now no means of reshipping all their cargos. Naturally M. Maisky had suggested that all the ships be re-routed – the twenty-four American vessels to Vladivostok and the ten British to the Persian Gulf – but this proved impossible. The Persian Gulf was congested through the flooding of roads and the railway near Khorramshahr and fully occupied with supplies from the United States. The route could accommodate only seven of the JW 54 ships carrying high-priority aircraft, tanks and explosives. The Pacific route took a further eight shipments of sisal rope, RAF spare parts and machinery made to Russian specifications. Two additional shipments to assembly plants in Gibraltar and Egypt cleared the 435 aircraft on Britain's account in this and the succeeding convoy. The remaining cargos, however, were unloaded onto British docksides. In May the SBNO reported that the RAF stores ex-Operation GRENADINE were in the process of being sorted prior to being either turned over to the Russians or utilized by the navy.

Chapter Eleven

Continuing British Service Personnel Problems in North Russia

In April 1943 the SBNO expressed to the Admiralty his hope that the relief of all naval ratings would take place as they became due; i.e. after serving nine to twelve months in North Russia.[1] Although no individuals had complained up to that time, he knew equally that none wished to stay any longer than necessary. New forms of administrative pressure were then gradually introduced by the Russians including, as the SBNO reported to London, a series of customs and passport regulations affecting British vessels and personnel which he thought were 'noxious and humiliating'.

Although no convoys would run again until November 1943, British service and Merchant Navy personnel remained in North Russia and their problems with the Russian bureaucracy persisted. Representations continued to be made to the Soviet government throughout the months of May, June and July on the subject of visas for service personnel entering and leaving Russia, while the Russians continued to insist there were far too many British service personnel in their country. Their treatment, particularly of those overdue to return to the UK and the conditions under which they were serving, remained a continuing concern of Admiral Fisher. On 21 May he signalled the Admiralty[2] requesting confirmation that every opportunity was being taken to send reliefs for the base personnel in North Russia in the destroyer being sent out with mail and stores etc. He emphasized that large numbers of naval personnel had by now been in North Russia for well over their twelve months, with some having been there about eighteen months. The Soviet government had pigeonholed nearly every naval relief application since January and there now appeared to be almost seventy outstanding. He considered either a new visa offensive ought to be launched and carried through to a satisfactory conclusion, or the naval personnel overdue for relief should be sent home now in the destroyer being sent with mail and stores. The Soviet government should then be informed that the convoys could not be restarted until facilities had been given for naval shore staffs to be brought up to full complement again. Otherwise he saw no prospect of these men ever being relieved before the end of the war, which was a very severe hardship and imposition on them. In his opinion, the withdrawal of personnel was well suited to the Russian organizational mentality and would be more certain of success. Admiral Fisher[3] requested the SBNO's North Russia comments and an early decision; the granting of visas was a matter affecting all three services, which the head of the mission was taking up with the ambassador.

The SBNO fully supported Admiral Fisher's views in his signal to the Admiralty on 22 May,[4] noting that the visa question was the bane of their existence. While under the present circumstances a small proportion of those now overdue could be spared without relief for a substantial period, their relief would be essential before the resumption of convoys etc. The SBNO requested as early notice as possible of personnel taking passage by the opportunity referred to above (the sailing of one destroyer with mail, stores, etc.) in order for returning personnel to assemble in the Kola Inlet and their exit visas obtained. The latter formality became akin to a major operation.

The head of the military mission in Moscow weighed into the debate two days later,[5] noting that personnel of all three services in North Russia had been sent on the understanding that they would be relieved after one year, to which the Russians had originally agreed. However, their relief had been impossible because Russia had withheld visas for these reliefs since January. Many personnel had now spent eighteen months in North Russia; this was unfair and as they knew it led to ill feeling with the Russians, he suggested that personnel due for relief should be sent home when passage was available. He went on to recommend that the Soviet authorities should be warned that when the time came to re-open convoys, this would not be possible unless they had granted visas for reliefs in good time. They must also grant visas for naval personnel to complete the establishment for operational duties. Army and Air Force establishments (numbers) had been progressively reduced, while the naval establishment had to be increased due to larger convoys and escorts. The strength of all three services was now below the agreed establishments. Visas were only being demanded for essential personnel. Relations with the Russian services were friendly, but the Russian Foreign Office was consistently obstructive. A threat to stop the convoys was the only action they would understand. Constant representation by all three services had produced no improvement and the head of the naval section had recently informed the Admiralty of the position and the ambassador informed that the matter was being reported to the chiefs of staff.

The Secretary of State for Foreign Affairs then raised the matter of visas again in his letter to the Soviet ambassador of 27 May, enclosing the formal Foreign Office response of 24 May to the ambassador's note of 22 February on the subject of visas for British service personnel proceeding to Russia on official business. The letter had offered assurance that no service personnel would be sent unnecessarily to Russia since they were too badly needed elsewhere, recognized the difficulties in providing accommodation in North Russian ports which would be taken into account in only applying for visas in absolutely essential cases, and expressed surprise that the presence of 300 to 400 personnel could be a source of unfavourable comment or insuperable difficulty. It also made the point that no difficulties were raised about granting British visas or facilities to members of the Soviet military mission or trade delegation, but equivalent advantages were not being granted to British citizens in Russia. It concluded by noting that the imposition of severe restrictions on British service personnel in Russia was hardly compatible with friendly relations, and Britain was apparently suspected of wishing to send to Russia for unspecified purposes people who were potentially dangerous and not really required for the duties intended. The note enclosed a list of personnel to be sent out on 31 May or 1 June by two destroyers sent to relieve naval personnel who had been in Russia for twelve to eighteen months who would return home in the same ships.

Although the earlier Russian reply of 22 February had given some ground in granting a number of visas that had previously been refused in October and November 1942, it had not agreed that the British government alone should judge the numbers of personnel required and had raised the issue that the principle (of reciprocity) of the numbers of British personnel employed in Russia and in the Soviet military mission in London should be equal. The Foreign Office note argued that the nature of the functions and operational roles of both groups were different in character and size, and even when convoys were suspended, the organization to protect convoys, unload supplies and look after RN and Merchant Navy personnel should be maintained at full efficiency and reliefs of personnel enabled so that the organization was in place to ensure the resumption of convoys was not delayed.

It had been planned to send out reliefs in the destroyers *Musketeer* and *Mahratta*; however, on 2 June the destroyers were ordered to return to Scapa Flow immediately to disembark all those passengers who had not been provided with visas for North Russia except for five DEMS (Defensively Equipped Merchant Ship) ratings on draft to merchant ships. The destroyers sailed again around midnight on the 2/3rd for Seidisfiord and would leave on 8 June for the Kola Inlet.

The Admiralty informed the SBNO on the 5th:

1. Naval reliefs have not been embarked in destroyers owing to objections of Soviet Government.

2. Admiral Fisher's 211716c May, Para 2. Note has been handed to Maisky pointing out numbers of personnel to be maintained in North Russia should be judged by operational requirements. Note suggests even when convoys are not running the base staff must be maintained at full efficiency. It is undesirable therefore to make drastic reduction at present. The Chiefs of Staff do not consider time is opportune to threaten unless visas are granted convoys will not be re-started.
3. SBNO North Russia's 221902b, May, Para 2. As many personnel as can be spared within the terms of Para 2, above are to be returned to UK as opportunity offers provided Ambassador to whom Foreign Office are telegraphing separately see no objections. We appreciate reliefs will be necessary before next convoy.

Russian Dismissal of Foreign Office Representations

The official Soviet government reply of 11 June to the Foreign Office letters of 24 and 27 May dismissed the Foreign Secretary's opinion on the principle of reciprocity and continued to argue that the volume of work carried out by the Soviet military mission and trade delegation in London was no less in volume than that carried out by the British military mission including the personnel in North Russia and the British personnel not gainfully employed. It also did not accept the argument that Soviet service personnel stationed in Britain received better treatment than British personnel in Russia, and continued to insist on adoption of the principles of reciprocity and equality set out in this and earlier correspondence. It argued that many British personnel had not performed any work for many months and were now redundant; by way of example it again cited Base Unit No. 126 at Archangel.

On 19 June,[6] the 30 Mission Moscow telegram to the War Office in response to an Air Ministry request of the 17th reported:

1. Account of shameful conduct over Visas is now on its way to you by air. Also mentioned in letter to CIGS.
2. Trouble over official mail is maddening but, in this case, entirely fault of home authorities. Each service has broken the agreement with Russians over mails at times, and trouble ensues. No trouble over official mails if rules are obeyed.
3. Hope to settle question of personnel mail in North Russia satisfactorily, but it required careful handling since Russians are technically within their rights, though they only recently insisted on them as part of general policy of vexatious formalities.

A Measure of Relief

However, some little progress was made. The SBNO's 22nd monthly report covering the period 1 to 30 June 1943 commented:

> Reliefs did finally reach North Russia in the destroyers *Musketeer* and *Mahratta*[7] which arrived in the Kola Inlet on the 12th of June with passengers, mail and stores, anchoring in Vaenga Bay so transfer of the Archangel and Moscow quotas could be made direct to and from the minesweepers *Britomart* and *Jason* who had come round from Archangel for the purpose. This was duly accomplished despite bad weather and the destroyers sailed in the evening of 12th June carrying in all between them 105 passengers. SBNO expressed gratitude to the Commanding Officers for their co-operation in embarking so many. Mails for the Kola Inlet were, however, not released as had been anticipated from preliminary arrangements, so the *Jason* was retained to accommodate the mail while negotiations proceeded. *Britomart* sailed for Archangel on the 13th with passengers, mail and stores.

Russian Reaction to Accusations of Mistreatment of British Service Personnel in North Russia

The Foreign Office submitted copies of the telegrams from the ambassador in Moscow together with a copy of the exchange of notes between the Foreign Office and the Soviet government to the Chiefs of Staff Committee on 3 July.[8] The committee was informed that the ambassador was unable to make much progress with Molotov, while the Soviet note completely rejected the 24 May proposals; i.e. that the whole question of visas be settled by a friendly arrangement in which each side would take note of the view of the other. It stuck to the argument that there should be equality of numbers between British and Soviet personnel and an upper limit should be imposed on these. The Foreign Office was of the view that any agreement to the principle of reciprocity, the factual basis for which was quite unreal, would simply further encourage the Russians in their view that the presence of British personnel in the Soviet Union represented dangerous elements whose numbers should be reduced, at almost any cost, to the bare minimum or even below it.

The Foreign Office sought the committee's comments on the draft it proposed to send to the British ambassador to instruct him as follows. Firstly to tell Molotov that the British government had received and studied the note of 11 June (see above) as well as the ambassador's report of his conversation with him and regretted, despite the Foreign Secretary's personal assurances, that the Soviet government maintained its position for a reciprocal limit on numbers of personnel in each other's country, the Soviet government's motives for which were not understood. Secondly, the impression given by the Soviet government's attitude and difficulties was taken to imply Soviet suspicion of the British people and the sincerity of a desire to collaborate. Thirdly, that Molotov be asked again to abandon the reciprocity proposal and deal with the matter on the basis suggested on 24 May. Finally, the ambassador was instructed to avoid argument on the points made in the Soviet note, but if pressed to say the position of No. 126 Base Unit at Archangel would be reconsidered, without prejudice to the general question of personnel and visas, in the light of General Martel's report.

The Chiefs of Staff Committee on 8 July,[9] after considering a letter from the Foreign Office covering a draft telegram to HM Ambassador, Moscow regarding the granting of visas for service personnel entering and leaving Russia,[10] instructed the secretary to circulate for their approval a redraft of the telegram to incorporate amendments and suggestions made during the discussion.

General Martel's Visit to the Northern Russian Ports

General Martel, Head of the British Military Mission in Moscow, was sent on a fact-finding visit to Russian northern ports[11] between 24 June and 6 July. His preliminary report[12] described very good relations between the Russian and British (military) authorities, but regarded the Russian civil authorities as putting every kind of obstruction in the way. He had met with leading civil officials in North Russia, but they were following policy evidently dictated from Moscow. His full report with the proposed minimum terms that he suggested should be accepted from the Russians was being sent by plane in the next few days; the ambassador had been fully consulted. General Martel judged that British service personnel had behaved remarkably well under great provocation except for a few minor cases and would continue to do so, but called for some urgent action to be taken with the Russian civil authorities as there was a limit to everyone's patience. Very little appeared in his view to have been done over this civil side during the past twelve months. He also advised that the Russian authorities now required all crews of Catalina aircraft arriving in North Russia to have both passports and visas.

This revised draft telegram was discussed by the committee on 12 July.[13] Further amendments were made pending the imminent arrival of General

Martel's report and the news that the crews of Catalina aircraft did not now require visas or passports.

The committee agreed the final draft and instructed the secretary to submit it to the Foreign Office for dispatch to the British Ambassador, Moscow, at the same time acquainting the Foreign Office that the chiefs of staff reserved the right to raise the matter afresh in the light of General Martel's report and/ or if the telegram failed to elicit a satisfactory reply.

The chiefs of staff replied on 12 July to the Foreign Office note of 3 July. Their comments substantially amended Paragraph 4, making the point that the British service personnel in North Russia constituted a military force operating on Russian soil in alliance with Soviet forces and as such were not ordinary foreigners. The efficiency of the force depended not only on the provision of adequate numbers of personnel to carry out the heavy work that occurred when operations were in progress, but also on maintaining a reasonable flow of new personnel to take the place of those due for relief.[14] There were numerous personnel due for relief and visas had been applied for their replacements, with 100 applications outstanding.

Diplomatic Negotiations in Moscow

The British ambassador in Moscow reported on 14 July[15] that he had spent two hours the previous evening discussing the matter of visas with M. Molotov (the Soviet Foreign Minister). The Russians had raised, as an issue of principle, the need for reciprocity in the numbers of Russian personnel in the UK and British personnel in North Russia 'which accepting practical needs for should be met', the Russians were clearly convinced that many British personnel had nothing to do. While they had rendered valuable service in 1941 and at the beginning of 1942, their usefulness was seen to have come to an end, with the Russians citing in particular Base Unit No. 126, some fifty men who had initially been instructing Russian personnel but who, now this work was complete, clearly had nothing to do.

M. Molotov was unconvinced by the arguments that these people were handling matériel arriving by convoys: while these were suspended they obviously had nothing to do, he argued; they had been idle when convoys were running and in any case the work they did was for the Russians themselves to do. Molotov then reverted to the question of reciprocity in numbers based on the size of the Soviet trade delegation in London. He was also intransigent on recognizing the differences between the work of the delegation in London and British personnel engaged on operational duties, with the latter requiring a larger number. Molotov was told this would make reciprocity difficult and a considerable measure of flexibility would be required. The discussion failed to agree on what numbers of personnel might be allowed under such terms. Told that convoys would be impossible to run if British personnel numbers were artificially reduced to an unacceptable level, Molotov reportedly remained intransigent and would not be drawn as to what formula could be adopted. It was agreed to revisit the matter after the head of the mission's visit to the North Russian ports.

The ambassador observed in a follow-up telegram the same day[16] that Molotov, although obstinate, was friendly but not much progress was made. Molotov remained wedded to the idea of reciprocity and his stance on the issue of visas fully based on the belief that most of the British staff in North Russia were redundant and their numbers should be substantially reduced, the basis for agreement being determined by the size of the Soviet trade delegation in London even though their role was not analogous to the number of British personnel in North Russia. He expected, however, that some concession would have to be made over the Movements Control Unit and Base Unit No. 126 if General Martel's visit confirmed they were doing work the Russians now preferred to do for themselves.

The Foreign Office responded in turn to these comments on 17 July. The reply circulated to the Chiefs of Staff Committee two days later[17] acknowledged the suggestion that the chiefs of staff should carry out a thorough examination of numbers to ensure that all service personnel were essential and fully occupied, the impression being that this Soviet accusation might well be the cause of all the difficulties over visas. It was also noted that the chiefs had omitted the reference in Paragraph 5 of the earlier draft to No. 126 Base Unit that the Russians had specifically contended was superfluous. Further advice was therefore sought for the ambassador on this point. Attention was also drawn to the assurance given on 24 May that only essential personnel would be sent to the Soviet Union.

Anglo-Soviet Perceptions

There is an argument to be had that the British authorities were not entirely blameless. In July 1943 the American Chargé d'Affaires expressed the view the friction was 'in large measure caused by the failure of British personnel to study to avoid [sic] unnecessarily injuring Soviet susceptibilities', but attitudes in London soured nonetheless. The attitude of the Russians in response to what they saw as inappropriate behaviour by the British service personnel in North Russia, particularly it would seem the Royal Navy, could perhaps be illustrated by a conversation M. Maisky had with the British ambassador in

Moscow in early July 1943 during which, the ambassador Sir A. Clark Kerr later reported, Maisky complained that the British government did not make sufficient allowance for what he called the 'inferiority complex' of the Russians. Maisky complained that the British 'made them feel like country cousins.' He added 'and they minded because they knew they were.... We expected them to be as grown up and as metropolitan as ourselves. They were not, and we should remember, for it was very important.' The ambassador pointed out: 'If there were anything in this theory, it belonged to the past.' M. Maisky, however, claimed we 'were still not treating his people as equals, as, for example, we treated the Americans.' He went on: 'Again I protested, but in my heart felt he was right. I feel we are still holding these people at arm's length.'[18]

General Martel's Report

General Martel had dispatched his report to London on 9 July, but it was not distributed by the War Cabinet Office to the Chiefs of Staff Committee for consideration until 21 July.[19] The fairly lengthy document concluded that the majority of the British service personnel deployed in North Russia were concerned with operational duties in connection with the convoys and had been reduced to a minimum by making full use of facilities offered by the Russians for ship repairs, etc. There were also army and RAF personnel who had been sent out to train Russians in operating equipment and aircraft and in supervising the unloading of ships. The numbers of these had been reduced and further reductions were proposed. The minimum number of British personnel required in the North Russian ports was assessed as 400. The current strength in July 1943 was below this number due to casualties and the inability to obtain reliefs for men sent home. The number would have to be restored to the minimum before the convoys could restart. General Martel recommended firstly the establishment of a small British military hospital at Archangel; secondly a set timescale for the granting of visas for reliefs for personnel; thirdly the removal of restrictions on official personnel on duty visiting British or American ships; fourthly that crews of merchant ships in port while conforming to the civil laws of the port be allowed unrestricted landing; fifthly mail to be passed without censorship or other restriction apart from customs; and finally he addressed a number of other points of minor detail.

Churchill Intervenes

On 25 July, Churchill wrote a minute to the Chiefs of Staff Committee[20] following receipt of two telegrams[21] from the head of the British Military Mission in Moscow in which he wrote:

See the various Telegrams about the ill-treatment of our people in North Russia. The only way to deal with this kind of thing is for ostentatious preparations to be made to withdraw the whole of our personnel without saying anything to them (the Russian authorities). Let a plan be made for this. As soon as the local Russians see we are off they will report to Moscow and will of course realise the departure of our personnel means the end of the Arctic convoys. If anything brings them to their senses, this will. If not, anyway we had better be out of it as it only causes friction. Experience has taught me it is not worthwhile arguing with Soviet people. One simply has to confront them with the new fact and await their reactions.

A particular issue was the stance adopted by the Russian authorities regarding jurisdiction over the trials of service and Merchant Navy personnel accused of having committed criminal offences in Russia.

The chiefs of staff discussed Churchill's minute[22] and draft telegram to General Martel[23] at their meeting the following day.[24] The record of the discussion explained:

The difficulties with the Russians fell under three heads, the trial of Service personnel and merchant navy personnel which were two distinct problems, and the question of Visas. If we were ostentatiously to make preparations for the withdrawal of the whole of our personnel in North Russia without saying anything to the Russian Authorities, we would be faced with the possibility of being obliged to withdraw all our personnel. In this event our action might be interpreted as a diplomatic defeat in as much as we had complied with Russian requests for a withdrawal of personnel; in addition we might have to withdraw certain personnel we wished to leave there; and thirdly as we could not bring back the merchant ships, we should be forced to choose between abandoning them or leaving the crews stranded.

It might be preferable to say frankly to the Russians that in view of the difficulties which had arisen we proposed to withdraw all our personnel in North Russia which were not actively employed at the present time. We should point out that this would probably delay the sailing of the next convoy, but this would be their loss rather than ours. Such an approach would avoid placing us in an embarrassing position as regards the personnel whom we wished to retain in Russia. We should also make it clear that before returning the convoy personnel to North Russia it would be necessary to arrive at a satisfactory agreement on the various points of difficulty.

Mr Dean (Foreign Office) said that we were not in a strong position as regards the sentenced merchant seamen since we could not legally claim that there was any alternative jurisdiction to which they were subject. As soon as the Foreign Office had obtained the precise facts they intended to make strong representations as to the severity of the sentences.

THE COMMITTEE:-
(a) Invited the Foreign Office in consultation with the Admiralty, War Office and Air Ministry to prepare in the light of their discussions a draft reply for consideration at their meeting on Thursday 29th July.
(b) Instructed the Secretary to despatch a telegram to General Martell explaining that the position of our personnel in North Russia was under urgent consideration and instructing him not to hand over Private Spencer or Sergeant Ryan to the Russian Authorities without further instructions.
(c) Took note that the Foreign Office, in consultation with the Ministry of War Transport, were taking up with the Russians the question of reducing the sentences on the two merchant seamen.

The situation was discussed again at the Chiefs of Staff Meeting on 29 July[25] when Sir Neville Syfret[26] handed round copies of a draft minute to Churchill prepared by the Admiralty as a result of consultation with the Foreign Office, War Office and Air Ministry. He said if the committee approved the conclusions reached he would welcome the opportunity to redraft the first two paragraphs before the minute went forward. There was general agreement with the course of action recommended and certain amendments to the draft were approved. The committee invited the Admiralty in consultation with the Foreign Office to prepare a revised minute to Churchill for circulation as soon as possible.

The secretary to the Chiefs of Staff Committee in a paper dated 11 August 1943[27] reported that the vice chiefs of staff had considered at their meeting[28] held on 29 July a minute from Churchill[29] on the subject of the ill-treatment of personnel in North Russia and subsequently, without further discussion, approved a note[30] by the secretary covering a report[31] for submission to Churchill under their signatures. Churchill had then authorized the dispatch of a message to M. Molotov on the lines of paragraphs 9 and 10 of the report and the Foreign Office had dispatched telegrams[32] accordingly. In addition, the Admiralty had telegraphed[33] Admiral Fisher.[34] The vice chief's paper, circulated as a series of annexes to the note for information and record purposes, reads as follows:

ANNEX 1
PRIME MINISTER
DIFFICULTIES IN NORTH RUSSIA

1. The Chiefs of Staff Committee have considered your Minute at Flag A on the ill-treatment of our people in North Russia, and their report on this complicated problem is attached at Flag B.

2. They fully agree with you that action on the lines you suggest should be far more effective than any form of argument; unfortunately we cannot afford to have our bluff called by the Russians, because the large majority of our naval and air personnel in this area are connected with current and impending operations irrespective of any North Russian convoys. The present position is outlined in paragraphs 2-4 of the attached report (FLAG B).

3. If, alternatively, we were to make a show of withdrawing the small number of men that can be spared while there are no convoys, this would be just about the number that the Russians have been pressing us to remove and would only lead them to suppose we had climbed down. This would do nothing to secure better treatment for our men, since the retention of the purely operational personnel would lead them to suppose that we were still considering the resumption of the convoys.

4. Apart from a direct threat not to resume future convoys unless our wishes are met, the Chiefs of Staff suggest that the only way of getting proper treatment for our men is to try to convince the Soviet authorities of the importance of the task in which they are engaged.

5. It is with the Soviet civil authorities that the main difficulty lies; the Service authorities are reported to be co-operative. The Chiefs of Staff therefore suggest that the question be taken up on the highest level, preferably in a personal message from you to Premier Stalin or, alternatively, through H.M. Ambassador who could convey your message from the Foreign Secretary to M. Molotov. Mr Eden, is, I understand, inclined to favour the latter method.

6. If you approve, the message to M. Molotov could be on the lines suggested in paragraphs 9 and 10 of the attached minute.

7. The position regarding the trial of Service personnel and Merchant seamen is outlined in the Note at Flag C on which action is already in hand.

Sgd. C.R. PRICE   2nd AUGUST 1943

ANNEX II
PRIME MINISTER
DIFFICULTIES IN NORTH RUSSIA

We were attracted by the proposals in your Minute d.141/3 because such action may weigh more with the Russians than any form of argument.

Unfortunately, however, our immediate requirements in North Russia for current and contemplated operations, quite apart from the question of future convoys, are a serious obstacle in carrying out the proposals.

2. The present position is as follows:
   (a) We have laboriously built up an organisation in North Russian ports which now meets operational needs. These ports are the nearest in Allied hands to the northern hide-outs of enemy main units, and the only ones from which regular air reconnaissance is practicable.

   The success of plans to destroy the enemy Heavy ships in September depends upon the existence of adequate facilities in North Russia and the retention there of all existing naval personnel except fifty officers and men who might be withdrawn if the base at Archangel were closed down.

   (b) But the presence in North Russia of 4 Allied Merchant vessels, with their 700 seamen, makes it impossible to close the Archangel base. These ships cannot be brought home until the dark period in November – and then only by means of a major operation – and they are now, at the request of the Russians, running cargoes between Archangel and the Kola Inlet.

   Three of H.M. ships (two minesweepers and one trawler) are established in North Russia to provide support and protection for the Merchant vessels. To withdraw all the service personnel would leave these men-of-war and Merchant vessels without maintenance, communication or hospital facilities in an unsympathetic country under severe climatic conditions and the enemy air. In short, so long as these ships are in North Russia, we must maintain the facilities both at Archangel and Murmansk.

   (c) The abandonment of the Y service would be a definite loss to our intelligence.

3. The result is, that so far as naval personnel are concerned, almost all are required for maintaining Merchant ship sailings or for operations against German main units. At best, we could perhaps

spare some 10 cooks, stewards, etc. at expense of the amenities for remaining personnel.
4. Of the small RAF party, only a very few are employed solely in connection with the convoys and could, therefore, be withdrawn. Of the Army Base Unit (totalling 57)[35] could, at a pinch, be withdrawn.
5. It would not suit us at all, therefore, to make ostentatious preparations for the withdrawal of all our people and then to have the Russians call our bluff.
6. If, on the other hand, we were to make a show of withdrawing the small number that can be spared while there are no convoys this would be just about the number that the Russians have already asked us to withdraw, and would only lead the Russians to suppose that we had climbed down. This would do nothing to secure better treatment for our men, since the retention of the purely operational personnel would make it plain that we were still intending the resumption of convoys. Even a warning that the withdrawal of these men would mean delay in the resumption of the convoys is unlikely to be effective, as the Russians would realise that the replacement of such a small number is not a difficult or lengthy operation.
7. Perhaps the major difficulty we have to overcome is that the Russians, in spite of repeated representations, have since last January been refusing all applications for Visas for Service personnel for North Russia. This means that men who are badly in need of relief cannot be released and the dispatch of the additional personnel required for our operations will be prevented.
8. Apart from a direct threat not to resume convoys unless our wishes are met, which is presumably not acceptable, we suggest that the only possibility of improving conditions for our personnel in North Russia and of solving this Visa problem is to convince the Russians of the importance of the work these men are doing.
9. The best course of action would be for you to address a message to President Stalin explaining briefly the difficulties we are having, that our men are really required for immediate operations quite apart from the convoys, and asking him to go into the whole question with his service Authorities. An alternative would be for the Foreign Secretary to send a similar message to M. Molotov through our Ambassador in Moscow.
10. The message to President Stalin or M. Molotov asking for help should, we think, lay a special emphasis on:

(a) Our need for permission to send reliefs, since the staleness of personnel is affecting their efficiency; the Soviet Authorities have refused Visas for all service personnel for the past six months.
(b) The importance we attach to our personnel in North Russia being dealt with for all minor offences by our own Authorities.
(c) Certain other difficulties, such as the vexatious regulations affecting the landing of personnel, mails and stores, and restrictions on the movement of personnel hindering the performance of their duties.

11. Whichever course is followed, we would, at the same, brief Admiral Fisher to explain fairly fully to the Head of Soviet Naval Staff the contemplated special activities, which we shall, in any case, have to mention to the Russians in due course.
12. As regards the trial of Service personnel and Merchant seamen for offences committed ashore, we think that you already know of the special difficulties to be faced in dealing with Merchant seamen. We therefore attach to this note an appreciation of the difficulties concerning jurisdictions.

Review of Numbers of Service Personnel in North Russia

As part of the attempt to break the deadlock over the numbers of service personnel in North Russia, Admiral Fisher signalled the SBNO on 15 August on behalf of the British ambassador. As the Russians were continually complaining of excessive numbers of personnel in North Russia especially when convoys were not running, the ambassador had asked for minimum numbers required assuming that they (the convoys) would not run for a period of about six months and no merchant vessels would remain in North Russia as at present. The SBNO was requested to signal numbers required in each of the following cases under headings of 'Scheme of Complement':

a. All requirements other than convoys to be met as at present; e.g. existing number of British Warships based in North Russia, readiness for reception in North Russian ports of warships for fuel and ammunition during operations east of Bear Island, intermittent air operations, intelligence liaison, supervision of repairs to damaged merchant vessels, maintenance of communications sufficient for above. Y activities[35] to continue.

b. All operational readiness being relaxed and establishments reduced to care and maintenance except Y. Improbable Admiralty would accept this.

2. It seems in either of the above cases, it would be essential to bring all establishments up to full strength about two months before convoys are restarted.

Unintended Consequences: The Azores Dimension

While this review was in hand the outcome of another seemingly unrelated set of circumstances in August 1943 prompted the Soviet authorities to demand resumption of the convoys. For some time the British and American governments had been planning a military occupation of the Portuguese Atlantic Islands (the Azores) as experience had shown that keeping even a single aircraft in company with an Atlantic convoy during the greater part of each day limited the operation of U-boats. However, in order to obtain maximum air protection it was necessary for convoys to follow a route that not only suffered from the disadvantages of bad weather and ice, but that inevitably became known to the enemy. This southerly route was devoid of air protection, but northerly and southerly routes having equal air protection would be a great advantage and consequently facilities in the Portuguese Atlantic Islands would be of outstanding value in shortening the war by convincing the enemy that he had lost the Battle of the Atlantic. Plans were therefore made for a military occupation of the islands but, in the event, British diplomatic efforts prevailed and on 15 August 1943 the planned invasion was cancelled.

Four days later, on the 19th, in a 'most secret and personal' message, President Roosevelt and Prime Minister Churchill jointly informed Premier Stalin:

> Following on decisions taken at 'Trident'[36] His Majesty's Government entered upon negotiations with Portugal in order to obtain naval and air facilities in a 'life-belt'. Accordingly His Majesty's Ambassador at Lisbon invoked the Anglo-Portuguese Alliance which has lasted 600 years unbroken and invited Portugal to grant the said facilities.
>
> Dr. Salazar has now consented to the use of a 'life-belt' by the British with Portuguese collaboration in the early part of October. As soon as we are established there and he is relieved from his anxieties we shall press for extensions of these facilities to United States ships and aircraft.
>
> The possession of the 'life-belt' is of great importance to the sea war. The U-boats have quitted the North Atlantic where convoys have been running without loss since the middle of May and have concentrated on the southern route. The use of the 'life-belt' will be of the utmost help in attacks on them from the air. Besides this there is the ferrying of United States heavy bombers to Europe and Africa, which is also most desirable.
>
> All the above is of most especially secret operational character.

This missive was, as we shall see later, to have some unintended consequences in prompting the Russians to seek resumption of the convoy programme.

Growing Discontent among Merchant Ship Crews in North Russia

Returning to personnel conditions in North Russia, Admiral Fisher, in a signal to the Admiralty on 19 August, reported as follows:

> Considerable discontent amongst crews of British Merchant vessels which have been idle for over six months. Supplies of fresh food inadequate, and increasing cases of stomach trouble. Clothing and boots are wearing out and survivors' stocks which have been drawn upon will not last beyond September.
>
> Even if basic items of stores are available to enable ships to stay until November or January, life will be reduced to bare subsistence. The continued idleness, likely to breed trouble on board and ashore with our allies. SBNO considers from every point of view no effort should be spared to get these ships home as soon as possible.

In his more detailed monthly report[37] the SBNO complained:

> This month has been one in which the state of British and US Merchant ships in North Russia has come to the fore. Originally planned to be sailed for the United Kingdom in September there have been indications the policy is to be amended in favour of leaving these ships out here for a considerably longer period. I pray and trust effect will not be given to this. There can be no doubt the personnel who man these ships are very discontented and the only wonder is there have not been more manifestations of this speaks volumes for the Masters and shore authorities who have done all in their power to keep the men occupied and provide what little recreation they can. Even as it is we have had a murder, more than one suicide, several Soviet citizens suffering from nose-bleeding, quite a number of mental cases and widespread stomach trouble.
>
> There was, too, the apparently inexhaustible supply of Soviet laws, one to meet any contingency (as required) to bolster up any move against us. I have asked for a copy of these laws on more than one occasion but so far have not been supplied with it.

Chapter Twelve

Russian Pressure for Resumption of Convoys

In late August the Russians began to press for the resumption of the convoys to North Russia. On 25 August, the Soviet Chargé d'Affaires delivered a letter to the Foreign Office in London requesting that the convoys restart, as had earlier been promised, in September. The Persian Gulf route had failed to reach the capacity of 240,000 tons a month rashly predicted by Churchill when he had cancelled the convoys in March (see above). Furthermore the letter claimed that the Pacific Route had disappointed expectations because of constant Japanese interference. In fact, the capacity of the various routes was not as low as the Russians claimed, although they were certainly below target.

The Foreign Office replied, citing operational considerations which made it impossible to restart the convoys in September. This response naturally infuriated the Kremlin. As the Commercial Secretary at the British Embassy in Moscow observed:

> The Soviet Government realised our decision to suspend Northern convoys (a) preserves both Merchant and naval ships from being sunk, and (b) makes them available for other work. They will not, however, accept the decision with good grace until they are convinced good use has been and is being made of these ships. They will only be convinced of this when a Second Front – as they interpret the phrase – has been established. Until then the suspension of convoys will continue to embitter the general relations between the two Governments.

The British Ambassador in Moscow, however, thought it would be politic to meet Soviet demands partway and halve the northern establishment (of personnel) when the convoys were not running. If the British personnel numbered only 160 in the idle months, he argued, the Russians might prove more co-operative when the convoys restarted. The chiefs of staff did not approve of either suggestion. Each of these would have involved a considerable diplomatic defeat since the chiefs of staff and War Cabinet had never accepted the right of the Russian government to dictate the number of men needed for duties in North Russia. Each proposal, furthermore, would have left unresolved the question of the twenty-four merchant ships and their 700 crew stranded in the northern ports since the cancellation of the convoys in the spring. Without the service establishment these men would be left without hospital services or communications with Great Britain. Finally, the Admiralty argued there was no month that could be described as idle.

Unbeknown to the Foreign Office, the C-in-C Home Fleet was about to launch an operation against the German surface vessels in the north for which the naval personnel in the Arctic were essential. Consequently the British government could at first only agree to make another ineffectual approach to the Soviet government in August and to withdraw a small number of service personnel in September. These were from the No. 126 Base Unit, sent in the early days of the protocols to assist with the arrival of supplies and whose usefulness had long since passed and would leave Russia on 5 October.

Signs of Progress with Treatment of British Service Personnel

By the end of August the SBNO had been able to report some progress in resolving difficulties with passes and mail, but none on the question of reliefs:

> August has seen some progress in the pass offensive. Such a document was needed for entering any establishment, docks etc. using the road and so on – a different pass for each. One thus accumulated, after varying degrees of difficulty, a considerable number of such documents; there was apparently no general pass. That the sentry could not in many cases read the pass did not really affect the issue; on occasions one of Messrs Gieves[1] Bills (duly receipted of course) had passed muster. At any rate British personnel we can now visit their own ammunition dumps, use the road from Murmansk to Vaenga, and visit the aerodrome at the latter (a great concession as British planes were using it), the only thing they could not as yet do was to use the only road out of Polyarny for exercise beyond the one-mile barrier. The presence of mines was the reason given, but this did not prevent local traffic using it and we persevere in our efforts to extend the limits of the concentration camp.
>
> The siege of North Russia had also been raised; two destroyers running the blockade had brought in mail and stores but no reliefs. The dearth of reliefs remained the most pressing problem. Of the 176 service personnel borne on 30 August, 152 were due or overdue for relief. The former number was now six fewer due to those sent home on 31 August without relief: three by Admiralty order and the remaining three on medical grounds (state of anxiety).

The situation was deteriorating, numbers were dropping, efficiency and morale were lower and with the best will in the world personnel were becoming dispirited due to the uncertainty of their position. These officers and men had given exceptionally good service and they fully realized the efforts being made to relieve them, but now the time had come to face the fact that with the dreary winter ahead it was more than probable that further men would have to be sent home on medical grounds. Nine months was the accepted limit of service in this climate, at this latitude and living on tinned food. The medical officers serving in North Russia had reported their concern in the above sense. Negotiations were now proceeding in Moscow to agree the total number of British required in North Russia, but whatever the agreed total, surely there was some means of bringing pressure to bear on the Russians to force them to allow say 100 reliefs to be sent out immediately so an equivalent number could be sent home? Some officers and men were nearing completion of their second year and many had served eighteen months here, which was double the time recommended as a limit. The situation was not improved when in September the Soviet Embassy in London announced that no more visas or special passes would be granted for British personnel to serve in North Russia. The Russians reiterated their argument that there should be equality of numbers between British servicemen in the Soviet Union and Russian representatives in the United Kingdom.[2]

Churchill Threatens to withdraw all British Service Personnel from North Russia

The larger issue of the size of the naval establishment in North Russia would, however, be deferred until Churchill, who had sailed for North America on 4 August for discussions with President Roosevelt and for the Quebec Conference, arrived back from the US in the battleship *Renown* at Greenock on the Clyde at 9.30 am on 19 September.[3]

During his absence, Churchill had sent a telegram on 5 September to the Foreign Secretary[4] in relation to General Martel's telegram of 28 August[5] in which he said:

Surely we should say to the Russians as soon as our special operation in the far North has been completed[6] we are willing, if you desire it, to withdraw all our personnel from North Russia. This of course will mean that no more convoys will come by the Arctic route. We should be sorry for this, as it is the best route and if the aforesaid operation succeeds it may become much easier.

Nevertheless we will certainly withdraw our personnel if that is your wish. There is no question of their remaining under present conditions.

2. Let me know what objections there are to this course from the Admiralty or Air viewpoint. I think myself it is the only way to get consideration.
3. What has happened to the two British merchant seamen who have been sentenced to long terms of penal servitude by Russian courts for trifling offences? They must not be forgotten.

Discussions on the Resumption of Convoys

Despite this impasse over treatment of British service personnel, consideration turned again to resumption of the convoys. On 12 September, the Minister of Production (Chairman of the Allied Supplies Executive) circulated a memorandum to the Chiefs of Staff Committee on delivery of supplies to Russia.[7] This advised that decisions about the opening of the Northern Route to Russia were now necessary as in the previous March the Russians had been told 'Provided HUSKY goes well, we should hope to resume convoys in early September providing the disposition of German main units permitted and the situation in the North Atlantic was such as to enable us to provide the necessary escorts and covering forces.'

The minister commented that the Admiralty's general attitude towards resumption remained unfavourable as long as the present German concentration (of heavy ships) remained, but went on to summarize the outstanding American and British commitments under the third protocol. He added that the Russians had been informed, through H.M. Ambassador, of the nature of an operation in mind for northern waters.[8] The reopening of the Northern Route largely depended on the success of this operation and convoys would not be restarted in September. The ambassador was being instructed to inform the Russians that the operational and strategic situation was too uncertain at present to give any decision. Further guidance was sought as to how any discussions on restarting the convoy should be handled.

American Pressure to Resume Convoys

The Chiefs of Staff Committee discussed the memorandum on 16 September.[9] Sir Neville Syfret reported that he had received a telegram from the First Sea

Lord informing him Mr Harriman was anxious that the convoys should be restarted as soon as possible. The Admiralty fully appreciated the importance of the convoys and were also desirous of recovering the twenty-four merchant vessels in North Russia. There would, however, be some difficulty in finding escort vessels suitably modified for the route while the presence of major units of the German fleet in North Norway had to be considered.

Sir Neville suggested the following replies to the questions in Paragraph 9 of the memorandum:

(a) Yes.
(b) No firm estimate can be given but it is recommended plans be made for sailing a convoy to North Russia assuming 1st December to be the first possible date of sailing from this country. The Committee approved the replies suggested by Vice Chief Naval Staff and instructed the Secretary to inform the Minister of Production accordingly.

Renewed Russian call for Resumption of the Convoys

This then was the situation when on 21 September M. Molotov made a peremptory demand for the immediate resumption of the northern convoys. The British ambassador in Moscow was sent for that evening by M. Molotov and handed a long memorandum on the subject. The ambassador reminded M. Molotov of the unhappy fate of the convoys the previous summer owing to the presence of German capital ships in the Norwegian fjords. If it was possible to dispose satisfactorily of the German fleet, convoys probably could be resumed without delay.

The full text of the exchange reported in a telegram dated 23 September 1943 from Moscow to the Foreign Office[10] read as follows:

Your Telegram No. 1198:
1. Mr Molotov sent for me on the evening of September 21st to hand me a long Memorandum about convoys.
2. After recapitulating substance of Mr Molotov's communication to Sir O. Sargent[11] of August 25th and our reply sent to him on September 6th, the Memorandum stated the Soviet Government had naturally borne in mind the proviso contained in Churchill's message of 30th March to Stalin, but the reasons given by His Majesty's Government for non-resumption of the convoys were not supported by facts. The Soviet Government wishes to remind his Majesty's Government:

(1) Of the statement contained in the joint message of August 19th from Churchill and President Roosevelt[12] about 'lifebelt' and the submarines of Germany abandoned the North Atlantic and were concentrating on the southern route; and

(2) Of the claim in joint statement issued by M.O.I. and US Bureau of Military Information on September 11th regarding naval losses in August, the enemy had not attempted to attack cargo ships in the northern part of the Atlantic and chances of attacks on submarines had been comparatively rare.[13]

These facts prove navigation conditions in the North Atlantic since May have not been dangerous for convoys proceeding to Northern Ports of Soviet Union.

3. This more favourable position, the increased naval strengths of the Allies and the elimination of the Italian fleet, which allowed the convoys to pass through the Mediterranean instead of around the Cape and thus set free escort ships for northern route, made a further postponement of convoys quite unjustifiable. The resumption was more necessary since the Soviet Union had this year received by the Northern Route less than one-third of last year's supplies (249,097 tons as against 764,337 tons).

4. His Majesty's Government's reference to the inadequate carrying capacity of Persian railways in Northern Zone only makes resumption of convoys more necessary as has been pointed out in the Soviet Memorandum of August 25th and the Soviet Government therefore maintained in deciding the question of resumption of convoys, due weight should be given to this fact, which is of the greatest importance to the whole question of Soviet supplies.

5. In view of the above circumstances and of the fact the Soviet Armies were now for the third successive month undertaking a wide and most strenuous offensive on almost the whole German front for the success of which every intensification and increase in supply of armaments and other material was important; the Soviet Government insisted upon the urgent resumption of convoys and expected His Majesty's Government to take necessary measures within the next few days.

6. Molotov made it clear the Soviet Government attached very great importance to the matter and in handing me this memorandum he repeated orally all its arguments, which countered with the obvious replies, reminding him of the unhappy fate of our convoys last summer owing to the presence of German capital ships in Norwegian fjords. If

we were able to dispose satisfactorily of German Fleet, I said I thought convoys could be resumed without delay.
7. Full text Memorandum goes to you by bag.

Churchill Considers Molotov's Demand

On 25 September[14] Churchill called a staff meeting to be held on the evening of 28 or 29 September to discuss the situation, noting:

> See Molotov's request in Clark Kerr's No. 1005. It is our duty if humanly possible to re-open these ARCTIC convoys, beginning in the latter part of November in accordance with the moon phase. We should try to run a November, December, January, February and March – total 5. The Admiralty and the Ministry of War Transport should prepare plans. I understand this is feasible. He added: 'Now the Russians have asked for the re-opening of these convoys, we are entitled to make a very plain request to them for the better treatment of our personnel in North Russia.'[15]

On 26 September the Cabinet Secretary also circulated to the Chiefs of Staff Committee[16] a copy of the Admiralty 'Note on the Resumption of Convoys for North Russia', prepared for the use of the British delegation to the forthcoming Tripartite Conference of Representatives of the USA, USSR and UK.[17] This note reviewed the background to the decision to suspend the convoys as set out in the prime minister's 30 March telegram to Stalin together with Stalin's reply, and went on to describe the current position as explained to the Russians. The German surface fleet concentration remained, and although HUSKY went well, the navy was now heavily committed to AVALANCHE.[18] The Russians had recently therefore been informed, through His Majesty's Ambassador,[19] that the convoys could not be restarted in September and their resumption largely depended on the success of operations (now imminent) to destroy the enemy main units,[20] all of which had been explained to the Russians. As far as commitments under the third protocol were concerned, it argued that there was an undertaking to supply shipping to augment Soviet tonnage 'so far as was necessary' for carrying the supplies promised. The Russians had asked for two-thirds of this to be sent by the Northern Route but had been told that no guarantee could be given about routes in the present circumstances. The maximum commitment for the Northern Route on the Russian demand for two-thirds would amount to some sixty or seventy ships, but for both for operational and supply reasons it would be more convenient to send these supplies if they were to go by the Northern Route in a greater number of smaller convoys than in two large ones.

There were also still the crews of the twenty-four Allied merchant ships in North Russia left behind in Russia after the last convoy. Some of these merchant ships had at Russian request been carrying Russian cargos between Archangel and the Kola Inlet. Recent reports concerning the morale of these crews made it very desirable that they should be brought back as soon as possible and the Commander-in-Chief, Home Fleet had it in mind to bring out about a dozen of the faster ships towards the end of October and the remainder later; provided, of course, that the operational risks justified this course of action.

In summary, the Admiralty note concluded, if the threat from the German surface units was removed the difficulty in restarting the Northern Route convoys would lie in providing naval escorts which must be specially prepared for Arctic service and could only be found at the expense of other naval undertakings. It fully acknowledged the necessity of running these convoys and bringing back the merchant ships now in Russian ports with every effort made to do so. Plans were therefore being prepared to enable a convoy to be run should the opportunity occur, with 16 November being the earliest possible date for doing so [JW 54].

Proposals for Resumption of the Convoy Programme

Churchill received a further brief from the vice chief of the naval staff on 26 September prior to the planned staff meeting containing specific but qualified proposals to resume the convoy cycle. Noting that conditions on the Northern Route were most favourable from the end of November to the end of January when it was dark, the ice was still well to the northward and, subject to anti-submarine escort vessels and destroyers being available and the general situation permitting, these were:

> To bring home in convoy (RA 54), in late October, those Merchant vessels capable of 10 knots or over at present in Russia, i.e. 12 out of the 23 there. Then in the third week in November to run a small convoy (JW 54) of 16 ships of 11 knots or over, to include one tanker and one store ship with the necessary fuel and special stores to enable subsequent operations to proceed.[21] Following this there would be an interval whilst this convoy is unloaded, then about 8th December a small convoy (JW 55) would be run, and RA 55 consisting of the unloaded ships of JW 54 brought home. Finally about 8th January further convoys, JW 56 and RA

56, would be run. After this as the weather conditions deteriorated and the ice came to the Southward, the cycle might have to be extended.

The C-in-C Home Fleet was, however, seemingly unwilling to make any firm commitment and advised Churchill that it would be unwise to make a definite promise now to Russia to run convoys for the navy might well be faced, when the time came, with a situation in the Atlantic and commitments in the Mediterranean that would prevent the collection of sufficient escorts. These proposals were not well received by Churchill; he regarded this appreciation by the VCNS as unsatisfactory and had it circulated to the Chiefs of Staff Committee for discussion at the staff conference to be held at 10.00 pm on Tuesday, 28 September.[22]

Churchill's minute of 27 September[23] calling the staff meeting read as follows:

Please see the attached from the VCNS, this is not satisfactory. Why cannot the November convoy be the full JW? This also applies to the December 8 convoy. We must try to run at least five full convoys before OVERLORD operations start. I do not agree the situation in the Atlantic or in the Mediterranean will be as strained as it was when we were running these convoys before. Naturally I am not going to make a solemn contract with Marshal Stalin, and we must safeguard ourselves against unfavourable contingencies, but I consider that November, December, January, February and March should each see a full convoy despatched.

Diplomatic Relations in North Russian Ports

Meantime the Chiefs of Staff Committee[24] received on 27 September another lengthy report from the head of the British Military Mission in Moscow dated 2 September and covering the period 5 July to 30 August. This included an update on relations with the Russians which reported no improvement in the situation since the previous report of 10 July; i.e. 'to the intolerable way in which we are treated by the Russian government over these domestic matters.' It went on to suggest that the stumbling block was the Russian government in Moscow over which the Russian military had no influence at all. The matter, while no doubt being dealt with in London, remained as urgent as ever.

The head of the mission had discussed with the ambassador the possible courses of action to deal with the situation. These were firstly to attempt to placate the Russians by agreeing to reduce the numbers of service personnel during the periods when convoys were not running (a gesture to reciprocity);

secondly, to threaten to stop the convoys; and thirdly, to treat the Russians in the UK in the same way as British personnel in Russia by introducing visas, censorship of mail, etc. The ambassador favoured the first option as during the recent quiet period the naval strength had fallen to 181 compared with the establishment of 278 that was calculated to be the number required to run the convoys at full strength. In addition, when convoys were not running, army and RAF numbers could also be reduced.

Chapter Thirteen

Negotiation on Renewal of the Convoy Programme

Roosevelt Consulted on Russian Demands

On 28 September, Churchill was again in correspondence with Roosevelt.[1] Paragraph 3 of his telegram read:

3. The Russians have demanded the renewal of the Arctic convoys. We are looking into this and I hope something may be possible between now and OVERLORD. Most Secret. We believe we have damaged *Tirpitz* (22 September) and that she will have to go back to Germany for docking & repair. If this should be so, it should give us 3 or 4 months' ease in the north.

That same evening, the Defence Committee (Operations) met to consider the two papers[2] submitted by the secretary to the Chiefs of Staff Committee[3] at Churchill's behest. Churchill stated when convoys to North Russia had stopped and the support groups been diverted to the Atlantic, it had not been the intention to discontinue these convoys altogether. The Persian route into Russia, although improved, was still inadequate and it had not been possible to open a 'second front' in 1942 or 1943. The Russian armies were now achieving great results and deserved all possible support. The Russian request to restart the convoys should be agreed, but before doing so British personnel deployed to North Russia must be given proper treatment. It was not enough to run convoys of sixteen ships. The aim should be to run up to five convoys between November and March, each of approximately fifty-five ships (American and British). There was also the question of the merchant ships now in North Russia. The vice chief of the naval staff had suggested bringing out only the fastest of these ships. Churchill insisted that all should be brought out. The C-in-C Home Fleet advised that the most suitable period for running the first convoy was between 15 and 25 November. It was not considered practicable to bring out all the ships now in Russia in one convoy owing to the shortage of sufficient escorts and the fact that the long hours of daylight would expose the whole convoy to considerable danger. If all were to be brought out, he suggested that the faster ships should leave with the first return convoy and the remainder at a later date when the hours of daylight would be shorter.

The Minister of War Transport reported that it would be necessary to start making preparations for the first convoy now, since a number of the ships would have to be modified. This could, however, be done in time for the convoy to sail in mid-November. The ministry could find some fifteen ships, and there was a large amount of American material already in this country waiting to go to Russia. The Americans should be able to find some twelve ships and these would be loaded in America. Including the oilers, stores ships and possibly a coal ship, the convoy would be made up to some thirty-five vessels. The US ships were of welded construction and the Americans did not consider that they required much stiffening. In order to ensure that the British ships were ready in time, he asked for special priority to be given to the work of stiffening them and also gave an assurance that all merchant ships included in future convoys to Russia would be capable of a speed of at least 10 knots.

Churchill then enquired what escorts would be necessary, noting that the enemy air strength in North Norway had been considerably reduced and also noting in view of the general pressure on his Air Force it would take the enemy some time to build it up again. Furthermore, one of the enemy's major naval units had left the area and it was possible that others would follow. The C-in-C Home Fleet advised that there were still a number of submarines in the area. The (size of) escort required would, of course, depend on the situation at the time the convoy started. The requirement was estimated as eight cruisers, twenty-four fleet destroyers, twelve escort vessels and four Hunt-class destroyers. This estimate, however, had been based on a smaller convoy, and if the size of the convoy was doubled the C-in-C estimated that approximately 50 per cent more escort vessels would be required, noting there was at the time a shortage of destroyers. Churchill pointed out that the support group diverted on loan to the North Atlantic when the convoys were stopped would have to be returned and suggested that new construction would be more than sufficient to meet the remaining requirement. He asked what support vessels were expected from this source by the beginning of November. The vice chief of the naval staff said that twenty-nine vessels including fifteen frigates and ten corvettes should be completed during this period.

The committee then considered the question of follow-up convoys. The Minister of War Transport said that some forty-seven (merchant) ships would be required to meet the full protocol requirements up to June 1944. There would be no difficulty in making up further convoys of thirty-five ships. Both the Americans and the Russians preferred the Northern Route and the

Negotiation on Renewal of the Convoy Programme 191

former had recently cut down supplies on the Vladivostok route, presumably owing to an increased Japanese threat against this route. If convoys of the size now proposed continued to be run, it was estimated that four convoys would complete delivery of our quota under the protocol. Churchill said he preferred to run four rather than five convoys. He did not intend to make any definite promise to the Russians, but to inform them that it was our earnest intention to run four full convoys at approximately monthly intervals staring in mid-November. He would make it clear that this was, however, conditional on British personnel employed in North Russia being properly treated, while any radical change in the situation in the Atlantic or in Northern waters might necessitate a change of programme. He fully realized the need for adequate escorts, but felt that these could be provided without any serious difficulty in view of the improved general naval situation and of the large number of escort vessels to be expected from new construction. He wished to be informed of the deliveries expected during the next five months of all types of naval vessels.

The committee agreed that

    (i)   As many as possible of the merchant vessels now in North Russia should be brought home in late October (Convoy RA 54).
    (ii) A convoy (JW 54) of about 35 ships (British and American) should be assembled in a UK port so as to be ready to sail by 15 November.
    (iii) The remaining Merchant vessels now in North Russia left over from Convoy RA 54 should be brought back by the escorts of JW 54.
    (iv) Further convoys, each of approximately 35 ships (British and American) should be sailed in December, January and February.

(b) To invite the Admiralty, in consultation with the Ministry of War Transport, to submit to Churchill a plan, as a matter of urgency, for putting (a) above into effect.

(c) The Ministry of War Transport should receive any special priority needed for stiffening of ships for the November convoy.

(d) The establishment of British personnel and equipment maintained in North Russian ports should be based entirely on operational requirements and should not be related to the numbers of Russian personnel in this country.

(e) To invite the Foreign Office in consultation with the Admiralty and Ministry of War Transport to prepare a statement to be presented to the Soviet Government explaining the resumption of the convoys

would be dependent on a settlement, satisfactory to us, of outstanding grievances regarding the treatment of our personnel in North Russia.
(f) Following approval by Churchill of the plan at (b) and of the statement at (e) above the Soviet Government would be informed of His Majesty's Government's intentions but not promises for the resumption of convoys to North Russia.

In his September report the SBNO noted:[4]

The general situation as regards merchant ships in North Russia was unsatisfactory as had been reported by signal. Every effort had been made to do what was possible in the way of recreation, provision of games, reading matter and so on during their enforced idleness but facilities are limited. He went on: There was no doubt what the personnel of these ships thought of our Allies – even the reddest of the red (in UK) drawn say from the Clyde district, have altered their views of Communism, these gentry (in Soviet Russia) now being among its most bitter opponents.

All provisions in North Russia had been pooled and issues made on a per capita basis to the merchant ships, canteen stores as far as they will go have also been issued to them, as has Services and survivors' clothing. There is no doubt that every effort should be made to get these ships away as soon as possible. The long dreary winter has commenced ...

Chapter Fourteen

Churchill's Preconditions for Resumption

Churchill responded at length on 1 October to Stalin's request for the reopening of convoys to North Russia:

> I have received your request for the reopening of convoys to North Russia. I and all my colleagues are most anxious to help you and the valiant armies you lead to the utmost of our ability. I do not therefore reply to the various controversial points made in Monsieur Molotov's communication. Since June 22nd, 1941, we have always done our best in spite of our own heavy burdens to help you defend your own country against the cruel invasion of the Hitlerite gang and we have never ceased to acknowledge and proclaim the great advantages that have come to us from the splendid victories you have won and from the deadly blows you have dealt the German armies.
> 2. For the last four days I have been working with the Admiralty to make a plan for sending a new series of convoys to North Russia. This entails very great hardships. Firstly the Battle of the Atlantic has begun again. U-boats have set about us with a new kind of acoustic torpedo which has proved effective against escorting vessels when hunting U-boats. Secondly we are at very full stretch in the Mediterranean building up an army in Italy of about 600,000 men by the end of November and also trying to take full advantage of the Italian collapse in the Aegean Islands and Balkan Peninsula. Thirdly we have to provide our share of the war against Japan in which the United States are greatly interested and whose people would be offended if we were lukewarm.
> 3. Notwithstanding the above it is a very great pleasure to me to tell you that we are planning to sail a series of four convoys to North Russia in November, December, January and February, each of which will consist of approximately thirty-five ships, British and American. Convoys may be sailed in two halves to meet operational requirements.[1] The first convoy will leave the United Kingdom about November 12th arriving in North Russia ten days later; subsequent convoys at about twenty-eight day intervals. We intend to withdraw as many as possible of the

merchant vessels now in North Russia towards the end of October and the remainder with the returning convoy escorts.

Churchill then added a further paragraph to avoid new charges of breach of faith from the Russians if efforts to help them proved in vain: '4. However I must put it on record that this is not a contract or bargain but rather a declaration of our solemn and earnest resolve. On this basis I have ordered the necessary measures to be taken for sending these four convoys of thirty-five ships.'

Churchill then proceeded to address the restrictions that the Russians continued to place on British service personnel in North Russia, saying the following:

5. The Foreign Office and Admiralty, however, request me to put before you for your personal attention, hoping indeed that your own eye may look at it, the following representations about the difficulties we have experienced in North Russia.
6. If we are to resume the convoys we shall have to reinforce our establishments in North Russia which have been reduced in numbers since last March. The present numbers of naval personnel are below what is necessary for our present requirements owing to men having to be sent home without relief. Your civil authorities have refused us all visas for men to go to North Russia even to relieve those who are seriously overdue for relief. Monsieur Molotov has pressed His Majesty's Government to agree that the number of British Service personnel in North Russia should not exceed that of the Soviet Service personnel and of the Trade Delegation in this country.

   We have been unable to accept this proposal since their work is quite dissimilar and the number of men needed for war operations cannot be determined in such an unpractical way.

   Secondly as we have already informed the Soviet Government we must manifestly be judges of the personnel required to carry out operations for which we are responsible; Mr Eden has already given his assurance that the greatest care will be taken to limit the numbers strictly to the minimum.
7. I must therefore ask you to agree to the immediate grant of visas for the additional personnel now required and for your assurance that you will not in future withhold visas when we find it necessary to ask for them in connection with the assistance that we are giving you in North Russia. I emphasise that of about 170 naval personnel at present in the North over 150 should have been relieved some months

ago but the Soviet visas have been withheld. The state of health of these men who are unaccustomed to the climate and other conditions makes it very necessary to relieve them without further delay.
8. We should also wish to send a small medical unit for Archangel to which your authorities agreed but for which the necessary visas have not been granted. Please remember that we may have heavy casualties.
9. I must also ask your help in remedying the conditions under which our Service personnel and seamen are at present finding themselves in North Russia. These men are of course engaged in operations against the enemy in our joint interest and chiefly to bring Allied supplies to your country.

They are, I am sure you will admit, in a wholly different position from the ordinary individuals proceeding to Russian territory.

Yet they are subjected by your authorities to the following restrictions which seem to me inappropriate for men sent by an ally to carry out operations of the greatest interest to the Soviet Union:
(a) No one may land from one of His Majesty's ships or from a British merchant ship except by a Soviet boat in the presence of a Soviet official and after examination of documents on each occasion.
(b) No one from a British warship is allowed to proceed alongside a British merchantman without the Soviet authorities being informed beforehand. This even applies to the British Admiral in charge.
(c) British officers and men are required to obtain special passes before they can go from ship to shore or between the two British shore stations. These passes are often much delayed with consequent dislocation of the work in hand.
(d) No stores, luggage or mail for this operational force may be landed except in the presence of a Soviet official and numerous formalities are required for the shipment of all stores and mail.
(e) Private service mail is subjected to censorship, although for an operational force of this kind censorship should in our view be left in the hands of the British Service authorities.
10. The imposition of these restrictions makes an impression upon officers and men alike which is bad for Anglo-Soviet relations and would be deeply injurious if Parliament got to hear of it. The cumulative effect of these formalities has been most hampering to the efficient performance of the men's duties and, on more than one occasion, to urgent and important operations. No such restrictions are placed upon Soviet personnel here.

11. We have already proposed to Monsieur Molotov that as regards offences against Soviet law committed by personnel of the Services and of ships of convoys, they should be handed over to the British Service authorities to deal with. There have been a few such cases, no doubt partially at any rate due to the rigorous conditions of service in the North.
12. I trust indeed therefore that you will find it possible to have these difficulties smoothed out in a friendly spirit so that we may each help each other and the common cause to the utmost of our strength.

Churchill regarded these (demands) as modest requests considering the efforts he was now to make and telegraphed Roosevelt again on 1 October:[2]

I send you herewith a Telegram we have received from Molotov last week, and the answer I have now sent. The running of these four convoys will be a great strain to us and also a valuable boon to them. We therefore thought it right to put before him the ill usage of our people, only a few hundred, during their stay in North Russia.

You will see that I have taken for granted the fact that you would wish to participate in the convoys, as so much of your stuff is waiting to be shipped and of your extreme regret at the time when we had to abandon the convoys.

Churchill then attached a copy of the ambassador's telegram (see above) and a copy of the telegram he had just sent to Stalin (see below).

The First Lord of the Admiralty wrote to Churchill on 11 October:

In Paragraph 6 of your recent Telegram to Stalin (T.1464/43), you emphasise we shall have to reinforce our establishments in North Russia before the convoys can be resumed. Our intention is to send the additional personnel in the destroyers, which are due to leave the UK on 21st October.

2. The Senior British Naval Officer North Russia whom we asked to state his requirements reports apart from the Archangel Hospital Unit, he wants 75 men of whom 13 are replacements for Army Base Unit No. 126 which has just been disbanded at Russian request. The remainder are either replacements for those sent home since last March without relief or are necessary additions to complement, a considerable number

are W/T operators and signal personnel on whose work the safety of the convoys may well depend.
3. The SBNO North Russia also stresses the point, which you made to Stalin; it is necessary for replacements to be sent for the 150 men who are now overdue for relief.
4. We are, of course, getting the men ready for embarkation but they cannot sail unless we first have Soviet permission for them to land in North Russia. Time is running short, and you may think it necessary to jog Stalin by informing him if the cycle of convoys is to begin on the 12th November, we must have his answer to your question regarding personnel in the course of the next few days.

The Azores Agreement

In what seemed at the time an unrelated development, Churchill informed the War Cabinet on 11 October that he intended to make a public announcement on the following day of an agreement that had been reached with the Portuguese government under which they would make available to the UK certain facilities in the Azores that would be of the greatest assistance in combating enemy U-boats. The details summarized in the War Cabinet Weekly Résumé for 7 to 14 October 1943 read:

AZORES
1. Portugal has granted Great Britain certain facilities in the Azores. As a result of diplomatic negotiations, followed by a visit to Lisbon of a British Services and Departmental Mission to discuss details, an agreement was signed on the 17th August which gave us unrestricted use of Lagens airfield on Terceira, the emergency use of Rabo de Peixe on San Miguel, and the unrestricted use of port and fuelling facilities at Horta, on Fayal.

A convoy with naval escort arrived off the Islands on the 8th. The force consists principally of RAF ground and administrative staffs, and military works companies for the development of the airfield. A temporary combined HQ has been set up at Angra (Terceira).

Portugal remains responsible for the defence of the Islands, with the exception of Lagens airfield, which a unit of the RAF Regiment will defend.

Stalin's Response to Churchill's Demands

Churchill had to wait some time for a reply from Stalin to his lengthy message of 1 October. He sent a telegram on 12 October to the British ambassador in Moscow[3] in which he complained:

> I have received no answer to my long Telegram of the 1st October about resuming the Arctic Convoys. If the cycle of convoys is to begin on November 12th we must have an early reply to our requests about personnel. Several dozens of WT operators and signals personnel, on whose work the safety of the convoys may well depend, are to leave the UK, together with about 150 reliefs for men due to return home, by destroyers sailing from the UK on October 21st. Pray therefore press for an answer. Meantime we are preparing the convoy in the hope the Soviets still want them.

Planning for the convoys had nevertheless gone ahead on the assumption that Churchill's high-level appeal would improve the situation in North Russia. However, after almost two weeks' delay, Stalin replied on 13 October, in what Churchill took to be an offensive manner since he clearly resented Churchill's refusal to make a binding commitment to run four convoys; the content was lengthy and the tone deprecatory. Stalin replied as follows:[4]

> I have received your message of October 1 informing me of your intention to send four convoys to the Soviet Union by the northern route in November, December, January and February.
>
> However, the information is depreciated by your further statement that the intention to send northern convoys to the USSR is 'not a contract or bargain', but merely a declaration which, I take it, may be renounced by the British side at any moment regardless of the effect on the Soviet armies at the front. I must say I cannot agree to this approach to the matter. The British Government's deliveries of munitions and other war cargoes to the USSR cannot be treated other than as an obligation assumed by the British Government, in accordance with the terms of a special agreement between our two countries, in relation to the USSR, which for more than two years has borne the tremendous burden of the struggle against Hitler Germany, the common enemy of the Allies.
>
> Nor can the fact be ignored that the northern route is the shortest, ensuring quickest delivery to the Soviet-German front of the munitions supplied by the Allies, and that unless that route is properly used the

USSR cannot get supplies on the required scale. As I have told you before, and as borne out by experience, shipment of munitions and other war materials to the USSR through Persian ports simply cannot make up for the shortage arising from non-shipment via the northern route of munitions and materials which, it will be readily understood, are needed to fully meet the requirements of the Soviet armies. This year, however, the shipment of war cargoes by the northern route has, for some reason or other, decreased considerably compared with last year, thus making it impossible to fulfil the plan for military deliveries and running counter to the appropriate Anglo-Soviet protocol on war supplies.

And so at the present time, when the Soviet Union is straining its forces to the limit in order to meet the needs of the front and ensure the success of the struggle against the main forces of our common enemy it would be impermissible to make supplies to the Soviet armies conditional on the arbitrary judgement of the British side. Such an approach cannot but be regarded as renunciation by the British Government of its obligations, as something in the nature of a threat to the USSR.

2. Concerning what you describe as controversial points in V.M. Molotov's communication, I must say that I see no grounds whatever for this comment. In my view the principle of reciprocity and equality advanced by the Soviet side for settling all visa matters affecting the personnel of the Military Missions is sound and really just. I am not convinced by the point that the difference in the functions of the British and Soviet Military Missions precludes the application of the above principle and that the numerical strength of the British Military Mission should be determined solely by the British Government.

This matter has already been dealt with in sufficient detail in the appropriate aide-mémoires of the People's Commissariat for Foreign Affairs.

3. I see no need for increasing the numbers of the British military personnel in the Soviet North, for the overwhelming majority of the British military personnel there now are not being used properly and have for months been doomed to idleness, something repeatedly pointed out by the Soviet side. As an example Base No. 126 at Archangel can be given, the abolition of which in view of its uselessness had been suggested more than once and to which abolition the British Government has only now agreed. I regret to say there are also instances of impermissible behaviour on the part of individual

British servicemen, who in a number of cases resorted to corruption in their efforts to recruit certain Soviet citizens for intelligence purposes. Facts such as these, which offend Soviet citizens, naturally give rise to incidents with undesirable complications.
4. With regard to the formalities and certain restrictions imposed in our northern ports, mentioned by you, it should be borne in mind that in a zone adjoining the front these formalities and restrictions are inevitable in view of the military situation in which the USSR now finds itself. Besides, they apply in equal measure to British and other foreign citizens as well as to Soviet citizens. Nevertheless, in this respect too, the Soviet authorities have granted British servicemen and seamen a number of privileges, of which the British Embassy was informed in March. It follows that your reference to numerous formalities and restrictions is based on inaccurate information.

As regards censorship and penalties in relation to British Service personnel, I have no objection to the censorship of private mail for the British personnel in our northern ports being handled, on a reciprocal basis, by the British authorities, nor to British personnel who have committed minor offences that do not involve judicial investigation being dealt with by the appropriate military authorities.

Churchill's reaction to this telegram was a characteristic mixture of aggression and generous impulse. 'He snorted as he read it,' Cadogan recalled, and at the end said 'I'll stop convoys.' However, Cadogan suggested another reply and Churchill calmed down.

The same day Churchill announced in the House of Commons that Portugal had agreed to Britain's request for certain facilities in the Azores to provide better protection for merchant shipping in the Atlantic. All British forces would be withdrawn from the Azores at the end of hostilities. The agreement would come into force immediately.

The British ambassador in Moscow forwarded the Russian reply to Churchill's message to the Foreign Office and the prime minister on 14 October, which read:

Your Telegram No. 1455.
I have now received from Molotov a copy of Stalin's answer to Churchill's message of October 1st.

The message seems to have caught Stalin in a rough mood, but I fancy I see more of Molotov's hand than of his in the reply, which apart from being discourteous leaves much in the air.

I suggest no answer be sent until the Secretary of State arrives in Moscow and has had time to feel his way a little, when we might submit some suggestions.

Renewed Negotiations in Moscow

Anthony Eden, the Foreign Secretary, was at the time in Moscow for the Foreign Secretaries' Conference[5] and on the 15th Churchill sent him the following telegram:[6]

> The offensive reply in my immediately following and been received to my Telegram No. 1453 about convoys. I sent you the reply, which I have drafted as you will be on the spot. I leave it to you to handle as you see fit. I do not think we should give way about the naval reliefs or Signallers.
>
> It would be a great relief to be freed from the burden of these convoys and to bring our men home from North Russia. If this is what they really mean and want we ought to oblige them.

On 15 October Churchill also sent the Foreign Secretary his draft reply to Marshal Stalin:[7]

1. It is impossible for His Majesty's Government to guarantee the four convoys mentioned can be run irrespective of the military situation on the seas. Every effort and heavy loss and sacrifice would, however, be made to do so if the Soviet Government attaches importance to the receipt of their cargoes. I cannot undertake to do more than my best and His Majesty's Government must remain the judge of whether any particular operation to be carried out by their forces is in fact practicable or not.
2. The running of these four convoys would be a very great burden to the Royal Navy and involves the diversion of much-needed Flotillas from the anti-U-boat war and from the escorting of troop and other important convoys. It also exposes the main units of the Fleet to serious risks. His Majesty's Government would be very glad to be relieved of the task of running the convoys if the Soviet government do not attach importance to the matter.
3. In particular the refusal of the request by the British Government in respect of the reliefs and a small increase in the few hundreds of British Servicemen in the North of the USSR, and in particular the Signals personnel on which the majority of these convoys to some extent

depends, raises an insuperable obstacle. His Majesty's Government would be very glad to withdraw the handfuls of Service Personnel from North Russia and will do so as soon as they are assured it is not in the interests of the Soviet Government to receive under the modest and reasonable conditions the British Government consider necessary.

The following day, Churchill telegraphed Roosevelt:[8]

Please see my No. 429 about Russian convoys. I have now received a Telegram from U.J., which I think you will feel is not exactly all one might expect from a gentleman for whose sake we are to make an inconvenient, extreme and costly exertion. I have sent the following suggested answer to Anthony for him to handle as he thinks best.

2. I think, or at least I hope, this message comes from the machine rather than from Stalin as it took 12 days to prepare. The Soviet machine is quite convinced it can get anything by bullying and I am sure it is a matter of some importance to show this is not necessarily always true.
3. I could not postpone or interrupt loading for more than a very short time – 24 to 30 hours at the very outside – and this again might not be long enough to attract attention. In doing even this I should jeopardise catching the convoy sailing date.
4. Two of the ships, which commence loading on Monday, are American, loading American cargo and I cannot stop them without American consent.

If an interruption of loading is to be carried out with any effect it must therefore be (a) after loading has been in full swing for a few days with every evidence of haste during the loading, and (b) after the Americans have been brought into line so American and British ships are stopped together.

I have spoken to the VCNCS on the possibility of postponing the convoy sailing date as a result of an interruption of loading. He tells me postponement cannot be entertained; if we cannot comply with the planned date the first half of the first convoy must be abandoned, which would reduce the November sailing to one party of about 18 ships.

Churchill had asked the Russian Ambassador F. Gusev, who had replaced Maisky as Soviet ambassador in September, to come and see him two days later on the 18th but before the meeting and, after consulting the Chiefs of

Staff Committee on the text of the draft, he telegraphed the Foreign Secretary who was now in Moscow:[9]

> It is a very good thing you are on the spot to deal with the convoy question. I am seeing the Soviet Ambassador at 3pm today, and propose to hand him back the offensive message from Stalin, saying I do not wish to receive it, as you will settle the matter in Moscow. You should not hand in my suggested reply, or take it at anything more than a guide.
>
> Further, the first convoy is assembling and leaves on November 12. The ships are being loaded, and I have not thought it right to interfere with this process, especially as it would involve the United States, who have sent their ships at our suggestion. I hope however in personal contact with Stalin may point out, first, the importance of these four convoys with the 140 cargos, and the efforts I have had to make to secure the necessary escorts; secondly; the small petty indulgences we ask in the treatment of our men in North Russia; thirdly our natural desire to be relieved of the burden of these convoys and bring our people back from North Russia; fourthly you could also disabuse his mind of any threat intended by my declining to make an absolute contract or bargain; all I wished to do was to reserve the final right of judging whether the operation was militarily practicable or could be attempted, having regard to the general situation in the Atlantic, instead being accused, as usual, of a breach of faith, and I must maintain this position.[10]

This was the first time Churchill had met M. Gusev who had succeeded M. Maisky. After an exchange of greetings and pleasantries, Churchill turned the discussion to Stalin's telegram. He told Gusev very briefly that he did not think this message would help the situation and it had caused him a good deal of pain; he feared any reply he should send would only make things worse. The Foreign Secretary was in Moscow and he (Churchill) had left it to him to settle the matter on the spot, therefore he did not wish to receive the message. Churchill then handed an envelope back to the ambassador. Gusev opened it to see what was inside and, recognizing the message, said he had been instructed to deliver it. Churchill replied 'I am not prepared to receive it', then stood up to indicate in a friendly manner that the conversation was at an end and ushered Gusev out.

After this meeting, Churchill again telegraphed Eden in Moscow:

> I am sending you in my immediately following a note I have made of my conversation with the Soviet Ambassador today.

2. In your talks about the convoys and the treatment of our men in North Russia you should keep up your sleeve the use of the argument about the *TIRPITZ* being disabled by the valour of our midget submarines. This undoubtedly makes it easier for us to undertake the convoys than at the time when my offer to Marshal Stalin was made, and consequently the probabilities of our being able to execute what we propose and intend to try have been much improved.[11]

Churchill informed the War Cabinet on the 18th.[12] Members had seen the reply from Premier Stalin to his telegram[13] announcing the intention to send four convoys and asking for better treatment for personnel in North Russia. Stalin's answer[14] had been couched in an unhelpful and grudging tone, and he (Churchill) had been sorely tempted to send a reply to the effect that if the Russians would not mitigate the ill-treatment of our personnel in North Russia, 'we should not send the convoys'. However, it was clearly right that we should send the convoys in the interests of the war effort if we could possibly manage to do so, and he had accordingly asked the Foreign Secretary to handle the matter in Moscow. In the meantime, he had seen the newly-appointed Russian ambassador M. Gusev and had handed back to him Premier Stalin's telegram, saying he was not prepared to receive it and Mr Eden would deal with the matter orally in Moscow. In further discussion, Churchill said he thought it would be a great advantage if the Russians delivered their messages in Russian and let us arrange for their translation. He felt sure the translations made were often very crude and the tone of the original was often lost in the process of translation.

On the following day Churchill telegraphed Eden:[15] 'War Cabinet endorsed my refusal to receive the peccant message from U.J., and both War Cabinet and COS Committee approved my 16.35 to you.'

The Foreign Secretary sent Churchill a progress report from Moscow on his discussion with his Russian counterpart on the afternoon of 19 October:[16]

When M. Molotov paid a courtesy call at this Embassy this afternoon, I took the opportunity to raise the question of convoys, which I told him you had instructed me to attempt to deal with whilst in Moscow. If M. Molotov also wished this matter to be taken up how did he think this could best be done? In my view I should see Stalin and put to him the position of His Majesty's Government in the matter. If agreement was found possible as a result of this discussion M. Molotov and I might perhaps then work out the many details which must be settled.

2. M. Molotov said in his reply his Government greatly values these convoys. They had sadly missed them. Northern Route was shortest and quickest way of getting supplies to the front while Russia was going through a difficult period. The German winter defensive line had to be broken. M. Molotov said he would speak to Stalin today and let me know what could be arranged about a meeting.

In a separate telegram the same day he added:

My attention has been drawn to the fate of the British Merchant seamen recently given severe sentences for an assault in North Russia upon a local Communist leader. I am most reluctant, and the Ambassador agrees with me, to promise resumption of convoys unless these unfortunate British seamen are released and handed over to our authorities for removal. I am convinced it would be totally repugnant to you, as it is to me, to allow these men to languish in a Soviet gaol while we are accepting these risks to British seamen in future convoys. I shall try what I can do by personal appeal to Stalin or Molotov.

Churchill telegraphed the Foreign Secretary again on the 20th:[17] 'On the basis of four convoys 130 to 140 cargoes we should ship about 860,000 tons. I worked hard for this, you know.'

The Foreign Office replied on the 21st to the telegram of 19 October from the ambassador in Moscow: 'Admiralty are anxious we should draw your attention to their view of all the difficulties under which we labour in North Russia, inability to send immediate reliefs is by far most serious and urgent.'

The Foreign Secretary reported to Churchill the same day: 'I hope to see Stalin tonight about convoys when I shall take up the whole question. Meanwhile I understand some destroyers are to sail today with a batch of men on board. I suggest that sailing should be held up a day or two.'

Churchill replied:[18] 'Reference the last paragraph of No. 49 Space. The sailing of the destroyers has been held up for twenty-four hours until 7 p.m. October 22nd in first instance.'

Progress was now being made. Discussions with Stalin and Molotov took place on the evening of the 21st, after which the Foreign Secretary reported:[19] 'Had preliminary talk with Molotov tonight on convoys – going was good. Am to see Molotov tomorrow in attempt to reach final agreement. Suggest destroyers be held another 24 hours.'

The following day the Foreign Secretary reported again:

My Telegram No. 50.
My talk with Molotov went well. He agreed to granting of Visas for fresh men we need and for reliefs, and to meet us on other matters connected with convoys. Visas will be given on their arrival in North Russia.

Destroyers may therefore sail at once.
Fuller report follows.

The Foreign Secretary's fuller report[20] received on 22 October detailed Eden's previous day's meeting with Stalin and Molotov. The conversation had roamed over a large variety of topics and lasted two and a quarter hours. After some preliminary exchanges of greetings, the Foreign Secretary had raised the question of convoys, saying he must explain how great a strain these placed on the Royal Navy. The passage of each one was a major naval operation that might require four cruisers and twelve destroyers for its immediate protection, in addition to which the entire Home Fleet would also have to come out to provide cover. To make available the necessary escorts it was necessary to reduce the naval strength in the Atlantic. Though it was true that anti-U-boat warfare was going better for Britain, the struggle was still a close-run thing.

The Foreign Secretary had shown Stalin a chart of the numbers of U-boats in service over the past three years, which proved their number was still near its peak. The reasons why Churchill was not prepared to promise he would carry out four convoys was because he did not wish to expose himself to reproach if, owing to some sudden development of the war, he could not in fact send all four. However, it was his earnest desire to make these convoys available and Stalin was told it was Churchill himself who had laboured hard to make the necessary arrangements and had now telegraphed to Eden he had calculated Britain should be able to send 130 to 140 cargos with about 860,000 tons of supplies and if the convoys were to be run he was anxious to start at once. Naval dispositions had been on this basis and it was intended to utilize the period during which the *Tirpitz* was out of action. The requirements in naval personnel had been reduced to what was considered the absolute minimum if convoys were to run and we must insist on the minimum. There were also other minor requirements which if general agreement was reached Eden wished to put to Molotov.

Stalin, who had nodded agreement to the description of the U-boat warfare, said his differences with Churchill were not about the difficulties of the operation but as to whether he was bound to do it. Churchill had implied that if Britain sailed any more of these convoys it would be as a gift. Stalin did not feel this was a true description of the position. On his understanding of it Britain was under an obligation to seek to deliver these goods. When he had sent his reply to Churchill, however, Churchill had been very much offended and would not accept Stalin's reply. Eden explained it had never been suggested that to sail these convoys was an act of favour or charity. Churchill had at all times been determined to make every effort to deliver these goods to an ally, but for the reasons explained could not pledge himself to a series of operations that he might not be able to carry out. Eden suggested Stalin himself must surely have confidence in the good faith of his ally and therefore it was not surprising if Churchill should have been hurt by the message. The marshal said this had not been intended.

After some further discussion Stalin said that he would not agree to increases in numbers of men. There were already very often sailors in Northern Russian ports with nothing to do and then they got into trouble with Russian sailors. The Russians might undertake running such convoys themselves. Eden replied that this was not possible. Stalin said if only our people in Northern Russia had treated his people as equals, none of these difficulties would have arisen, and if our people would treat his people as equals we could have as many personnel as we liked. After some further argument it was decided that Molotov and Eden would meet on the following day when Molotov would be given a list of British requirements to see whether agreement could be reached. Eden reported the next day that he had received a message from Molotov on the evening the two imprisoned British sailors had been pardoned.[21]

In consultation with Molotov, Eden eventually hammered out an arrangement satisfactory to both British and Soviet governments. It was agreed that the 320 servicemen[22] in the northern ports should not be increased by more than 10 per cent without the knowledge of the Soviet government. Eden conceded the size of the establishment should be reduced when the convoys were interrupted in the spring. Molotov in turn agreed that visas should be provided within these limits and accommodation should be made available in an Archangel hospital to allow British casualties to be treated by their own medical personnel. The Kremlin also accepted that there would be less rigorous censorship of mails and British personnel committing offences should be handed over to their own authorities.[23] In token of this, Stalin had as mentioned granted a pardon to the two sailors already serving sentences in Soviet prisons.[24] This agreement resulted in considerably improved relations in the northern ports.

The head of the British Military Mission in Moscow signalled to the Admiralty on 23 October:

Urgency of additional staff and reliefs for North Russia has been fully appreciated and acted upon by Foreign Secretary with whom I have had several meetings. It was one of main issues discussed at his first meeting with Molotov and then with Stalin and these discussions have been most encouraging.

2. Minor vexations have been put forward but not yet in detail. In his message to Prime Minister, Stalin agreed to permit censorship of service mails by British authorities on basis of reciprocity but arrangement remains to be settled definitely.

The destroyers with the reliefs for the British service personnel in North Russia finally sailed on 23 October under Operation FR, which would also provide the escort for the return convoy RA 54.

Churchill telegraphed the Foreign Secretary on the following day:

I am so glad at the turn events have taken. If you think fit, say to Stalin you have received these very words from me:

It is one of my chief desires to send the largest possible quantity of cargoes to North Russia in the new convoy cycle, for which I will do everything in my power. The disablement of the *Tirpitz* is a great help. On the other hand, we lost 6 destroyers yesterday in the Aegean and Atlantic and this is where the shoe pinches. The Admiralty are very reluctant to pledge themselves to the later convoys absolutely irrespective of the situation in the Atlantic. All I can say, therefore, is I will do my utmost. If I fail, Mr Stalin may reproach me with having failed but not with having broken faith. I cannot make a lawyer's contract; I think it at least four to one we shall run the whole cycle.

You should send for the Admiral in North Russia or any other officers who can throw light on this suggestion our sailors do not treat the Russians as equals. This is very odd, as in Great Britain the Russians are treated as more than equals and with exceptional deference and goodwill. If ordinary sailors or workmen are irritated about their letters, hospital treatment etc., they will very likely be rude. You should say the most careful propaganda and the strictest orders will be given to ensure relations of mutual goodwill and respect between all ranks in North Russia. On the other hand how could he justify a Russian regulation which made the British naval commander of our forces in Archangel or Murmansk ask Soviet permission and have a Soviet guide or escort before leaving a British warship in his own boat to visit one of his own British Merchant ships?

Churchill's Preconditions for Resumption 209

Churchill was now able to report to the War Cabinet on 25 October:[25] 'The news received from the Secretary of State for Foreign Affairs shows the Moscow Conference is proceeding very well on all points. It looks as if we should receive satisfaction in regard to the treatment of British personnel in North Russia.'

The SBNO reported Operation FR – the passage of Russian light craft from Iceland – was completed with the arrival of the eight destroyers with Captain D3 in *Milne* (SO) in the Kola Inlet on 28 October. With these destroyers came a large draft to complete North Russia to full complement and provide reliefs. The results of the Moscow Conference not having filtered through to the local officials (after six days) and despite the explanation given, permission to land was refused. The next day, however, all was well and disembarkation of personnel and stores commenced, somewhat hampered by the fog that did not clear until 31 October.

Chapter Fifteen

Resumption of Convoy Cycle: November 1943 to April 1944

The cycle of supply convoys to North Russia, suspended in March 1943, resumed in November 1943 after a gap of some eight months, beginning with Operation FS. The first convoy of the new cycle, the westbound convoy RA 54A, left Archangel during the forenoon of 1 November.[1] The first eastbound convoy of the new cycle, JW 54A, sailed from Loch Ewe for Murmansk and Archangel on 15 November 1943. However, the danger from German heavy ships in Northern Norway had not yet passed.

Battle of the North Cape

During a conference with Hitler on 19 December, Admiral Dönitz obtained agreement for the *Scharnhorst*, provided the chances of success seemed reasonable, to attack the next Russian convoy that could be located. However, given the cessation of the convoys during the summer months there had been little opportunity to conduct operations and as a result the German naval units had seen little activity. Thus the German naval staff issued orders in November stating: 'The functions of the ships remain unaltered. Against this traffic (the Arctic convoys) both the Northern Task Force (essentially the *Scharnhorst* and the destroyers) and the U-boats are to be employed.'

Admiral Kummetz, the Task Force commander, preferred to wait for the completion of repairs to the *Tirpitz* and restrict himself to forays with the destroyers. Dönitz also reinforced the two U-boat flotillas in Norway. With Kummetz on leave in Germany, Rear Admiral Bey commanding the destroyers was given the task of attacking the convoy JW 55B that sailed from Loch Ewe on 20 December.

The Sinking of the *Scharnhorst*

The attack on JW 55B failed with the sinking of the *Scharnhorst* on 26 December by the convoy cover force. On 27 December Churchill telegraphed Stalin the news: 'The Arctic convoys to Russia have brought us luck. Yesterday the enemy attempted to intercept with the battlecruiser *Scharnhorst*. The Commander-in-Chief, Admiral Fraser, with the *Duke of York* (a 35,000-ton battleship) cut off the *Scharnhorst*'s retreat and after an action sank her.'

Stalin replied to Churchill: 'I send you personally, also to Admiral Sir Bruce Fraser and the valiant sailors of the *Duke of York*, my congratulations on this splendid blow.'[2]

Roosevelt also sent his congratulations on the evening of the 27th: 'The sinking of *Scharnhorst* has been great news to all of us. Congratulations to the Home Fleet.'

The four convoys in this cycle passed through a total of fifty-four merchant ships without loss.

Reduced Threat from German Surface Forces

The German attempt to attack JW 55B led to the loss of their last operational capital ship in Norway. Thereafter unless and until the *Tirpitz* returned to active service, the Allied Arctic convoys would face no serious threat from *Kriegsmarine* surface forces. By the end of 1943, several new factors combined with the weather conditions provided the convoys with a better chance of getting through to Murmansk without incurring excessive losses. Firstly, the bulk of the German Air Force had been withdrawn from Northern Norway and redeployed in the Mediterranean. Secondly, the inclusion of escort carriers within the convoys provided a new and effective method of keeping U-boats at a distance. Thirdly, on 22 September, the *Tirpitz* had been mined and severely damaged by two British midget submarines that penetrated the Altenfjord; the only remaining German capital ship, the *Scharnhorst*, was sunk on 26 December; and finally British radar development had advanced more rapidly than that of the Germans. All these factors gave the convoy escorts a greater advantage during the long Arctic winter nights when reconnaissance by planes and U-boats was difficult or impractical.

German Reassessment of the Operational Situation

Group North, in a further assessment of the operational situation submitted on 8 January, reported as follows:

> The last three PQ convoys passed Bear Island passage at intervals of about one week, PQ 25 (according to the numbering given at the time) on 6 February according to dead reckoning. The first two convoys were relatively small (about 15 steamers) and together corresponded roughly

to the strength of earlier PQ convoys, while the last convoy, both as regards the number of steamers and the light escort forces, corresponded to earlier convoys. A returning QP convoy had not been observed since 25 January.

The purpose of the enemy's changed convoy tactics was not evident, but the following possibilities were suggested:

1. As a result of agreements reached and a planned large-scale offensive which would consume great quantities of material, the delivery of supplies to Russia was to be speeded up, and the period of darkness in Arctic waters exploited to the full.
2. The enemy intends, by a quick succession of convoys, to exhaust our forces both as regards manpower and boats available, so that our power to attack will be lessened with each successive convoy.
3. Owing to Russia's urgent need for supplies, the first convoy sailed earlier than was originally intended and was really meant to form one large convoy together with the second one.
   c. We must still expect that PQ convoys and corresponding QP convoys will continue to run at short intervals.

In commenting on operations by the German Air Force and U-boats, Group North went on to report:

a. *Luftflotte* 5 has done everything to comply with the requests of the Navy for reconnaissance flights against PQ convoys and – so far as was necessary – against QP convoys.

   The fact that, of the last three convoys, the first was intercepted by U-boats only on reaching the Bear Island passage, the second by a meteorological aircraft, and the third by another meteorological aircraft about half a day's run west of Bear Island passage shows that air reconnaissance with the available forces does not ensure the early interception of convoys – the last two successes were merely a lucky chance.

b. So long as air interception of convoys is not certain, the main burden of reconnaissance remains with the U-boats. This implies that at any given time there would always have to be at least six boats in the Bear Island passage, and if, as is desirable, the patrol line were to be moved further to south-west, the number required would be correspondingly greater. Apart from the boats at sea, a large number of boats in port, at operational readiness, would be needed to ensure successful attacks against the frequently running convoys.

The report ended with the following comment:

a. A further increase in Northern Waters U-boats is considered necessary. Attention is drawn to the fact that combat strength would not rise in direct proportion with an increase in boats, as the maintenance capacity in Northern Waters would soon be exhausted, so that long passages for repairs in home ports would become necessary.
b. It is requested to apply to the C-in-C of the Air Force, Operational Staff, for the reinforcement of *Luftflotte* 5 so that convoy reconnaissance may be extended.

Churchill Promises an Extra Convoy

The convoy planning continued, and Churchill wrote again to Stalin on 17 January:

> I find I can work in an additional Arctic convoy,[3] twenty ships, mostly United States, leaving the United Kingdom about March 15th to March 18th without prejudice to our main operations.
> I hope this will be agreeable to you.
> January 17th, 1944

Stalin replied three days later:

> Thank you for informing me of your decision to send an additional convoy of 20 ships to the Soviet Union in mid-March over and above those provided for earlier. They will be of great value to our front.
> January 20, 1944

Return of the U-Boat Threat

The War Cabinet Weekly Summary for 20 to 27 January 1944 reported: 'Early on the 26th a convoy[4] to N. Russia was attacked by at least six U-boats when east of Bear Island. Three ships have been sunk and HMS *Obdurate* (a destroyer) was torpedoed but is proceeding with the convoy.'

German Navy Review of the Strategic Situation

The *Kriegsmarine* was unhappy with the outcome of the latest operations. The experience led Group North to request on 30 January an increase of

U-boat strength in Northern Waters in view of the general strategic situation. Ten U-boats had been temporarily withdrawn from Northern Waters at the beginning of September. One was lost and had not been replaced and another had been detached for open-water firing, leaving only eleven available for operational use. Due to restricted dockyard capacity half of these were in refit, thus never more than six U-boats were at a state of readiness. The Luftwaffe had also been considerably weakened by the withdrawal of units; half of the bomber force had been withdrawn. No striking success from surface forces could be expected because of restrictions on their offensive operations against convoys, especially those whose escorts were equal to our forces in strength.

In commenting on the failure to disrupt the convoys, the War Diary explained:

> The attack on PQ 21 has shown once again the escorts of all Russian convoys were very strong. It was, therefore, particularly difficult for U-boats in such small numbers to break through the ring of escorting vessels to come within attacking distance of the Merchant ships. Only an increased number of boats could offer any prospects of deflecting the escort vessels and making success more likely.
>
> Supplies to Russia had been sent at a greater rate during December and January than was expected and Russian air units and naval forces had recently been reinforced in the Northern Area.

Group North's further comment on the situation read:

> The enemy attaches great importance to the increase of war materials for the Russians in the Northern Area. With corresponding strengthening of the northern sector of the Russian front a large-scale offensive might become possible, combined with a major landing in Northern Norway. Hence the strengthening of all our forces, particularly of the Luftwaffe and U-boats, is essential both for success in offensive operations, viz. attacking of Russian supply convoys and for successful defensive action; viz. defence against enemy landing. Hence request is urgently made to increase U-boat strength, at least to the old number of 23 boats.

Admiral Northern Waters endorsed Group North's request and called for twenty-three U-boats to be allocated to Captain U-boats by April for the use of Admiral Northern Waters, noting firstly the prospects of success against PQ convoys, always strongly escorted, were slight with only a few U-boats of which only six at a time were at operational readiness; secondly the reinforcement of Russian air and naval forces; and thirdly the importance of U-boats in preventing landings.

Admiral Northern Waters, also noting that the obvious increase in PQ traffic might perhaps be intended for a Russian offensive in the northern area, suggested replacements could possibly be made at an earlier date as desired by Group North, but acknowledged this could only be decided by C-in-C U-boats, who had the overall picture of the situation and knew the prospects of success.

The Additional Convoy

Churchill informed Stalin on 9 February 1944:

> 4. I have now succeeded in arranging with the British Admiralty and the American War Shipping Administration for another additional convoy of ships to go to North Russia in March. I should hope that the actual number of ships would be 18 or 20, nearly all of which are American. Although this does not increase the amount of supplies due under the Protocol, it conveys them to you a good deal quicker and along the northern route, which I understand you greatly prefer to the Persian. The Arctic convoys have been getting through well and the U-boats were much knocked about on the last occasion by our escorts. Every good wish.

Stalin acknowledged the message on 11 February: 'The Soviet Government is grateful to you for the information on the despatch of another additional convoy to the USSR in March. Please accept my best wishes.'

U-Boat Attacks Frustrated

The first part of the next convoy operation, Operation FX, the passage of eastbound convoy JW 57 to North Russia, took place during the last week of February. Determined German attempts to intercept the convoy and inflict heavy losses failed. The convoy suffered no loss or damage.

The German Naval Staff War Diary reported: 'Again U-boat Command noted the weather, depth-charge and hydrophone pursuits and enemy air activity dispersed the U-boats and hampered their attacks, with the unsatisfactory result of the Operation attributable mainly to the very strong escort provided for the convoy.'

The second part of Operation FX (the passage of RA 57 from North Russia) which sailed from the Kola Inlet on 2 March and arrived at Loch Ewe eight days later was completed with the loss of one merchant ship sunk and the cost of three U-boats destroyed.

Captain U-boats Norway regarded the outcome of the operations against JW 57 and RA 57 (identified as PQ 30 and QP 26), as unsatisfactory. His Situation Report of 8 March calling for a change in tactics complained:

> The unsatisfactory results of the attacks on the last two convoys as well as the U-boat losses incurred compel us to alter our tactics for the future. As long as we did not need to reckon with such strong carrier-borne and land-based air defences as accompanied PQ 30 and QP 26, interception of the convoy in the early-morning hours with a subsequent hauling ahead in preparation for night attacks was thought to be successful. However, as recent experience has shown, as soon as there is strong, enemy air cover it is useless to maintain a surfaced disposition in the daytime as it only leads to losses. Moreover [he went on], the boats are quickly forced to submerge by aircraft and anti-submarine units and in many cases have no time to transmit the first shadowing report which is of extreme importance for operational control.
>
> In future it will therefore be necessary, especially off the enemy's coasts, to order U-boats to take up submerged positions during daylight. Extensive air reconnaissance will continue to be of extreme importance. Submerged positions are also important in preventing the patrol line from being observed. Air reconnaissance, particularly on the night and day before the convoy comes within range of the patrol line, must be so strong in numbers that any evasive action taken by the convoy and major variations in course will be observed without fail. Moreover, during the first night of the operations an air shadower must be continuously with the convoy to transmit beacon signals.
>
> The U-boat patrol line must be placed and manoeuvred in such a way that at nightfall the convoy will be in its immediate vicinity, not more than 30-40 miles away.
>
> By the elaboration of beacon signal methods and their increased use, as in the Atlantic, all the U-boats must be enabled to attack early during the night. (Establishment of the convoy's position by the U-boat with the help of two position lines. Reception of beacon signals from shadower from various geographical directions.) The first night is decisive for the success of the whole operation.

At dawn, the U-boats must withdraw to a safe distance from the convoy and haul ahead. In case of strong enemy air cover, any of the boats that are too close to the convoy must at first remain submerged for their own protection. But this entails that such boats will not be in position during the following night and will take correspondingly longer before they will be able to attack again. During the summer months of continuous daylight in the Arctic (30 April to 15 August), U-boats will only be able to operate in submerged attacks. During daytime, they will either haul ahead or remain submerged.

Chapter Sixteen

Suspension of Convoys Before OVERLORD

On 9 March Churchill and Roosevelt messaged Stalin: 'The Russian convoys are being run up to the last minute before "OVERLORD" with very heavy destroyer escorts.'

German Review of Effectiveness of U-Boat Operations

Group North/Fleet commented two days later in the *Interim Conclusions* on the operation against QP 26 (RA 57):

> The measures taken by U-boat Command were adequate to the needs of the situation. The transmission of an estimated position as a guide for the U-boats in the absence of shadowers' reports or in case of obvious mistakes in fix in the reports of convoy positions had proved satisfactory. Once again, U-boat operations had been very ably supported by the German Air Force, so far as their forces and types of aircraft permitted and the weather allowed them to operate. The successes gained, as could be foreseen after the conclusion of operations against PQ 30, were regrettably small. The causes of this comparative failure, apart from strong anti-submarine measures by enemy naval and air forces, were the increasing periods of daylight and adverse weather conditions.
>
> As regards possible improvements, it was recognised the even closer cooperation between the German Air Force and the U-boats, as suggested by Captain U-boats, Norway might increase the chances of success. The same held for the proposed improvements in shadower technique and the bringing up of U-boats. Moreover, improvements in navigation, especially through radio beacon bearings, were regarded as most important measures to increase our successes. Navigational conditions and fixes were evidently better than in the last convoy operation.
>
> So far as future operations were concerned it was recognised the prospects of U-boat successes would decrease further with increasing and then continuous daylight. In order therefore to achieve satisfactory results a maximum number of U-boats should take part in convoy operations.

This can be attained by abandoning operations against QP convoys and employing only a small number of U-boats on continuous sea patrol. The main task of reconnaissance must then fall more than ever on the German Air Force. Only after the air reconnaissance had intercepted a convoy should the U-boats put out from the operational ports and be drawn up in positions as deeply staggered as possible in order that they may remain undetected. Even then, without the allocation of bombers and long-range fighters, great successes against convoys could hardly be expected.

Group North/Fleet concluded:

In spite of the vigorous and energetic action of the U-boats, which was beyond all praise, and good support from the German Air Force, the operation remained unsuccessful. The cause for this must not be sought in those who took part, or those who directed the operation, but in the very difficult conditions which prevailed.

Churchill telegraphed Stalin on 10 March:[1] 'You will be glad to hear that the latest Russian convoy has now got safe home and that four U-boats out of the pack that attacked it were certainly sunk on the voyage by the escort.'[2]

The War Cabinet learned on the following day[3] that a large convoy[4] had arrived in North Russia without any loss or damage.

Stalin replied to Churchill on the 13th: 'Thank you for your information about the latest convoy, which has delivered badly-needed cargoes to the Soviet Union. I was deeply satisfied to learn from your Telegram that the convoy sunk four enemy U-boats en route.'[5]

Taking the Battle to the Enemy: Proactive Convoy Defence

Arrangements were now made to further strengthen the offensive capacity of the convoy air and surface escorts with the addition of two escort carriers and two support groups.

The first part of the next operation – Operation FY, the passage of JW 58 to North Russia – took place at the end of March. The convoy of forty-six merchant ships[6] sailed from Loch Ewe for North Russia on the 27th and included the US cruiser *Milwaukee* being transferred to the Russian Navy as part of an agreement over the disposal of the surrendered Italian fleet. The Murmansk section arrived at the Kola Inlet without incident on the 4th and the White Sea Section in Archangel on the 6th.

With the safe arrival of so many merchant ships, the destruction of three U-boats (plus a fourth incidental kill) and six shadowing aircraft, JW 58 was regarded as one of the most successful Arctic convoys.

The German Reaction to Strengthened Convoy Protection

Meantime the *Kriegsmarine* remained unhappy about the outcome of their attacks on the convoys due to the continued presence of aircraft carriers in the through escort. During a conference on 12/13 April between Hitler, Dönitz, Jodl and Göring, Dönitz argued that enemy carrier-borne aircraft prevented U-boats from approaching convoys, but it would be easy to combat these carriers with Norwegian shore-based aircraft. Göring agreed only to arrange the necessary ground organization to enable him to send bombers to North Norway when required for each operation, while Dönitz argued unsuccessfully for permanent bomber forces to be allocated for the purpose. This lack of aircraft to conduct anti-shipping operations would remain a fundamental weakness in the Germans' capability to conduct offensive operations against the convoys.

End of the 1943/44 Convoy Cycle

JW 58 and RA 58 were the last convoys to be run in the spring of 1944 before the cycle was suspended during the summer months. The overriding demands of Operation NEPTUNE (the naval element of the invasion of Normandy) on available fleet escorts meant that it was impossible to run another JW convoy in the time available before D-Day. There were, however, still forty-four merchant ships lying empty in North Russian ports and it was decided, given the suspension of the convoy cycle and the need to release naval assets for OVERLORD, to bring all these back to the UK as quickly as possible and send a strong naval escort through to the Kola Inlet as quickly as possible to cover the operation.

The recovery operation, Operation FZ, took place at the very end of April. As there was no corresponding outward-bound convoy, the escorts sailed direct from Scapa Flow to the Kola Inlet and returned with the convoy after a five-day turnaround. The object of the operation was to bring out the large number of empty merchant ships lying in Russian ports together with the USN crew of the USS *Milwaukee* transferred to the Russian Navy and 1,430 Russian naval personnel to crew ex-RN warships in UK ports awaiting transfer to the Red Fleet. The convoy of forty-four merchant ships plus an escort oiler left the Kola Inlet on the 28th. No battle squadron or cruiser force covered the convoy as the German surface threat was now confined to destroyers. The American and Russian naval passengers were landed in the Clyde on the 5th. The merchant ships dispersed and arrived at Loch Ewe and the Clyde on 6 and 7 May respectively, having lost one merchant ship to U-boat attack.

During the 1943/44 winter cycle, a total of 197 merchant ships set out for North Russia. Of these seven returned and three were sunk, while five of the fifty who made the return journey were lost.

Results of 1943/44 Winter Convoy Cycle and Plans for Resumption following OVERLORD

On 3 May 1944, Churchill sent Stalin a summary[7] of the results achieved during the 1943/44 winter convoy cycle. This read as follows:

> Last autumn I gave instructions for a convoy cycle consisting of four convoys, each of about 35 British and American ships, to be sailed to your northern ports and I was later able to add two additional half convoys of 20 ships each to the original programme, making a total of 180 ships which were expected to carry about one million tons dead-weight of cargo. The outward cycle has now been completed and I take pleasure in reporting to you the results of the efforts we have made.
>
> 2. Excluding rescue ships, the Royal Navy has convoyed 191 ships to your northern ports comprising 49 British and 118 United States dry cargo ships, one crane ship to aid in discharge, 5 ships with United States military cargoes and 18 tankers. In dead-weight tons the cargo carried consisted of:
>
> | | Tons |
> | --- | --- |
> | British | 232,600 |
> | American | 830,500 |
> | Aviation spirit, alcohol and fuel oil | 171,500 |
> | United States army stores | 25,000 |
> | A total of | 1,259,600 |
>
> 3. In spite of heavy attacks launched by a vigilant enemy, the Royal Navy succeeded in bringing safely to your ports all but three of the ships despatched; in doing so I am glad to tell you that our losses were only two destroyers sunk and one fighter aircraft shot down, for which the infliction on the enemy of the loss of the *Scharnhorst*, 8 U-boats and

5 aircraft is fair compensation. Also we have damaged seriously the *Tirpitz* in this part of the world.
4. All this has been very successful and it rejoices my heart that these weapons should reach your gallant armies at a time when their great victories are occurring. The moment we have got over the crisis of 'OVERLORD' I shall be making plans to send you more. I have already given directions for the matter to be studied so that we can make another convoy engagement with you if the course of battle allows. I expect really heavy sea losses in this particular 'OVERLORD' battle, where warships will have a prolonged engagement with shore batteries and all vessels will be in great danger from mines. We think we have got the U-boat and enemy aircraft pretty well mastered, but the little 'E' boats will be a danger at night with their great speed. I felt I owe it to Mr Lyttelton, Minister of Production, who has been largely in charge of this business of Arctic supplies to make you acquainted with the fact that we have succeeded beyond our hopes.

Good wishes.
May 3rd, 1944

Deterrent Effect of Escort Carriers on U-Boat Operations

The German naval staff continued to remain concerned about the negative effect the presence of aircraft carriers in northern waters was having on U-boat operations. The subject resurfaced at a meeting on 4 May, when in discussing PQ convoys it was recognized that the weakness of the German Air Force allowed the escorting enemy carriers to remain unmolested. Dönitz suggested that the torpedo flights would be more useful in northern waters than in the Mediterranean, with which Hitler agreed.

Stalin's Appreciation

Stalin replied to Churchill on 8 May, noting:

Your message of May 3 received.
    The organisation of the convoys which delivered their cargoes to Soviet northern ports is indeed worthy of recognition and approval. I thank you for the exceptional attention you have devoted to this matter. Would you mind if the Soviet Government were to confer an Order on Mr Lyttelton for his great services? We would gladly award decorations

to others as well, who have distinguished themselves in organising and sailing convoys.

I am pleased to learn from your communication that you have issued instructions to study the question of sending the further convoys of which we are still badly in need.

I realise how much your attention is now riveted to 'OVERLORD', which is bound to call for tremendous exertion, but which also holds out the promise of tremendous gains for the entire course of the war.

Best wishes.
May 8, 1944

In a further update to Stalin on 24 May, Churchill included the news: 'I am hoping to make you a renewed programme for Arctic convoys, but I must see first what we lose in destroyers and cruisers in the sea part of "OVERLORD".'
Stalin recorded his appreciation two days later:

I welcome your readiness to resume later the programme for Arctic convoys.

Thank you for your congratulations. We are preparing might and main for new major operations.
May 26, 1944

Although the convoy programme was suspended until 15 August 1944, planning continued. Churchill next wrote to Stalin on 17 June:[8]

I am hoping to resume northern convoys to Russia about August 10th. I have communicated with President Roosevelt and he is in full agreement. We hope to have about thirty Merchant ships loading in the near future of which two-thirds will be American. The regular official correspondence will pass through the usual channels.

Stalin responded four days later:[9] 'Thank you for the news that you and the President plan to resume northern convoys to the Soviet Union about August 10. This will help us considerably.'

Impact of Fuel Shortages on German Air Force Capability

By June 1944, as a result of the critical fuel situation, the German Air Force was no longer able to carry out reconnaissance of enemy convoy routes in northern waters and in the Arctic Ocean to the extent they had previously, with the German Naval Staff War Diary reporting on 1 June: 'Reconnaissance of an estimated day's run is to be limited to those cases where there were definite indications of the approach of a PQ or QP convoy.'

The Final Correspondence with Stalin

Several weeks passed before the next exchange of telegrams between Churchill and Stalin took place on 20 July, when Churchill informed Stalin:

> The first convoy of the new cycle starts in August. Thereafter I am planning to run a regular stream of convoys which will not be given up unless I show you good reason that I must have the destroyers elsewhere. I do not think it will occur.
>
> Presently we may come by shorter routes.

This was to be the last recorded exchange of correspondence between Churchill and Stalin, who replied: 'I was pleased to learn from your message about the August convoy, to be followed, as you write, by a new cycle of convoys, which we need badly.'

Chapter Seventeen

The Final Convoy Cycle

The new convoy cycle commenced in August 1944 with Operation VICTUAL which covered the passage of convoys JW 59 and RA 59. JW 59 of thirty-three merchant ships[1] left Loch Ewe on 15 August accompanied by a number of other vessels being delivered to the Russian Navy.

The convoy was attacked by U-boats on 21 August 220 miles south-west of Bear Island when the minesweeper *Kite* deployed astern of the convoy was torpedoed and sunk. All thirty-three merchant ships of JW 59 arrived safely in the Kola Inlet at 6.00 am on the 25th. During the passage U-boats were sighted on twenty-three occasions, but the effective anti-submarine air patrols meant that none was allowed closer than 40 miles from the convoy. Aircraft from the two carriers flew for 444 hours in the U-boat area and made fourteen attacks on U-boats at distances between 50 and 75 miles from the convoy without incurring any losses.

The *Kriegsmarine*, however, claimed the operation against the convoy a total success with

> One cruiser of the DIDO class,[2] one auxiliary aircraft carrier and four destroyers sunk. Further claims included one probable hit scored each on a destroyer and frigate, the sinkings of which were probable and two further hits might be possible on the searching group. The main target of the operation was the nucleus of the convoy, which was not reached through lack of German air reconnaissance and strong air protection [of the convoy] from carriers. After heavy destroyer losses in previous convoys the enemy was understood to counteract the use of *Zaunkönig*[3] by stronger air protection and maintaining a cautious attitude in the closer surroundings of submarines. This proved convoy reconnaissance should only be carried out by planes really much stronger in combat should a successful submarine operation be guaranteed. Our own air reconnaissance suffered many losses.

As was often the case, these claims were very much exaggerated and bore no relation to the reality.

Detection of Convoys

The German naval authorities in Norway had been alerted to the resumption of the convoys, as confirmed by the War Diary entry for 4 September:

> According to a Naval Command, Norway Report of 4th September, observations in the area of the Bear Islands, Norway since 29th August have suggested the presence of QP convoys, as a PQ convoy had arrived at Murmansk and Archangel on either the 26th or 27th August (JW 59). It was assumed the attack on the *TIRPITZ* by carrier-based planes on 29th August served the purpose of keeping her immobilised. The assumption was confirmed by an observation report of a meteorological plane on 3rd September of the sighting of a convoy with carrier, cruiser and destroyer escort. At present Admiral, Norway did not expect any more danger from carriers in the Arctic Ocean.[4]

The German Reaction to Increased British Air Activity

The inclusion of aircraft carriers in the convoy escort was continuing to exercise increasing pressure on the German forces. At a conference on the 'Situation in Norway' held with the chief of the German naval staff at 11.00 am on 17 September, Naval Command Norway emphasized the strikingly increased air activity of the enemy over the area of the Arctic coast. The command's Situation Report confirmed noticeable enemy pressure in the northern area and read in part:

> The gains of the enemy in the western and southern parts of Europe were making available strong air and naval forces. The effect on the entire Norwegian area was already noticeable in the increase of the enemy activity. The knowledge of the conditions created as the result of the desertion of Finland and of the withdrawal of the 20th, Army Command was offering an incentive for warfare on a large scale in the Norwegian area, particularly along the Arctic coast. Anglo-American naval and air operations in connection with outflanking Russian landings were to be expected. The presence of a British battleship in the Vaenga Bay, attack on the task force by a four-engined formation making use of Russian air bases, news about two PQ convoys or enemy formations, extensive reconnaissance and attacks by enemy submarines and air force against our sea communications, together with certain unusual observations made by radio and radar, could all be considered as signs of a coming major enemy operation.

Naval Staff, Operations Division, informed the admiral at the Führer Headquarters, Armed Forces High Command, Operations Staff, High Command, Army and High Command, Air, Operations Staff, and added 'View of the situation is shared by Naval Staff.'

The German Naval Staff expected the convoys to be resumed in late September and the Naval Staff War Diary for the 24th contains the following entry:

> Presumptions concerning PQ or QP convoys have not been confirmed for the time being but it must be expected that they are under way. Likewise it must be expected enemy combat groups would suddenly appear off the coast for the purpose of carrying out limited assignments. According to statements made by prisoners the Anglo-American vessels detected in ports of the Arctic Ocean (one battleship, one cruiser, six submarines) were handed over to Russia and were sailing with Russian crews. The small number of ships in Scapa Flow as established by radio interception could give rise to the assumption of a PQ convoy being at about the Bear Island on 22 Sept. The presence of combat and carrier groups in Northern Waters was to be presumed. On the basis of experiences made so far attacks against the coast were, therefore, not out of the question.

Convoy Propaganda

Press reports lauding the success of the convoys appeared in the national and international press on 28 September. The article published in *The Times* is shown below:

> THURSDAY, 28 SEPTEMBER 1944
> Convoy Heroes.
> The law that the convoy must get through has nowhere applied more grimly or gloriously than on the Arctic passage. The Germans, in control of Norway and northern Finland, have made the most resolute efforts to stop supplies. The losses of the Royal Navy have not been light. The Merchant ships of the Allied nations have suffered, sometimes grievously. The Admiralty states that in the last six months alone nearly 1,250,000 tons of war equipment and material have been delivered; more than 98 p.c. of the supply ships reached their destination under the sure shield of the Allied warships. This is an enterprise of vital importance to the common victory. It is right that the scale of British help to Russia and the

keeping open of the Arctic supply line against the worst hazards should be known to the peoples of both countries.
London
Times.

The westbound convoy RA 60 comprising thirty-two merchant ships including two fleet oilers and one rescue ship sailed from the Kola Inlet on the 28th. The convoy was intercepted by a U-boat and two merchant ships were sunk. These were the only losses suffered by the convoy, which arrived in Loch Ewe on 4 October.

German Failure to Disrupt Convoys

The continued lack of success in operations against the convoys troubled the German Naval Staff, with the War Diary entry for 1 October complaining:

> No Russian convoys had been running for some time, one had been sighted at the end of August by U-boats, which attacked, sinking one auxiliary aircraft carrier, one cruiser of the Dido class and five destroyers, besides damaging one battleship or heavy cruiser. The U-boats were strongly attacked but managed to break through the defences to fire their torpedoes. It seemed remarkable U-boats in Northern Waters had not yet been fitted with *Schnorkel* in view of these successes.

This lack of success was raised again on the 5th when the German Naval Staff acknowledged:

> The submarine actions against the latest PQ and QP convoys had yielded no success worth mention, since the PQ Convoy[5] was not attacked and the QP Convoy[6] attacked too late by only one submarine. Almost without any loss and at times in a distance of between 40 and 50 nautical miles, the enemy transported most important supply goods and a vast tonnage along the Norwegian coast.

The German Naval Staff then asked the High Command Air, Operations Staff to

> Examine whether it could not still be made possible to provide stronger air reconnaissance and also a sudden action of strong bomber formations (II and III Battle Group 40) in such particularly favourable opportunities.

In the interest of the entire warfare, the Naval Staff deemed it hardly bearable to leave their own inshore waters to the enemy without having made at least the attempt to destroy the ships and the cargo.

However, by early October fuel shortages were further restricting Luftwaffe operations in Norway. On the 9th, the Air Force General Commanding in Norway was ordered

> to increase the reconnaissance activity as far as possible within the limit of the available fuel supplies after the PQ Convoys had been detected. Unfortunately, it would not be possible to put into action the suspended bomber formations in the area of Norway. There was no fuel available with the exception of a threatening danger north whereby action would be taken without any regard to the fuel situation.

The German Naval Staff War Diary situation update for 12 October read:

> The supply traffic between England and Russia resumed in August 1944 after an interruption of four months with two couples of convoys so far in a space of four weeks. The PQ convoys had left from England around the middle of the month, and the QP convoys from Murmansk towards the end of the month two days after the arrival of a PQ convoy. Under maintenance of the so far existing traffic schedule, the departure of PQ (34)[7] from England would have to be expected in the middle of October, and the departure of QP (31) from Murmansk with the end of October.
>
> The departure of four submarines from Narvik and three submarines from Hammerfest had been provided for 14th October for the escort during the transfer of the *TIRPITZ*. Subsequently, the boats were to occupy the patrol line against the PQ convoy expected on about 20 Oct.[8] The Naval Command, Norway believed on the 15th the Carrier unit had been put into action for disturbing the shipping routes or was building a wing protection for the simultaneously sailing PQ convoy.
>
> By the 16th, 15 submarines had been placed at the disposal of the PQ convoy in Northern Waters on a position south-west of the Bear Island. Twelve boats of these had been put into position as group Panther; the other three were serving as advanced observers for the convoy and carrier radio traffic.
>
> It was reported on the 20th the PQ Convoy had not been detected again. The boats of the Group Panther[9] were ordered early that day to operate against several smoke clouds which had been reported. At 16.22,

the air reconnaissance reported one cruiser and four freighters on a southeast course. The boats had orders in case that they did not come into an encounter with the enemy to interrupt the operation against this unit at 04.00 on 21st October and to occupy with high speed the patrol line in the Barents Sea west of Novaya Zemlaya to off the coast of Murmansk.

For submarines, the concentration point of action of the entire submarine force was to be seen already now in the Northern Waters where 20 boats were at sea at present on the 21st under the newly-started operation against a new PQ or QP Convoy; these boats were standing so closely to the coast that they might come into action, if necessary, against landing operations as quickly as from the ports; six other submarines were being repaired.

The greatest danger for our withdrawal movements in the Northern Area was to be seen in air raids from Russian airfields or from British aircraft carriers, while the weakness of our defence against landings originates from the lack of air forces for reconnaissance and battle action.

On the 27th, it was declared the reconnaissance of Murmansk would be decisive for submarine employment and PQ spotting and QP assembling. The German Naval Staff called for the GAF to execute adequate reconnaissance, if need be operating with BF 109 plane, Ba/R2 of the 1st Close Reconnaissance Airplane Group 32. It was also noted the Air Force Operations Staff had reported two torpedo groups of Bomber Group 26 were being transferred to Bardufoss and Banak assigned to fight aircraft carriers escorting PQ convoys.

The Contribution of Aircraft Carriers to Convoy Defence

The presence of aircraft carriers within the convoy formations was an increasing cause for concern, with the German High Command, Naval Liaison Office noting on 27 October:

1. With remarkable exceptions the appearance of carriers comes surprisingly as the carriers keep wireless silence and there was no air reconnaissance for early spotting.
2. Fighting of aircraft carriers in these areas would only be possible with numerous submarines. If that ought not to be mere successes by chance then it would be necessary to send the boats out in the right time (that is to say very early) against the carriers, because effect could only be expected when the enemy with his fast carriers would run in our submarine position. Owing to their surplus of speed

no operating behind these carriers would be possible. Therefore, submarine operations against these carriers would only promise any results in case required air reconnaissance would be available. The only true employment of submarines in Northern Waters would be against enemy convoys. There would be no results if operating with these few submarines against fast carrier groups in this wide area.
3. In the present situation Naval Staff saw the only possibility of fighting such carrier groups with the Air Force.

There was also at this time a reaffirmation of the *Kriegsmarine* priorities. The tasks in order of priority were stated on 27 October as follows:

Protection of the coasts of the Reich against enemy landing operations;
Protection of the sea routes along the German coasts;
Protection and control of the western and central part of the Baltic Sea and of Baltic Sea Entrances as supposition for the possession of a base without no creation of a submarine force would be possible;
Establishment of an offensive submarine force;

and finally

Protection of the sea route to Norway and along the Norwegian coasts as supposition for the possession and defence of Norway.
In case the matériel situation would no more allow the completion of these tasks they had to be abandoned in reverse sequence of their priority.

The German Naval Staff had been pressing the Luftwaffe for some time to increase the strength of the 5th Air Force in Norway. The War Diary for 27 October noted that Air Force Operations Staff had reported the transfer of two torpedo groups of Bomber Group 26 to Bardufoss and Banak assigned to fight aircraft carriers escorting PQ convoys.

Further Press Reports

A communiqué describing the experiences of JW 64 and RA 64 issued by the Admiralty on 18 February and published in a number of newspapers the following day read:

MONDAY 19 FEBRUARY 1945
HOW CONVOYS FIGHT WAY TO RUSSIA[10]
LONDON, Sun. (AAP).

ALLIED convoys voyaging to Russia and back to Britain still work under the greatest difficulty and danger. In Summer, when approaching northern latitudes, they proceed in almost unceasing daylight, which makes them the target for enemy aircraft, and in Winter the only daylight they see is about three hours of poor dusk.

The Admiralty today tells the story of one of these convoys. The official account says:

Combined action by HM ships and naval aircraft prevented strong forces of U-boats and torpedo-carrying aircraft from launching even one attack against an important convoy which recently made the double passage from the United Kingdom to North Russia and back.

During the course of these operations, which were carried out in weather of extreme severity, one naval aircraft was lost. At least two U-boats were destroyed, and two torpedo-carrying aircraft and one reconnaissance aircraft was shot into the sea. Several other enemy aircraft were damaged.

The convoy was under the command of Rear Admiral R.R. McGrigor, in escort carrier *Campania*, whose aircraft made the first contact with the enemy. A U-boat, which was sighted on the surface, was attacked with depth-charges, but the enemy submerged, making it impossible to observe results.

Later the corvette *Bamborough Castle* detected another U-boat and carried out sustained attacks. Shortly afterwards a large quantity of oil and much wreckage welled to the surface. This U-boat is considered to have been destroyed. About the same time a number of contacts were obtained by an outer screen of escort ships, indicating that a strong force of U-boats was attempting to converge on the convoy.

While these U-boats were being attacked, enemy reconnaissance aircraft appeared, and were engaged by fighter aircraft operating from HMS *Nairana*. One Blohm and Voss 138 aircraft was shot into the sea, and the remainder of the enemy force was driven off.

Towards nightfall, and in weather which reduced visibility to a few hundred yards, two waves of Junkers 88 torpedo-carrying bombers attempted to approach the convoy simultaneously, and from different directions. Twice the enemy aircraft were driven off, and although several launched or jettisoned their torpedoes, none of the escorts was damaged.

Later the enemy apparently was reformed, or was reinforced, and attempted to approach the convoy from three separate directions. Again the aircraft were driven off.

During the course of these engagements, two Ju 88 aircraft were shot down by gunfire, one by HM cruiser *Bellona*, and one by the combined fire of destroyers. Four survivors were picked up and made prisoners.

One fighter aircraft which was last seen pursuing a Ju 88 failed to return to HMS *Nairana*.

Several uneventful days followed, until aircraft on patrol from HMS *Nairana* sighted a U-boat on the surface and attacked, forcing the enemy to submerge. Later aircraft from HMS *Campania* attacked another U-boat with depth-charges, which were seen to straddle the enemy.

Further press reports appeared on 2 April:

2 APRIL 1945
ALLIED CONVOY HOME FROM RUSSIA AFTER
DESPERATE ARCTIC BATTLE[11]
LONDON, Sunday. Returning from a North Russian port after delivering a record cargo of war supplies for the eastern front, an Allied convoy had to fight its way through heavy seas, U-boat packs, Nazi torpedo and dive-bombers, and torpedo boats to reach Britain. Despite almost continuous attacks, 94 per cent of the ships in the convoy reached port.

The convoy had an uneventful trip from Britain to Russia with its tanks, trucks, planes, ammunition and food for the Red Army, but immediately it started on the home run the Nazis attacked.

Gales at 70 miles an hour lashed the ships, and waves 60 feet high crashed down on the slippery decks, two days out of the Russian port, and the Nazis had to give up the attack temporarily. Twice the convoy was scattered, and twice Home Fleet escorting warships under the command of Rear Admiral R.R. McGrigor, CBE, DSO and Bar, shepherded the ships into formation again.

Torpedo and dive-bombers screamed down on the convoy through a hell of flak sent up by the warships and AA gunners on the Merchant ships, and depth-charges kept the U-boats below the surface.

Day after day the battle went on until patrol bombers from Britain took over the protection of the convoy and dispersed the U-boat packs.

Only six per cent of the ships in the huge convoy was lost. A corvette was hit by a torpedo and sank; almost all the crew were lost in the heavy

seas. At least one U-boat was destroyed and 12 Nazi torpedo and dive-bombers were shot down.

More than 6,000 men of the Home Fleet manned the cruisers, destroyers and corvettes that escorted the convoy, which was made up of British and American vessels.

A second report read:

CONVOY REACHES RUSSIA INTACT[12]
LONDON, Sunday: Despite persistent, sustained attacks by enemy planes and underwater craft in the North Sea, another large convoy, without loss, has fought its way through to Russia. The enemy lost at least one U-boat and 12 aircraft. Attacks by both torpedo-carrying aircraft and U-boats were maintained during the return passage to the United Kingdom. Although some losses were suffered, 94 per cent of the ships reached their destinations safely. During these operations the British corvette *Bluebell* was torpedoed and sunk.

Weather of exceptional severity was encountered during the voyage. Storms, with gusts which at times reached 80 knots, twice scattered the convoy, but each time it re-formed.

The *Lark* and the *Alnwick Castle* detected and attacked with depth-charges a U-boat which was on the surface. Both ships opened fire and the U-boat sank vertically, stern first. One survivor was picked up. Five hundred Norwegians who were recently evacuated by Royal Navy destroyers from the enemy-occupied island of Soroy made the passage to the United Kingdom in ships of this convoy.

Also on 2 April, the First Lord of the Admiralty made a speech in which he presented his assessment of the overall success of the Arctic convoy programme.

2 APRIL 1945
677 Ships Got To Russia
LONDON: Convoys to Russia represented one of the great sea operations of the war, declared the First Lord of the Admiralty, Mr Alexander; speaking at a luncheon in honour of the Russian armed forces. Mr Alexander said that under British naval command, and with an almost entirely British naval escort, 739 loaded cargo ships sailed for the north of Russia and 677 arrived. The Royal Navy lost two cruisers, five destroyers, eight escort ships and an Oiler. An escort aircraft carrier and seven destroyers were damaged. Casualties included 95 officers and 1,561

men of the Royal Navy killed and also many hundreds of British and Allied Merchant seamen. The fact that the battleship *Royal Sovereign*, as well as some destroyers and submarines and the American cruiser *Milwaukee*, were handed over to Russia some time ago has hitherto been kept secret at the request of the Soviet Government.

The naval correspondent of the *Daily Telegraph* says that the Soviet Navy has now a considerable fleet in the Arctic where, presumably, the ships still are because the Germans dominate the entrance to the Baltic. The *Royal Sovereign* is one of many British battleships fitted with external anti-torpedo bulges, reducing their speed to about 20 knots. The usefulness of these warships to the Soviet has been increased by the destruction of the *Tirpitz* and the *Scharnhorst*.

The Penultimate Convoys

The penultimate convoy JW 66, with twenty-seven merchant ships including three escort oilers and one rescue ship, sailed from the Clyde on the 16th under Operation ROUNDEL and arrived safely without incident in the Kola Inlet on the 25th. However, the return convoy RA 66 with twenty-six merchant ships, including three escort oilers, one rescue ship and two Norwegian relief ships, the penultimate return convoy from North Russia experienced what was to be the last convoy battle of the war.

RA 66 set out from the Kola Inlet on 29 April. In anti-submarine operations off the Kola Inlet, a U-boat[13] was sunk during the engagement and another U-boat[14] torpedoed the destroyer *Goodall* which blew up and sank. The abandoned hulk of the *Goodall* was scuttled the next day by gunfire from the frigate *Anguilla*; the *Goodall* became the last major warship of the Royal and Dominion Navies lost in the war against Germany in what was also to be the last confirmed U-boat success in the northern theatre. During the 29th, three frigates detected, tracked down and sank two U-boats in what was the last encounter between U-boats and warships of the Royal Navy during the Second World War. Convoy RA 66 arrived safely in the Clyde on 8 May 1945.

The Final Convoys

The last operation to escort convoys to and from North Russia, Operation TIMELESS, took place between 12 and 30 May 1945, soon after the German surrender.[15] JW 67 of twenty-six merchant ships including one escort oiler, one rescue ship and two Norwegian relief ships left the Clyde on 12 May and reached the Kola Inlet on the 20th. Three days later the return convoy RA 67 of twenty-five merchant ships including two escort oilers and one rescue ship set out and on the last day of the month sailed up the Firth of Clyde, Scotland. Both convoys arrived at their destinations without incident.

This brought the saga and sacrifice of the convoys to North Russia to an end. All trade shipping convoys ceased at midnight on Monday, 28 May 1945. The official Admiralty announcement as reported on the morning of 29 May read as follows:

CONVOYS GO: SHIPS BURN ALL LIGHTS
LONDON, Tues – Trade shipping convoys in the Atlantic and other non-combat areas ceased at midnight last night.

Announcing this, British Admiralty says that ships already listed for trade convoys will now sail independently.

At night they will burn navigation lights at full brilliancy and need not darken other lights.

Convoy system for Merchant shipping was put into operation immediately after the declaration of war, and was based on the experience of unrestricted U-boat warfare of the last war.

During this war, however, owing to the danger of air attack and the pack technique of U-boats, the system was much enlarged.

Small ships added greatly to the safety of convoys.

After describing the war in the Atlantic the article continued:

Russia-bound convoys were also subjected to fierce attacks from German land-based aircraft, U-boats and E-boats.

Many a heavy battle has been fought in Arctic waters, but 88 per cent of supplies for Russia were safely delivered.

These convoys were always in danger, also from attack by large surface warships.

It was on a marauding trip that the German battlecruiser *Scharnhorst* met her doom at the hands of the Royal Navy.

Finally on 11 June 1945, Stalin sent the following message to President Truman:

On the third anniversary of the Soviet-American Agreement on the Principles Applying to Mutual Aid in the Prosecution of the War against Aggression, I beg you and the Government of the United States of America to accept this expression of gratitude on behalf of the Soviet Government and myself.

The Agreement, under which the United States of America throughout the war in Europe supplied the Soviet Union, by way of Lend-Lease, with munitions, strategic materials and food, played an important role and to a considerable degree contributed to the successful conclusion of the war against the common foe – Hitler Germany.

I feel entirely confident that the friendly links between the Soviet Union and the United States of America, strengthened in the course of their joint effort, will continue to develop for the benefit of our peoples and in the interests of durable cooperation between all freedom-loving nations.

J. STALIN

Churchill, it appears, received no equivalent communication.

Chapter Eighteen

Retrospection and Reflection

Churchill, Roosevelt and Stalin

In his role as prime minister and Minister of Defence, Churchill presided over the War Cabinet, the Defence Operations Committee and exercised supervision and direction of the Chiefs of Staff Committee. He was therefore personally involved in the key decisions that shaped the development, planning and implementation of the Arctic convoys and the political and diplomatic exchanges that influenced the evolution of the convoy programme; for example, in pledging aid to Russia in June 1941 without consulting his War Cabinet and in promising to send a convoy every ten days without apparent recognition of the practical implications of doing so.

Despite his antipathy towards the Communist regime, Churchill recognized the pragmatic need to support Russia against German aggression and in doing so relieving pressure on the Western Front. Even in the latter years of the war he remained committed to providing military assistance to Stalin, expressing a strong sense of duty to fight the convoys through whatever the cost. In reality, faced with the level of losses in PQ 17 and PQ 18 he had to temper his aspirations, but commenting on the possible cancellation of PQ 18 in the summer of 1942 he felt 'this would be a very grave decision and was inclined not to lower but on the contrary to raise the stakes, on the principle of "In defeat, defiance".'

While Roosevelt corresponded directly with Stalin on a number of strategic issues, it was primarily left to Churchill to act as the intermediary in communications between the three on the convoy programme.

As we have seen, he was at times in the early days and months overambitious in the promises he made to Stalin in terms of the ability of the Royal Navy and the Ministry of War Transport to find sufficient escorts and merchant ships to support his intentions and the scale of diversion of scarce military supplies to satisfy Stalin's demands. He also received repeated demands for the opening of a Second Front to relieve pressure on the Russian forces.

These demands in turn resulted in greater involvement of the United States, with Churchill frequently appealing to Roosevelt for additional naval escorts, to Stalin for more protection for convoys and the increasing flow of

American aid with American ships which later comprised the majority of the convoys and threatened to overwhelm the Royal Navy's capabilities, leading to pressure from both Washington and Moscow for enhancement of the shipping programme to clear the backlogs without practical assistance from either.

Churchill regarded Britain as being under an obligation to send material to the Russians and declared maintaining contact with Russia and keeping the Russian forces resupplied as one of the three or four most important vital war objectives, but his aspirations were also tempered by the harsh reality of the demands imposed by other operational imperatives and threats and the challenges these presented. For example, he had to accede to the advice of the Admiralty and the War Cabinet in the face of threats presented first by the arrival of the *Tirpitz* in Norway in early 1941 followed by the German heavy ships as a 'fleet in being' in 1943 which lead to cancellation of the early 1943 convoys, and having to divert scarce Royal Naval escorts to protect the Atlantic convoys in 1942 and also to support operations in the Mediterranean and later in Normandy in the summers of 1943 and 1944.

Churchill also became embroiled in diplomatic disputes with the Russians over the treatment of British service personnel in North Russia and the planned deployment of RAF bomber squadrons to North Russia for convoy protection under Operation GRENADINE and in the failure of the 1942/43 winter convoy cycle to deliver the promised volume of shipments, the consequences of which caused him great resentment. In January 1943 he complained:

> (Maisky) is not telling the truth when he says I promised Stalin convoys of thirty ships in January and February ... Maisky should be told that I am getting to the end of my tether with these repeated Russian naggings and that there is not the slightest use trying to knock me about any more.

Meantime the plans to deploy RAF aircraft to North Russia in early 1943 – Operation GRENADINE – for convoy protection encountered political opposition from the Russian authorities in a dispute and became inexorably entangled with the political and diplomatic estrangement from Soviet authorities over the treatment of British service personnel in North Russia. Continued Russian intransigence failed to impress Churchill, who was at the time minded to suspend the convoy programme altogether. He also became involved in the bitter recriminations within the War Cabinet and chiefs of staff as to who was responsible for the debacle which was mainly a British misunderstanding with Churchill seeking to distance himself from any blame.

A more serious breakdown in relations was averted when news of deployment of German heavy ships in Northern Norway led to cancellation of the March convoy and redeployment of the escorts to protect the Atlantic convoys following the serious shipping losses incurred in early March. After a series of consultations with Roosevelt, Churchill informed Stalin that the March and May convoys had been postponed as Operation HUSKY, the invasion of Sicily planned for July/August 1943, had prior claim on all available escorts and assured Stalin that the convoys would be restarted early in September if enemy dispositions and the Atlantic situation allowed. This came as unexpected and unwelcome news to Stalin, who replied 'circumstance cannot fail to affect the position of the Soviet troops.'

The diplomatic exchanges over the accusations of mistreatment of British service personnel in North Russia continued. Churchill intervened in July 1943 when he complained to the chiefs of staff:

> See the various Telegrams about the ill-treatment of our people in North Russia. The only way to deal with this kind of thing is for ostentatious preparations to be made to withdraw the whole of our personnel without saying anything to them (the Russian authorities). Let a plan be made for this.

In the event Churchill was persuaded to let the matter rest for the time being.

Reports of the treatment of British service personnel in North Russia continued to arrive in London from Moscow. In August the Russians began to press for the resumption of the supply convoys to North Russia when the Soviet Chargé d'Affaires delivered a letter to the Foreign Office asking for convoys to restart in September as Churchill had promised.

However, in early September Churchill, reacting to these latest reports from Moscow, wrote to the Foreign Secretary:

> Surely we should say to the Russians 'As soon as our special operation in the far north has been completed, we are willing, if you desire it, to withdraw all our personnel from North Russia. This of course will mean that no more convoys will come by the Arctic route.
>
> We should be sorry for this, as it is the best route and if the aforesaid operation succeeds it may become much easier.
>
> Nevertheless we will certainly withdraw our personnel if that is your wish. There is no question of their remaining under present conditions.'
>
> 2. Let me know what objections there are to this course from the Admiralty or Air viewpoint. I think myself it is the only way to get consideration.

There the matter rested again until in late September the Soviet Foreign Minister sent for the British ambassador in Moscow and 'insisted upon the urgent resumption of convoys' to which his government attached 'very great importance' in view of the fact it had so far received via the Northern Route less than one-third of the previous year's supplies. By the Allies' own admission, he said, the shipping position had improved. Roosevelt and Churchill had stated on 19 August that Germany's submarines had abandoned the North Atlantic in favour of the southern route; since then Italy and its battle fleet had surrendered unconditionally. In such circumstances the continued postponement of the Northern convoys was 'quite unjustifiable'.

Despite the unresolved personnel issues, Churchill was initially receptive to the request, stating 'It is our duty if humanly possible to reopen these Arctic convoys, beginning in the latter part of November ... We should try to run a November, December, January, February and March convoy – total, five.' The Defence Committee agreed. Despite the reservations of the Admiralty, it was decided to plan four Arctic convoys in the winter. Churchill, however, would make this conditional on the 'settlement, satisfactory to us, of outstanding grievances regarding the treatment of our personnel in North Russia'.

In his reply he told Stalin that the convoys would be resumed. There would be one each month, he hoped, from November to February, each of thirty-five British and American ships, adding that this is not 'a contract or a bargain, but rather a declaration of our solemn and earnest resolve.' Furthermore, Churchill called for the removal of the many inappropriate restrictions placed on British servicemen 'sent out by an ally to carry out operations of the greatest interest to the Soviet Union' adding, by way of a thinly-veiled threat: 'The Russian attitude at present makes an impression upon officers and men alike which is bad for Anglo-Soviet relations, and would be deeply injurious if Parliament got to hear of it.'

Planning for the convoys went ahead on the assumption that this high-level appeal would improve the situation in North Russia, but after almost two weeks' delay Stalin replied in an 'offensive manner'. Churchill took offence at the critical and negative tone of Stalin's response to this demand and once again considered stopping the convoys. He returned Stalin's message to the Russian ambassador, refusing to accept it.

Nevertheless, as a conciliatory gesture he allowed the first of the planned convoys to sail, but delegated to the Foreign Secretary Anthony Eden, who was in Moscow for a conference, the task of reaching a diplomatic resolution with Stalin and Molotov, Eden's Soviet opposite number.

Fortunately this conference in Moscow from 19 to 30 October proved to be an 'unqualified success'. Molotov went out of his way in his first meeting with Eden on 19 October to stress how greatly the Soviet Union valued the convoys, and two days later Stalin told the Foreign Secretary that his message had not been meant to cause offence. His differences with the prime minister, he said, were not about the character of the operation of the convoys but about whether these were a 'gift' or an 'obligation'.

In consultation with Molotov, Eden eventually hammered out an arrangement satisfactory to both British and Soviet governments and the convoys were resumed during the winter of 1943/44.

The convoy cycle was temporarily suspended after March 1944 as the overriding demands of Operation NEPTUNE (the naval element of the invasion of Normandy) on available fleet assets made it impossible to run another JW convoy in the time available before D-Day. Churchill then informed Stalin: 'I am hoping to make you a renewed programme for Arctic convoys, but I must see first what we lose in destroyers and cruisers in the sea part of OVERLORD.'

Then in early May Churchill sent Stalin a brief résumé of the results of the winter convoy cycle, adding: 'The moment we have got over the crisis of OVERLORD I shall be making plans to send you more. I have already given directions for the matter to be studied so that we can make another convoy engagement with you if the course of battle allows.'

OVERLORD delivered the opening of the Second Front in Europe Stalin had long called for. Now, in a series of cordial diplomatic exchanges, Stalin thanked Churchill for the news that Churchill and President Roosevelt planned to resume northern convoys to the Soviet Union on about 10 August. Churchill wrote: 'The first convoy of the new cycle starts in August. Thereafter I am planning to run a regular stream of convoys which will not be given up unless I show you good reason that I must have the destroyers elsewhere. I do not think it will occur.'

The final convoy cycle commenced on 15 August 1944 with JW 59 and ran uninterrupted until 6 May 1945.

The convoys, while offering some protection to the merchant ships through strength in numbers were, as we have seen, frequently at risk of attack from German U-boats, aircraft and surface vessels, while the weather conditions also presented a significant hazard. The Admiralty 'Foreword to the C-in-C Home Fleet's Despatches on Convoys to North Russia' published in the *London Gazette* on 13 October 1950 eloquently explains these factors (see 'Analysis and Conclusions').

Churchill later wrote:[1]

It is true that the Russian entry into the war diverted the German air attack from Great Britain and diminished the threat of invasion. It gave us important relief in the Mediterranean. On the other hand, it imposed upon us most heavy sacrifices and drains. At last we were beginning to be well equipped. At last our munitions factories were pouring out their supplies of every kind. Our armies in Egypt and Libya were in heavy action and clamouring for the latest weapons, above all tanks and aeroplanes. The British armies at home were eagerly awaiting the long promised modern equipment which in all its ever-widening complications was flowing at last towards them. At this moment we were compelled to make very large diversions of our weapons and vital supplies of all kinds, including rubber and oil. On us fell the burden of organising the convoys of British and still more of United States supplies and carrying them to Murmansk and Archangel through all the dangers and rigours of the Arctic passage. All the American supplies were a deduction from what had in fact been, or was to be, successfully ferried across the Atlantic for ourselves. In order to make this immense diversion and to forgo the growing flood of American aid without crippling our campaign in the Western Desert, we had to cramp all preparations which prudence urged for the defence of the Malay peninsula and our Eastern Empire and possessions against the ever-growing menace of Japan.

Without in the slightest degree challenging the conclusion which history will affirm that the Russian resistance broke the power of the German armies and inflicted mortal injury upon the life-energies of the German nation, it is right to make it clear that for more than a year after Russia was involved in the war she presented herself to our minds as a burden and not as a help. None the less we rejoiced to have this mighty nation in the battle with us, and we all felt that even if the Soviet armies were driven back to the Ural Mountains Russia would still exert an immense and, if she persevered in the war, an ultimately decisive force.

Churchill's last published words on the Arctic convoys appear on p.422 of Volume VI of his *History of the Second World War: Triumph and Tragedy*, in which he writes: 'Allied help to Russia deserves to be noted and remembered.'

Churchill then gave an account of losses and values of supplies carried to Russia in the convoys[2] and concludes: 'Thus we redeemed our promise, despite the many harsh words of the Soviet leaders and their harsh attitude towards our rescuing sailors.'

Appendix

Analysis and Conclusions

Introduction

The first (eastbound) supply convoy from Britain to North Russia, code-named 'Dervish', sailed from Liverpool for North Russia on 18 August 1941 and the last, JW 67, from the Clyde on 12 May 1945. The first (westbound) return convoy from North Russia, QP 1, sailed from Archangel on 28 September 1941 and the last, RA 67, on 23 May 1945.[1]

Although Churchill had promised Stalin that the convoys would be sent every ten days, this appears to have been one of Churchill's more grandiloquent gestures that failed to anticipate the practical difficulties and dangers that could accompany such a venture. In the event, despite post-war assertions recorded in Hansard that the work was 'never interrupted',[2] the convoy programme did not run continuously or at regular intervals during the war, the frequency and size of each convoy being determined by wider political and military constraints including competing strategic military objectives and the strength of the German opposition they faced. Rather they ran in a number of distinct phases or cycles, mirroring the effects of these constraints.

The Early Convoys

The first continuous convoy cycle ran from August 1941 to September 1942, but within this time frame there were distinct variations in the pattern of enemy activity which inflicted higher casualty rates during certain months than others and so this cycle has been divided for discussion into two main phases: the first covering the period from August 1941 to March 1942 ('Dervish' to PQ 11) and the second, in two parts, the period from March to September, PQ 12 to QP 8 and PQ 13 to QP 15.

Phase One: August 1941 to February 1942

During the first phase, between August 1941 and February 1942, twelve convoys containing ninety-three merchant ships sailed to North Russian ports and six convoys with sixty-seven merchant ships returned. Of those ninety-three eastbound, one returned to port and one was sunk, while of the sixty-seven westbound, two returned to North Russian ports and one was sunk. The only two merchant ships lost were both stragglers from convoys: the first sunk by a U-boat and the second by a German destroyer. Of the naval escorts, the RN destroyer *Matabele* was sunk in convoy PQ 8, while the German navy suffered no losses.

The Germans made little attempt to interfere with the passage of the convoys during this period, largely due to a lack of sufficient military resources in northern waters and competing military priorities elsewhere. One merchant ship, a straggler from a convoy, was sunk by a U-boat. The German navy suffered no losses.

However, by the beginning of 1942, the German High Command had come to recognize the strategic significance of the flow of supplies to North Russia and begun to reinforce their naval and air forces in Northern Norway.

Phase Two: Part One, March 1942

During the four weeks between 23 February and 20 March 1942 only one eastbound convoy – PQ 12 – and one westbound convoy – QP 8 – of seventeen and fifteen merchant ships respectively sailed between 1 and 12 March. Only one merchant ship from QP 8 was sunk, but the events that occurred during these four weeks marked a watershed in what had gone before and what would follow with changes in tactics and operations adopted by both the British and German navies and the subsequent shift in the direction and intensity of German efforts to disrupt the sea line of communications to North Russia. PQ 12 became the first convoy to North Russia to be the target of a planned attack by German heavy surface forces following the deployment of the heavy ships to Northern Norway.

On 14 March 1942, Hitler decided to make the Arctic convoys a strategic target of major importance linked directly to the campaign in Russia as the Anglo-American deliveries of war supplies were, he declared, 'sustaining Russian ability to hold out.' He added: 'It is necessary that maritime communications over the Arctic Ocean between the Anglo-Saxons and Russians, hitherto virtually unimpeded, should henceforth be impeded.'

This directive was followed by Admiral Raeder's declaration on 31 March of the commencement of an all-out offensive against convoys carrying vital British and American war goods to Russia. His statement immediately followed the British Admiralty announcement that a strongly-escorted convoy (PQ 13) had reached Murmansk despite three air and sea attacks. German newspapers promised that the German navy and Air Force would take necessary steps to close the Murmansk route. A German naval spokesman said the attack was the first act in the Battle for the Arctic.

Phase Two: Part Two, March to September 1942

From March 1942 until the end of that year, the convoys became exposed to increasingly heavy air and U-boat attacks as well as potential attack by surface forces following the deployments of German heavy surface units and destroyers to Northern Norway. The Royal Navy's ability to protect the convoys was at the same time very limited. The ongoing lack of naval escorts and limitations on the endurance of the destroyers restricted the ability of the escorts to protect the convoys and to proactively hunt and destroy U-boats. The deployment of the German heavy surface warships against the convoys, while perceived by the Admiralty as a major threat, was, however, constrained by shortages of fuel and the severe operational restrictions placed on their use by the German high command.

Of the 6 eastbound convoys of 179 merchant ships, 20 returned to port, primarily due to weather conditions, and 159 went on to North Russian ports. Fifty-two merchant ships and two naval auxiliaries were sunk. Two-thirds of the merchant ships lost were American (including Panamanian-flagged ships). Convoys PQ 17 and PQ 18 together accounted for two-thirds of all the losses incurred during this period; the highest loss rates for the whole of the convoy programme.

Initially German attention had focused on the eastbound convoys to North Russia, but in late April instructions were issued for the westbound convoys to also be attacked. The returning convoys then fared little better. Of 149 merchant ships, 5 turned back to North Russia and of the 138 who went on, 15 (11 per cent of the total) were sunk or wrecked, 5 of these part of QP 13 which ran into a British minefield off Iceland, and in addition one naval auxiliary was sunk. In total eight RN warships and one Polish submarine were also lost. During this phase the German navy lost two destroyers and six U-boats (see Table Six).

First Temporary Suspension of the Convoy Programme: September to December 1942, Operations TORCH and FB

After the severe losses sustained in PQ 17 and PQ 18, and in the face of the competing demand for naval resources to support the invasion of North Africa (Operation TORCH), the convoys were suspended between September and

December 1942, although one return convoy was run in November to bring back a number of the merchant ships stranded in North Russia.

During this period, thirteen merchant ships were sailed singly from Iceland to North Russia under Operation FB. Of these only five arrived safely, three turned back, one was wrecked on the coast of Spitsbergen and four were sunk either by aircraft or U-boat attack; an attrition rate of 39 per cent. This Allied operation was judged a failure and one not to be repeated. The Russians sailed a further eight merchant ships independently for Iceland: of these, seven arrived safely with one intercepted and sunk by a German destroyer. The Russians also organized a further programme of independent sailings of twenty-five merchant ships between December 1942 and January 1943, of which three were lost.

Phase Three: December 1942 to March 1943

The third phase of sailings resumed in late December 1942 when sufficient naval escort forces were found to provide the level of protection then thought necessary. After some debate on the risks involved, it was decided to sail each convoy in two sections, each of about sixteen merchant ships, with an interval of seven days between the sailing dates of each section. This phase turned out to be a short cycle of only four eastbound and three westbound convoys before the cycle was again suspended as a result of the redeployment of the German heavy ships to Northern Norway. The four eastbound convoys included seventy-three merchant ships, of which eight were forced to return to port and one wrecked on arrival in the Kola Inlet; none were sunk by enemy action. The three eastbound convoys of fifty-two merchant ships suffered greater losses, with four merchant ships sunk by U-boats and one foundered. As all the torpedo and heavy bombers of the German Air Force had been withdrawn to the Mediterranean in October 1942, it had been left to the U-boats and surface forces to mount most of the attacks, but on New Year's Eve convoy JW 51B was attacked by the pocket battleship *Admiral Lützow*, heavy cruiser *Hipper* and five destroyers deployed under Operation *REGENBOGEN* ('Rainbow Order'). In the action that followed the German destroyer *Friedrich Eckoldt* and RN destroyer *Achates* were sunk. This engagement came to be called the Battle of the Barents Sea. The RN minesweeper *Bramble* was also lost in a separate action. One Russian destroyer was also lost.

Suspension of Sailings: March to November 1943, Operation HUSKY

By this time the strengthened arrangements for convoy protection had begun to take effect and the rate of merchant shipping losses at last began to decrease. The continuation of this convoy cycle was, however, threatened firstly by the dispute between the British and Russian governments over the Russian objections to the proposal to deploy RAF squadrons in North Russia for convoy[3] protection, and secondly by British objections to the perceived ill-treatment by the Russian authorities of British service personnel in North Russia leading up to the point where Churchill was minded in early March to stop the convoys completely. These threats were, however, rapidly overtaken by news of the concentration of German heavy ships in Northern Norway and the refusal of the Royal Navy to run further convoys while this potential threat remained. There was also a pressing need for all available home fleet escorts to be sent to the Mediterranean in June 1943 for Operation HUSKY, the invasion of Sicily. As a consequence the convoys were suspended in March 1943 and not resumed until November of that year.

Phase Four: November 1943 to April 1944

After some lengthy political manoeuvring, the convoy cycle resumed in November 1943. The convoys were by now much larger, of up to forty merchant ships each, the maximum deemed manageable on the route. Some 197 merchant ships sailed for North Russia in 8 convoys during this phase of the programme: 7 of these ships returned to port, but of the remaining 190 only 3 were lost; a significant reduction over previous sailings. The 7 return convoys again included 197 merchant ships, although 4 of these had to return to port for various reasons and only 2 of the remaining 193 were lost, both to U-boats. The Royal Navy lost two destroyers, both sunk by U-boats, during convoy operations in January and February 1944, but as the measures to counter the U-boat threat gained strength, the Royal Navy and RAF sank a total of sixteen U-boats between January and May before the return of RA 59 in May brought this particular convoy cycle to a close.

Convoys Suspended: May to August 1944, Operation OVERLORD

The convoy programme remained suspended during the summer of 1944 while all available naval resources were committed to Operation OVERLORD, the D-Day landings.

Phase Five: August 1944 to May 1945

The convoys resumed in August with JW 59. The convoys run during this cycle were slightly larger ones of around thirty to thirty-five merchant ships.

Analysis and Conclusions 249

As the sinking of the *Scharnhorst* during JW 55B left the Germans with no effective heavy ships in North Norway, battleship cover for the convoys was no longer required and effort now focused on countering the U-boat threat.

During this period the threat to the convoys from enemy air attack was very much reduced, but there remained a strong concentration of U-boats, while five German destroyers were still at Altenfjord. Once the risk from the *Tirpitz* was neutralized after the damage inflicted by the RAF bombing on 15 September (Operation PARAVANE[4]) and given the reduced air threat, there was concern that the Germans would increase U-boat operations. However, the reinforcement of the 5th Air Force following the return of torpedo-bombers to Northern Norway in December 1944 and the strengthening of the U-boat force following redeployments from the Atlantic and the loss of bases in Western France intensified both the air and U-boat threat. This was accompanied by the adoption of new tactics and increasing efforts by the German navy to disrupt the convoys, in particular the concentration of U-boat Wolf Packs off the entrance to the Kola Inlet where the restricted waters and poor ASDIC conditions made anti-submarine operations difficult.

In the absence of the surface threat, the emphasis in convoy protection was focused on countering that from the U-boats and the Luftwaffe. The results of the change in tactics adopted were significant: despite the very determined efforts by the strengthened German Air Force, only one of the six merchant ships sunk from both east- and westbound convoys was sunk by a torpedo-bomber, while five were accounted for by U-boats. Of the 249[5] merchant ships that sailed in 9 convoys to North Russia during this phase, none returned to port and only 2 were lost. Some 223 merchant ships sailed in 9 westbound convoys; none returned to port, but 6 were sunk, one by aircraft and 5 by U-boats. Of the latter, two were sunk on their way to join the departing convoy.

Despite the significant reduction in losses of merchant ships, the cost to the Allied navies, particularly the Royal Navy, in countering these more determined attacks was high. As a result of the intensified efforts by the U-boats to disrupt the convoy traffic, six Allied warships were sunk for the cost of twelve U-boats.

The convoys to North Russia finally came to a close in May 1945 with the arrival of JW 67 and the return of RA 67 to the Clyde on the 30th. On completion of this final phase there were twenty-four merchant ships still in North Russian ports, but these returned independently during the following weeks.

A master list of all convoys by Convoy Identification Code, ports and dates of arrival and departure is given in Table One.

The convoys, while offering a degree of protection to the merchant ships through strength in numbers were, as we have seen, frequently at risk of attack by German U-boats, aircraft and surface vessels, while the weather conditions themselves also presented a significant risk. The Admiralty 'Foreword to the C-in-C Home Fleet's Despatches on Convoys to North Russia' published in the *London Gazette* on 13 October 1950 noted the following:

> The Russian convoy routes, in contrast to the complete freedom of movement of the Atlantic routes, were restricted to the east and south by an enemy-occupied coastline of Norway and to the west and north by ice fields. The convoys themselves were subject to attack by surface forces over a large part of their 2,000-mile passage, to air attack for 1,400 miles and to U-boat attack throughout their entire run. The severe Arctic weather added to their navigational difficulties during winter months, but they ran a greater risk of attack between March and September owing to the continuous daylight of the Far Northern summer. Nevertheless, in spite of these very adverse conditions, under British command, and almost entirely under British naval and air escort, forty outward and thirty-five homeward-bound Russian convoys made the passage during a period of nearly four years.

Convoy Sailing Programme

CONVOY CODE	DEPARTED PORT	DEPARTED DATE	ARRIVED PORT	ARRIVED DATE	NOTES
'Dervish'	Hvalfjörður Iceland	21 August 1941	Archangel	31 August 1941	
QP 1	Archangel	28 September 1941	Scapa Flow	10 October 1941	
PQ 2	Liverpool	13 October 1941	Archangel	30 October 1941	
QP 2	Archangel	3 November 1941	Kirkwall, Orkney	17 November 1941	
PQ 3	Hvalfjörður	9 November 1941	Archangel	22 November 1941	
PQ 4	Hvalfjörður	17 November 1941	Archangel	28 November 1941	
QP 3	Archangel	27 November 1941	Dispersed	3 December 1941	
PQ 5	Hvalfjörður	27 November 1941	Archangel	13 December 1941	
PQ 6	Hvalfjörður	8 December 1941	Murmansk	20 December 1941	
PQ 7A	Hvalfjörður	26 December 1941	Murmansk	12 January 1942	
QP 4	Archangel	29 December 1941	Dispersed	9 January 1942	
PQ 7B	Hvalfjörður	31 December 1941	Murmansk	11 January 1942	
PQ 8	Hvalfjörður	8 January 1942	Archangel	17 January 1942	
QP 6	Murmansk	24 January 1942	Dispersed	28 January	
PQ 9/10	Reykjavík	1 February 1942	Murmansk	10 February 1942	
PQ 11	Loch Ewe Kirkwall	7 February 1942 14 February 1942	Murmansk	22 February 1942	
QP 7	Murmansk	12 February 1942	Dispersed	15 February 1942	
QP 8	Murmansk	1 March 1942	Reykjavík	11 March 1942	
PQ 12	Reykjavík	1 March 1942	Murmansk	12 March 1942	
PQ 13	Reykjavík	20 March 1942	Murmansk	31 March 1942	
QP 9	Kola Inlet	21 March 1942	Reykjavík	3 April 1942	
PQ 14	Oban	26 March 1942	Murmansk	19 April 1942	
QP 10	Kola Inlet	10 April 1942	Reykjavík	21 April 1942	
PQ 15	Oban	10 April 1942	Murmansk	5 May 1942	
QP 11	Murmansk	28 April 1942	Reykjavík	7 May 1942	

252 Allied Convoys to Northern Russia 1941–1945

CONVOY CODE	DEPARTED		ARRIVED		NOTES
	PORT	DATE	PORT	DATE	
QP 12	Kola Inlet	21 May 1942	Reykjavík	29 May 1942	
QP 13	Archangel	26 June 1942	Reykjavík	7 July 1942	
PQ 17	Reykjavik	27 June 1942	Dispersed	4 July 1942	
AUGUST SAILINGS POSTPONED					
PQ 18	Loch Ewe	2 September 1942	Archangel	21 September 1942	Reykjavik no longer convoy assembly point
QP 14	Archangel	13 September 1942	Loch Ewe	26 September	
QP 15	Kola Inlet	17 November 1942	Loch Ewe	30 November 1942	
CONVOY CYCLE SUSPENDED DURING OPERATION TORCH. INDEPENDENT SAILINGS: OPERATION FB					
WINTER CONVOY CYCLE 1942/43					
JW 51A	Loch Ewe	15 December 1942	Kola Inlet	25 December 1942	
JW 51B	Loch Ewe	22 December 1942	Kola Inlet	4 January 1943	Battle of the Barents Sea
RA 51	Kola Inlet	30 December 1942	Loch Ewe	11 January 1943	
JW 52	Loch Ewe	17 January 1943	Kola Inlet	27 January 1943	
RA 52	Kola Inlet	29 January 1943	Loch Ewe	9 February 1943	
JW 53	Loch Ewe	15 February 1943	Kola Inlet	27 February 1943	
RA 53	Kola Inlet	1 March 1943	Loch Ewe	14 March 1943	
JW 54 CANCELLED AND CONVOYS SUSPENDED UNTIL NOVEMBER DUE TO DEPLOYMENT OF GERMAN HEAVY SHIPS IN NORWAY AND OPERATION HUSKY					
WINTER CONVOY CYCLE 1943/44					
RA 54A	Kola Inlet	1 November 1943	Loch Ewe	14 November 1943	
JW 54A	Loch Ewe	15 November 1943	Kola Inlet	24 November 1943	Convoys sailed in two parts under mid-winter policy
JW 54B	Loch Ewe	22 November 1943	Archangel	3 December 1943	
RA 54B	Archangel	26 November 1943	Loch Ewe	9 December 1943	
JW 55A	Loch Ewe	12 December 1943	Archangel	22 December 1943	
JW 55B	Loch Ewe	20 December 1943	Archangel	30 December 1943	Battle of the North Cape
RA 55A	Kola Inlet	22 December 1943	Loch Ewe	1 January 1944	
RA 55B	Kola Inlet	31 December 1943	Loch Ewe	8 January 1944	

Convoy Sailing Programme

CONVOY CODE	DEPARTED		ARRIVED		NOTES
	PORT	DATE	PORT	DATE	
JW 56A	Loch Ewe	12 January 1944	Archangel	28 January 1944	
JW 56B	Loch Ewe	22 January 1944	Kola Inlet	1 February 1944	
RA 56	Kola Inlet	3 February 1944	Loch Ewe	11 February 1944	
JW 57	Loch Ewe	20 February 1944	Kola Inlet	28 February 1944	
RA 57	Kola Inlet	2 March 1944	Loch Ewe	10 March 1944	
JW 58	Loch Ewe	27 March 1944	Kola Inlet	4 April 1944	
RA 58	Kola Inlet	7 April 1944	Loch Ewe	14 April 1944	
RA 59	Kola Inlet	28 April 1944	Loch Ewe	6 May 1944	
CONVOYS SUSPENDED DURING OPERATION NEPTUNE/OVERLORD: THE D-DAY LANDINGS					
JW 59	Loch Ewe	15 August 1944	Kola Inlet	25 August 1944	
RA 59A	Kola Inlet	28 August 1944	Loch Ewe	5 September 1944	
JW 60	Loch Ewe	15 September 1944	Kola Inlet	23 September 1944	
RA 60	Kola Inlet	28 September 1944	Clyde	5 October 1944	
JW 61	Loch Ewe	20 October 1944	Kola Inlet	28 October 1944	
RA 61	Kola Inlet	2 November 1944	Loch Ewe Clyde	9–11 November 1944	
JW 61A	Loch Ewe	31 October 1944	Murmansk	6 November 1944	Repatriation of Russian prisoners of war. Not supply convoy
RA 61A	Kola Inlet	11 November 1944	Clyde	17 November 1944	See above
JW 62	Loch Ewe	29 November 1944	Kola Inlet	7 December 1944	
RA 62	Kola Inlet	10 December 1944	Loch Ewe Clyde	19–20 December 1944	
JW 63	Loch Ewe	30 December 1944	Kola Inlet	8 January 1945	Ceased to be an ocean convoy assembly point on 7 January 1945
RA 63	Kola Inlet	11 January 1945	Loch Ewe Clyde	21 January 1945 23 January 1945	
JW 64	Clyde	3 February 1945	Kola Inlet	15 February 1945	
RA 64	Kola Inlet	17 February 1945	Loch Ewe Clyde	28 February 1945 1 March 1945	
JW 65	Clyde	11 March 1945	Kola Inlet	21 March 1945	
RA 65	Kola Inlet	23 March 1945	Clyde	1 April 1945	

254　Allied Convoys to Northern Russia 1941–1945

CONVOY CODE	DEPARTED		ARRIVED		NOTES
	PORT	DATE	PORT	DATE	
RA 66	Kola Inlet	29 April 1945	Clyde	8 May 1945	Germany surrendered on 8 May 1945, VE Day
JW 67	Clyde	12 May 1945	Kola Inlet	20 May 1945	
RA 67	Kola Inlet	23 May 1945	Clyde	30 May 1945	
ALL CONVOY SAILING PROGRAMMES CEASED AT MIDNIGHT ON 28 MAY 1945					

Notes

Chapter One
1. W.M. (41), 62nd Conclusions, Monday, 23 June, 5.00 pm.
2. Hansard, House of Commons, Volume 372, debated on Tuesday, 24 June 1941. Columns 971-974.
3. Hansard, Lords, Volume 119, debated on Tuesday, 24 June 1941. Column 486.
4. Churchill to Stalin, 8 July 1941.
5. Churchill, *The Second World War*, p.465.
6. Operation EF, 24 July to 7 August conducted by carriers *Victorious* and *Furious* was a failure. Of twenty-four aircraft launched by *Furious*, thirteen were shot down and eight damaged.
7. Operation GAUNTLET, 19 August to 10 September 1941.
8. HMS *Adventure*.
9. Operation BENEDICT.
10. This initial shipment was sent in Convoy 'Dervish'.
11. W.M. (41), 76th Conclusions, 31 July at 12.15 pm (CAB/65/19/12).
12. For a report on the outcome of the conference see W.P. (41) 238, 8 October 1941 (CAB/66/19/11).
13. This was actually Convoy 'Dervish'.
14. Churchill, *The Second World War*, Volume III, p.461.
15. The protocol was renewed on 1 July 1942, 1 July 1943 and 1 July 1944.
16. Translates as 'He gives twice who gives promptly'.
17. W.M. (41), 100th Conclusions.
18. A report of the proceedings of the Moscow Conference which resulted in the signature of the Confidential Protocol dated 2 October 1941 between Great Britain, the United States and the USSR and signed by Lord Beaverbrook as Chairman of the British Mission was circulated to the War Cabinet on 8 October. The protocol, which provided for material aid to Russia over a period up to 30 June 1942, included a list of seventy types of matériel and equipment requested by the USSR and details of their availability.
19. Hansard, Volume 374, Thursday, 23 October 1941, Column 2005.
20. Hansard, House of Lords debate, 23 October 1941, vol. 120, cc385-40.
21. The Southern Route.
22. 500 miles south-east of Moscow to which the British Embassy Staff were evacuated on 15 October 1941 from Moscow following the threat of German capture of the city.
23. This is borne out by convoy commodores' and masters' reports of shifting cargos causing damage and matériel being lost overboard.
24. *Z-23*, *Z-25* and *Z-27*.
25. *U-134* and *U-454*.
26. *U-131*.
27. *The War at Sea, 1939–1945: The Defensive*, Volume 2, *The Period of Balance*.
28. *Z-23*, *Z-24*, *Z-25* and *Z-27*.
29. *Z-26* had returned to port with engine trouble.
30. At the entrance to the White Sea.
31. ADM 199/1104.

Chapter Two

1. In naval warfare, a 'fleet in being' is a naval force that exerts a controlling influence without ever leaving port. Were the fleet to leave port and face the enemy, it might lose in battle and no longer influence the enemy's actions, but while it remains safely in port, the enemy is forced to continually deploy forces to guard against it. A 'fleet in being' can be part of a sea denial doctrine, but not one of sea control.
2. 'Dervish' plus PQ 1 to PQ 6.
3. Churchill, *The Second World War*, Volume VI, *The Hinge of Fate*, p.98.
4. War Cabinet, 26 January 1942, W.M. (42), 11th Conclusions.
5. See 'British Policy and Strategy Towards Norway, 1941–45: "The Zone Of Destiny"'.
6. This was not actually the case at the time of the report but applied from 1 March (PQ 12) onwards; still, it was a reasonably intelligent assumption.
7. Ob.d.M. B.Nr. 605/42 Gkdos. Chefs. Dated 14 March 1942. Führer Directives and other top-level directives of the German armed forces, 1942–45.
8. Telegram Number 48: Churchill to Roosevelt.
9. The concept of a 'force in being'.
10. There were actually six, but PQ 9 and 10 were combined in a single sailing.
11. Supplement to the *London Gazette*, 17 October 1950: Extract from Despatch Covering the Period 1 April to 30 June 1942. Home Fleet, 2 August 1942.
12. D.O. (42) 37, dated 8 April 1942.
13. W.M. (42), 47th Conclusions, 13 April 1942.
14. It would later be confirmed that two had been lost.
15. W.M. (42), 48th Conclusions, Minute 4, 14 April 1942.
16. W.M. (42), 48th Conclusions, Minute 4. Confidential Annex, 14 April 1942.
17. For further details see 'German Attacks on the Murmansk Run'.
18. W.M. (42), 50th Meeting, 20 April 1942.

Chapter Three

1. W.M. (42), 52nd Meeting.
2. PQ 14.
3. W.P. (42), 178, 26 April 1942, Post Protocol Supplies to Russia.
4. Telegram 141.
5. Fleet Admiral Ernest King, Commander-in-Chief United States Fleet and Chief of Naval Operations.
6. Churchill, *The Second World War*, Vol. IV, *The Hinge of Fate*, p.231.
7. Telegram 85, dated 1 May.
8. PQ 16 was the first to contain thirty-five merchant ships.
9. W.M. (42), 56th Conclusions.
10. Churchill includes a paraphrased version of this message in Vol. IV, p.233.
11. *The War at Sea 1939 to 1945*, Volume 11, Chapter V, 'Home Waters and the Arctic. 1st January-31st July 1942', p.130.
12. W.M. (43), 64th Conclusions. Minute 2, Confidential Annex (18 May 1942, 5.30 pm).
13. PQ 16.
14. W.M. (42), 68th Conclusions.
15. Telegram 89, Extract.
16. Telegram 91, Extract.
17. R152 dated 31 May 1942.
18. Code name for the build-up of US forces in the United Kingdom.
19. 'Dervish' to PQ 16.

Chapter Four
1. Operation HARPOON.
2. W.P. (42) 265, dated 22 June 1942.
3. The Archangel section of twelve ships left on 26 June and the Murmansk section of twenty-three ships twenty-four hours later.
4. Churchill, *The Second World War*, Vol. IV, *The Hinge of Fate*, p.237.
5. D.O. (42), 14th Meeting.
6. Sailed 27 June. Arrived, scattered, 4 July.
7. Excluding three rescue ships and two fleet oilers.
8. W.M. (42), 91st Conclusions.
9. Most of the nominated merchant ships were already loaded, assembled in Iceland and awaiting sailing instructions.
10. Churchill, *The Second World War*, Vol. IV, *The Hinge of Fate*, p.238.
11. *British Foreign Policy in the Second World War*, p.198.
12. Telegram 113.
13. Telegram 166, dated 15 July 1942.
14. PQ 16.
15. W.M. (42), 95th Conclusions.
16. 23 July 1942.
17. W.M. (42), 96th Conclusions.
18. Following Operation TORCH.
19. W.P. (42) 317, 27 July 1942.
20. Member for Kingston and Hull.
21. Member for Seaham, County Durham.
22. Hansard, House of Commons Debate, 29 July 1942. Volume 382, Columns 487-9. Merchant Navy Shipping Protection Gun Armament.
23. Telegram No. 124.
24. Sir Ronald Campbell, British Minister to the United States.
25. The first naval personnel had arrived in North Russia in August 1941 in Naval Party 100.
26. W.M. (48), 101st Conclusions, Minute 1.
27. Post-war analysis failed to confirm any of this.
28. For which read First Sea Lord.
29. Commander of the Cruiser Cover Force.
30. Again post-war evidence shows that Hamilton was unfairly made to take the blame for others' failings.
31. Should be 1 May.
32. War Cabinet. W.M. (42), 102nd Conclusions, 3 August 1942.
33. W.P. (42) 337, dated 3 August 1942.
34. W.M. (42), 103rd Conclusions, dated 4 August 1942.
35. This contained significantly more detail than the original draft (see text in italics).
36. Hansard, House of Commons Debate, 17 December 1946. Volume 431, Columns 1777-81.
37. Extract from the *London Gazette*. Despatch Covering Period 1 July to 30 September 1942. Home Fleet, 3 January 1943.

Chapter Five
1. W.P. (43) 344.
2. W.M. (42), 107th Conclusions, Minute 1 (7 August 1942, 5.00 pm).
3. TULIP No. 59.
4. Confidential Annex (11 August 1942, 12.15 pm).
5. Telegram REFLEX No. 68.

6. The operation to carry supplies to Malta in August 1942.
7. German Naval Staff Operations Division War Diary.
8. W.M. (42), 124th Conclusions.
9. Telegram No. 186.
10. P.M. Personal Minute D154/2.
11. Projected US plan for a major Allied landing on the coast of German-occupied Northern France (1942).
12. W.P. (42) 417, 17 September 1942.

Chapter Six
1. W.M. (42), 172nd Conclusions.
2. Since 1940, Hitler had been convinced that the British intended to invade Norway.
3. One of Churchill's pet projects which did not carry the support of the chiefs of staff.
4. For a comprehensive account of JUPITER see *British Policy and Strategy Towards Norway, 1941–45* by Chris Mann (published in 2012 by Palgrave Macmillan).
5. Telegram 151.
6. Telegram 154.
7. Telegram T. 1242/2 No. 153, dated 22 September 1942.
8. Prime Minister's Personal Telegram, Serial No. T.1245/2. Former Naval Person to President, Personal and Most Secret, No. 154.
9. Telegram No. 187, dated 26 September.
10. Telegram No. 155, dated 28 September.
11. Telegram 189, dated 5 October.
12. The proposal to deploy an Allied Air Force in the South Caucasus was not accepted by the Russians, ostensibly because of the large numbers of Allied personnel that would have had to be supported. See Churchill, *The Second World War*, Vol. IV, *The Hinge of Fate*, p.852.
13. Telegram 157.
14. W.M. (42), 132nd Conclusions.
15. Telegram No. 189.
16. W.M. (42), 134th Conclusions.
17. W.M. (42), 135th Conclusions, Minute 1, Confidential Annex (7 October 1942, 12.30 pm).
18. Telegram No. 160, serial No. T. 1303/2.
19. 7 October 1942. To the Former Naval Person from the President, Telegram No. 192.
20. In response to Roosevelt's 192. W.M. (42), 135th Conclusions, Minute 1.
21. Prime Minister's Personal Telegram to the President, No. 160, serial No. T. 1303/2.
22. W.M. (42), 136th Conclusions.
23. Telegram 166, dated 8 October.
24. Telegram 167, dated 8 October.
25. This had said 'Further to paragraph one of my message of September 30th, my later information shows that the German plans for sending shipping to the Caspian by rail have been suspended.'
26. W.M. (42), 145th Conclusions.
27. Island of Novaya Zemlya.

Chapter Seven
1. The Peoples' Commissariat for Internal Affairs, which included the Border Force.
2. Churchill, *The Second World War*, Vol. IV, *The Hinge of Fate*, pp.515-516.
3. RN Auxiliary Hospital, Vaenga continued to operate until its closure on 21 July 1945.
4. Now invalided as a result of his experiences.
5. This example again illustrates Churchill's propensity to alter dates and facts, ostensibly for security reasons.

6. Debate on the Address, *House of Commons Debate, 11 November 1942, Vol. 385, Column 28.*
7. W.P. (42) 525, 13 November 1942.
8. Admiralty File ADM 233/249.

Chapter Eight
1. W.P. (42) 525, dated 13 November.
2. Personal Minute Ref. M/529/2.
3. Note 2, ibid.
4. D.O. (42), 17th Meeting.
5. Telegram 166, dated 8 October.
6. D.O. (42), 18th Meeting.
7. 23 November Meeting D.O. (42), 18th Meeting.
8. See C-in-C Home Fleet Despatch covering the period 1 October to 31 December 1942, dated Home Fleet, 4th March 1943, published as a supplement to the *London Gazette*, 17 October 1950, 5151.
9. 23 November D.O. (42), 18th Meeting.
10. Note 8, ibid.
11. Dates for these exchanges vary between different sources, but wherever possible dates recorded in Cabinet Minutes have been taken as correct.
12. W.M. (42), 162nd Conclusions, Monday, 30 November 1948.
13. Two returned and two were sunk.
14. W.M. (42), 169th Conclusions.
15. Sailed 15 and 22 January.
16. W.M. (43), 1st Conclusions, 4 January.
17. W.P. (43) 12, dated 7 January 1943.
18. JW 51B, arrived 4 January 1943.
19. The engagement came to be known as the Battle of the Barents Sea.
20. GEN. 1/1st Meeting.
21. PREM 3/393/8, 4 January 1943.
22. Telephone conversation of 6 February.
23. Minute No. M.20/3, 9 January.
24. President Roosevelt's Special Advisor and Emissary to Prime Minister Churchill.
25. Sir Alan Brooke, 16 January 1943.

Chapter Nine
1. The deployment of thirty-two Hampden bombers from 144 and 155 Squadrons (sixteen from each) to Northern Russia in September 1942.
2. JW 53 sailed on 15 February.
3. Masking Beacon = Meacon: long-wave jamming apparatus denying direction-finding signals to enemy aircraft.
4. Air 277, dated 20 February.
5. Signal OZ 526, dated 22 February.
6. Air 395, dated 23 February.
7. Deputy Chief of Naval Staff.
8. D.O. (43) 5, Air Protection of Convoys to Russia.
9. D.O. (43), 1st Meeting.
10. C.O.S. (43), 46th Conclusions, Minute 2, dated 22 February.
11. Rear Admiral M. Dolinin was responsible for the military bases in the White Sea and was the official consignee for supply shipments.
12. W.M. (43), 35th Conclusions, War Cabinet, 25 February 1943, Supplies to Russia: Air Protection of Convoys.

13. Telegram No. 144, Foreign Office to Moscow, dated 26 February.
14. It later transpired that RAF personnel classified by the Russians as 'operational' were allowed to come and go as they pleased with no passports, visas or restrictions whatsoever, whereas naval parties were treated as having 'mission' status; i.e. non-operational.
15. There are suggestions that the general attitude of the Royal Navy personnel in their dealings with their Russian counterparts coupled with an inherent sense of inferiority on the part of the Russians especially as how they perceived themselves as being treated was a significant factor.
16. W.M. (43), 36th Meeting, 1 March 1943, Convoys in Russia: Air Protection.
17. Signal from the SBNO.
18. Telegram No. 132.
19. Head of the Soviet Military Mission in London, 1941–44.
20. 'I will notify your Department directly', Churchill issues an order on the subject.
21. Permanent Under Secretary Ministry of War Transport.
22. Personal Minute M.133/3.
23. See Annex III to C.O.S. (43), 36th Meeting.
24. W.M. (43), 38th Conclusions, 8 March 1943.
25. C.O.S. (43), 36th Meeting, Minutes, 9 March 1943.
26. C.O.S. (43), 60th Meeting, 10 March 1943.
27. C.O.S. (43) 116 (O).
28. British Ambassador to Moscow 1942 to 1946.
29. Note 26, ibid.
30. C.O.S. (43), 38th Meeting, Item 9.
31. This related to the handling of mail, visa requirements, special certificates for technical equipment and Customs and Immigration regulations and restrictions relating both to personnel and stores.
32. As perceived by the Royal Navy, but not necessarily by the Russians.

Chapter Ten

1. Minute by Prime Minister, Serial No. D.51/3. C.O.S. (43) 124 (O), 13 March.
2. 11 March. On forthcoming military plans and Operation VULCAN to clear the Axis forces out of North Africa.
3. Kåfjord, Norway, some 500km north of Narvik.
4. C.O.S. (43) 194.
5. D.O. (43), 3rd Meeting, dated 16 March, 10.30 pm.
6. Dated 16 March and attached as Annex 1 to minutes.
7. President Roosevelt's representative.
8. Ironically the very reason that the convoy was ordered to disperse.
9. This appears somewhat disingenuous as on other occasions destroyers had been refuelled by fleet oilers or from other heavy warships.
10. Also known as Altafjord.
11. This stratagem tried with PQ 17 proved wholly unsuccessful.
12. In fact the German naval staff had an effective capability of predicting and detecting convoy movements.
13. Telegram T. 102/20.
14. ANFA 3rd Meeting, Minute 2.
15. W.M. (43), 22nd Conclusions, 18 March, 6.00 pm.
16. Allied operation in Tunisia, North Africa, 16 to 27 March 1943.
17. Telegram T.1312, 19 March.
18. Telegram T.263, dated 20 March.

19. W.M. (43), 44th Conclusions, Minute 2, 22 March 1943, 5.30 pm.
20. Prime Minister's Personal Telegram T364/3, dated 25 March.
21. A. Cadogan, Minute dated 22 March.
22. Cable C 274.
23. Dated 28 March.
24. Telegram T404/3, dated 30 March.
25. JW 54.
26. W.M. (43), 46th Conclusions, Minute 2, Confidential Annex.
27. Note 10, ibid.
28. W.M. (45), 48th Conclusions, Minute 2, Confidential Annex (5 April 1943, 5.30 pm).
29. Telegram No. 460/3.

Chapter Eleven
1. The first draft of naval personnel – Naval Party 100 – British Naval Base Personnel, Northern Russia and Murmansk-Polyarny August 1941. Naval Base Party 200 was established at Murmansk.
2. Signal 211716/C.
3. Previously the SBNO, North Russia. Left on 12 April 1943 to take up duty as Head of Naval Section of the British Mission to Moscow.
4. Signal, SBNO to Admiralty (221907/B).
5. Signal, 30 Mission, Moscow, 240930/Z.
6. Signal 19111245.
7. *Matchless* and *Musketeer* with stores and passengers left Scapa Flow for North Russia on 3 June and arrived at Seidisfiord on 4 June; sailed 8 June.
8. C.O.S. (43) 187, 3 July 1943.
9. C.O.S. (43), 151st Meeting, 8 July 1943.
10. Note 8, ibid.
11. Archangel, Murmansk, Polyarny and Grażyna, between 24 June and 6 July.
12. 30 Mission, Moscow Signal 08/1744, July 1943.
13. C.O.S. (43), 113th Meeting.
14. It is conceivable that the Russians failed to understand this approach.
15. Telegram number 485.
16. Telegram number 486, dated 9 June 1943.
17. C.O.S. (43) 202, dated 19 July.
18. *British Foreign Policy in the Second World War*, p.243.
19. C.O.S. (43) 204, dated 21 July 1943.
20. C.O.S. (43) 214.
21. Telegram 9522, 18 July, and Telegram 9544, 23 July.
22. Note 20, ibid.
23. C.O.S. (43) 212.
24. C.O.S. (43), 118th Meeting, 26 July 1943.
25. C.O.S. (43), 119th Meeting, Minutes, 29 July 1943.
26. Vice Chief of the Naval Staff.
27. C.O.S. (43) 461 (O).
28. C.O.S. (43), 119th Meeting 11, Minute 1.
29. C.O.S. (43) 214, PM Minute of 25 July.
30. Annex I.
31. Annex II.
32. Nos 1057 and 1058 of 8 August.
33. Nos 302340 July and 070155 August.

34. Senior British Naval Officer, North Russia.
35. Intelligence-gathering.
36. The Casablanca Conference.
37. Dated 7 September 1943.

Chapter Twelve
1. Gieves & Hawkes, military tailors.
2. Chronology of difficulties in Northern Ports, 28 September 1943, ADM 199/606.
3. Various sources including photographs in the IWM Archive cite the 20th, but the Admiralty War Diary and other official sources clearly state the 19th.
4. Telegram, Welfare No. 628.
5. Telegram, Military 9798.
6. Attack on the *Tirpitz*.
7. C.O.S. (43) 526 (O).
8. Note 7, ibid.
9. C.O.S. (43), 218th Meeting (O).
10. FO 954/3B/485.
11. Permanent Under Secretary of State, Foreign Office.
12. Most Secret and Personal Message from President Roosevelt and Prime Minister Mr Winston Churchill to Marshal J.V. Stalin, dated 19 August 1943.
13. The joint statement issued by the prime minister and president on 10 September reporting on the August 1943 anti-U-boat campaign.
14. C.O.S. (43) 583 (O), dated 25 September.
15. Prime Minister's Personal Minute M.600/3.
16. C.O.S. (43) 584 (O).
17. Foreign Secretaries' Conference.
18. Invasion of Italy.
19. Presumably the 25th August letter.
20. Operation SOURCE: X-craft attack on the *Tirpitz*.
21. There was a need to replenish stocks for the ships in North Russia and for the return convoy.
22. C.O.S. (43) 590, Annex II.
23. Prime Minister, Personal Minute, Serial No. 603/3, dated 27 September.
24. C.O.S. (43) 265.

Chapter Thirteen
1. Telegram No. 425.
2. C.O.S. (43) 583 (O); C.O.S. (43) 590 (O).
3. Churchill in *The Second World War*, Vol. V, *Closing the Ring*, p.292 gives the date of the meeting as the 29th (he was given to altering dates, etc.). There is no mention of the *Tirpitz* in the minutes of the meeting. The following text on p.263 is also not an accurate description of events.
4. SBNO 25th Monthly Report: 1 September to 30 September 1943 (extracts).

Chapter Fourteen
1. There were, in the event, seven convoys: JW 54A, JW 54B, JW 55A, JW 55B, JW 56A, JW 56B and JW 57.
2. Telegram No. 429.
3. Telegram T.1600/3.
4. Telegram T.1625/3.
5. Foreign Secretaries' Conference: Moscow 19 to 30 October 1943.
6. Telegram No. 1628/3.

7. Telegram No. 1630/3.
8. Telegram No. 459.
9. Telegram T.1660/3.
10. Telegram T.1659/3, 17.10.1943.
11. Telegram T.1660/3, 18.10.1943, CAB 65/40/5.
12. W.M. (43), 142nd Conclusions, Minute 3.
13. Telegram T.1464/3.
14. Telegram T.1625/3.
15. Telegram T.1402.
16. Telegram T.1667/3, FO 954/3B/514.
17. Telegram T.1674/3.
18. Telegram T.1687/3.
19. Telegram T.1143, FO 954/3B/516.
20. Telegram 143.
21. Churchill, *The Second World War*, Vol. V, *Closing the Ring*, p.294.
22. There was also a hospital unit which brought the total establishment to 383.
23. 30 Mission to Admiralty. Cable 061652C, 7 November 1943, ADM 199/606.
24. Churchill, *The Second World War*, Vol. V, *Closing the Ring*, p.261.
25. W.M. (43), 145th Conclusions.

Chapter Fifteen
1. Leaving the eight slowest ships to follow at the next opportunity.
2. Sent on 27 December; received on 29 December.
3. JW 58 eventually comprised forty-seven merchant ships.
4. JW 56A.

Chapter Sixteen
1. Telegram 252.
2. JW 57.
3. W.M. (44), 47th Conclusions.
4. JW 58.
5. Telegram 253.
6. The *Gilbert Stuart* straggled and returned.
7. Telegram 261.
8. Telegram 282.
9. Telegram 283.

Chapter Seventeen
1. Including one rescue ship and one replenishment oiler.
2. Actually HMS *Kite*.
3. Acoustic torpedoes.
4. This appears to have been a rather naïve assumption.
5. JW 60.
6. RA 60.
7. The change in convoy codes from PQ to JW had never been recognized.
8. JW 60.
9. This 'Wolf Pack' operated from 16 October to 10 November 1944.
10. JW 64/RA 64.
11. RA 64.
12. JW/RA 64. This particular article confuses two convoys.
13. *U-307*.

14. *U-286*.
15. 7 May 1945.

Chapter Eighteen
1. Winston Churchill, *The Second World War*, the classic one-volume abridged version.
2. In fact an unattributed extract from Admiralty Despatches published in October 1950.

Appendix
1. After 'Dervish' each eastbound and westbound convoy was assigned an individual alpha-numeric identification code: PQ/QP up to September 1942 and JW/RA from December 1942 until the end of the war.
2. Hansard, House of Commons Debate, 17 December 1946, Volume 431, Columns 1777-81.
3. Operation GRENADINE.
4. The attack conducted on 15 September 1944 by RAF bombers from an airfield in North Russia rendered the *Tirpitz* unfit for combat and unable to be repaired as it was no longer possible for the Germans to sail the battleship to a major port.
5. Excludes four Norwegian relief ships which did not go through to North Russia.

Bibliography

Churchill, Winston, *History of the Second World War*, Volumes I to VI.
Maisky, Ivan, *The Maisky Diaries: The Wartime Revelations of Stalin's Ambassador in London* (Yale University Press, 2016)
Mann, Christopher, *British Policy and Strategy Towards Norway, 1941–45* (Springer, 2012)
Roosevelt, Franklin D., *Papers as President: Map Room Papers, 1941–1945* (Franklin D. Roosevelt Presidential Library & Museum)
Roskill, Captain S.W., DSC, RN, *The War At Sea: 1939–45*, Volume I: *The Defensive*; Volume II, *The Period of Balance*; Volume III, *The Offensive, Part 1: 1 June 1943–31 May 1944* (1960); Volume III, *The Offensive, Part 2: 1 June 1944–15 May 1945* (1961) (London, HMSO, United Kingdom Military Series)
Sokol, A.E., *German Attacks on the Murmansk Run* (US Naval Institute)
Admiralty CB 4051: History of U-Boat Policy 1939–1945
Churchill and Roosevelt: The Complete Correspondence, Volumes 1 to 3 (Collins, 1988)
The Führer Conferences on Naval Affairs (HMSO, 1948)
The Führer Directives
German Naval Staff Operations Division War Diaries
Hansard Records, hansard.parliament.uk
Supplement to the *London Gazette*, 17 October 1950: 'Convoys to North Russia:
Correspondence between the Chairman of the Council of Ministers of the USSR and the Presidents of the USA and the Prime Ministers of Great Britain during the Great Patriotic War of 1941–1945'.
War Cabinet Minutes and Conclusions (The National Archives)

Index

Achates, HMS (Destroyer), 105, 247
Admiral Scheer, KMS (Heavy Cruiser), 18, 49, 117
Aid to Russia,
 alternative means of assistance, 51
 reduced supplies, 46
 US/Soviet Mutual Aid Agreement, 48
Aircraft carriers – contribution to convoy defence, 230
Alexander, A.A., First Lord of the Admiralty, 145, 234
Anglo-American Mission to Moscow, 7–11, 13
Anglo-Russian relations, deterioration in, 92, 113
Archangel, problems, 13–14, 16
Arctic, 3, 12, 14, 18, 36, 40–2, 45, 47, 52, 62, 73, 75, 79, 83, 88, 100, 129, 158, 171, 180–1, 185–6, 189, 198, 210–13, 215, 217, 220, 222–3, 226–8, 233–6, 238, 240–3, 245, 250
 Battle for the, 21–3, 25, 246
Atlantic Conference, 6–7
Augusta, USS (battleship), 6
Azores Agreement, 177, 197, 200

Barbarossa, Operation, 1
Barents Sea, 23, 51, 55, 60, 64, 69, 71, 102, 141–2, 145, 148, 151, 153, 155, 158, 230
 Battle of, 247
Beaverbrook, Lord, Minister of Production, 7–9, 11, 13
Bluebell, HMS (Corvette), 234
Browne-Cunningham, Sir Andrew, Admiral of the Fleet, 78

Casablanca Conference: implications, 109
Churchill, Winston, Prime Minister and Minister of Defence,
 pledges military aid to Stalin, 1–2, 4–5, 7–8, 10, 12–13
 on cancellation of convoys, 43–4
 informs Stalin of resumption of convoy programme, 44
 consequence of prohibitive losses, 55, 111, 137, 146
 inquiry into PQ 17 disaster, 58–9, 61–6
 consults Roosevelt on resumption of convoys, 59–61
 informs Stalin of preliminary arrangements to run convoy to Archangel in early September, 69, 71–2
 informs Stalin PQ 18 has started, 71
 Operation TORCH, 72, 77, 79–81
 Operation JUPITER, 79
 on cancellation of PQ 19, 82–3
 informs Stalin of independent sailings, 86–7
 closure of British Military Hospital at Vaenga, 90
 requests further PQ convoys be run, 96–8
 resumption of convoys, 96, 98
 request to Roosevelt for extra escorts declined, 101
 correspondence with Stalin on future convoys, 101–102, 104, 107
 undiplomatic exchanges with Stalin, 107
 accuses Maisky of disinformation, 107–108
 advises Stalin of revised sailing programme, 108–109
 attends Casablanca Conference, 109–12
 sees convoys as sound military dividend, 110–11
 threatens stoppage of convoys if the scale of German attack becomes too heavy, 148–56

Index 267

burden borne by Russian armies an unequalled contribution to the common cause, 160
Azores Agreement, 177
threatens to withdraw British service personnel, 181
sets out pre-conditions for resumption, 181–6
Soviet demands for resumption of convoys, 183–5, 189–92
on ill-treatment of British personnel in North Russia, 185, 189, 203–204, 208–209, 239
treatment of Stalin's response, 204, 207
on sinking of *Scharnhorst*, 210–11
promises Stalin an extra convoy, 213, 215
proposes resumption, 221–2
Operation OVERLORD, implications, 221–2, 242
last exchange with Stalin, 224
receives no thanks from Stalin, 237

Convoys

Convoy Cycle August 1941–September 1942
Convoy proactive defence, 219
Convoy protection, Admiralty review, 25
Dervish (first convoy), 10, 244
JW 54, 113, 142, 143, 147–53, 157, 161, 186–7, 191
PQ 1, 10
PQ 6, 15
PQ 14, 27, 29
PQ 16, 35, 42, 45
RA 54, 142, 186, 191, 208
PQ 17,
  postponement, 47
  convoy disaster, 49
  German Naval Staff assessment, 50
  aftermath, 51
  joint Anglo-Soviet inquiry, 58
  political fall-out, 59
  ongoing recriminations, 62
  proposed press statement, 64
  House of Lords debate, 158
PQ 18,
  possible resumption, 59
  plans for, 68
  postponement, 70
  strategic implications, 73
  suspension, 77
PQ 19/PQ 20 cancellation, 77–8
programme outcome, August 1941–December 1942, 104
sailing programme, Admiralty review May 1942, 42

1942/43 Winter Convoy Cycle
resumption of convoys, November 1942, 96
programme January–March 1943, 103
progress of winter convoy cycle, 104
planned programme January–March 1943, 105

Summer 1943 Convoy Programme
future of May (1943) convoy, 137
further debate on May 1943 convoy, 139
March 1943 convoy suspension, 141
suspension of convoys prior to invasion of Sicily, 143
effects of suspension on Moscow Protocol, 161
Churchill intervenes, 170

1943/44 Convoy Cycle
Russian pressure for resumption, 179
discussions on resumption, 181
American pressure, 182
renewed Russian demands, 183
Churchill considers Molotov's demand, 185
proposals for resumption, 186
negotiation on resumption, 189
Roosevelt consulted on Russian demands, 189
Churchill sets preconditions for resumption, 193
Stalin responds to Churchill's demands, 198
renewed negotiations in Moscow, 201
convoy cycle November 1943–April 1944, 210
the additional convoy, 215
outcome of convoy cycle, 220–1

1944/45 Convoy Cycle
final convoy cycle, 225
penultimate convoys, 235
final convoys, 235

Dönitz, Karl, Grand Admiral German Navy, 18, 141–2, 148, 210, 220, 222
Duke of York, HMS (Battleship), 211

Escorts, convoy shortages, 14, 28, 98, 111
  Churchill's request for extra convoy escorts rejected by Roosevelt, 97
Eden, Anthony, British Foreign Secretary, 34, 52, 76, 91, 146, 148, 152–4, 173, 194, 201, 203–207, 241–2
Edinburgh, HMS (Cruiser), 37, 63, 102
El Almirante (SS) American, 15
Escort carriers, effect on operations, 73

Fisher, Douglas, Rear Admiral, Head of Naval Section, British Mission to Moscow, 162, 172, 176, 178
Foresight, HMS (Destroyer), 63
Forester, HMS (Destroyer), 63
Fraser, Sir Bruce A., Vice Admiral RN, C-in-C Home Fleet, 211
Führer Conference, 15, 17, 18, 23, 70, 210, 220, 226
Führer directives, 14, 16, 22
Future convoy programmes, 34, 78, 98, 101, 103, 105, 134, 139, 152, 157, 173–4, 190, 205

German Naval Activity
  initial military response, 12
  further military response, 14
  reinforcement of northern Norway, 14
  military intervention, 15
  strengthening of forces in Norway, 16
  deployment of heavy ships to Norway, 18
  strengthening of U-boat force in Norway, 18
  deficiencies in capability, 19
  deployment in Norway, 20
  knowledge of convoy routes, 20
  review deployment of heavy surface forces, 24
  limitations on naval operations, 25
  shortfalls in military capability, 36
  failure of initial operations, 40
  military response, 45
  naval staff analysis of supplies to Russia, 47
  September 1942 convoy: German assumptions, 70
  concentration of heavy ships in Norway, 141
  reduced threat from, 211
  reassessment of operational situation, 211
  review of strategic situation, 213
  reaction to strengthened convoy protection, 220
  reaction to increased British air activity, 226
  detection of convoys, 226
  failure to disrupt convoys, 228
Goodall, HMS (Frigate), 235
GRENADINE, Operation, 113–40
  Anglo-Russian diplomatic relations, 113
  errors and misunderstandings, 114
  confiscation of radio monitoring equipment, 114
  Russian opposition, 115
  ongoing political debate, 118
  Grenadine again, 124
  Churchill's reaction, 129
  Grenadine misunderstandings, excuses, blame, 130
  the Russian problem, 136
  recriminations, 138
  America enters debate, 139
  German capabilities, 142
Gusev, Fedor, Soviet Ambassador to Britain, 202–20

Hampden Bombers (RAF), 91, 110, 113, 115, 117, 123, 131, 133, 135–7, 141–2
Harriman, Averell, 7–9, 13, 32, 35, 107, 139, 143–4, 146, 160, 183
Hazard, HMS (Minesweeper), 15
Hitler, Adolf, 1, 15, 17, 18, 22, 27, 198, 210, 220, 222, 245
Hopkins, Harry, Roosevelt's special envoy to Britain, 2, 4–6, 32, 35, 111
Hussar, HMS (Minesweeper), 63

Independent sailings, North Russia, Operation FB, 77–9, 81–8

Index

Invasion of Sicily, 80, 98, 101, 143, 147, 149, 240, 248
Ismay, Hastings, Major General, Chiefs of Staff, 10, 19, 41, 54, 132, 136, 137, 143

King, Ernest, Admiral USN, 24, 29, 36–8, 41, 53, 82, 97
King George V, HMS (Battleship), 37
King's Speech, debate on, 92
Kite, HMS (Sloop), 225

Leathers, Lord, Minister of War Transport, 34–5, 134–5, 139
Luftwaffe operations, 20–1, 26, 73, 214, 229, 231, 249
  impact of fuel shortages on capability, 223

Maisky, V., Soviet Ambassador to Britain, 7, 42, 57–8, 60, 83, 87, 91, 107–108, 118–19, 139, 156–7, 160–1, 165, 169–70
Matabele, HMS (Destroyer), 245
Merchant ship crews stranded in north Russia – growing dissent, 178
Merchant shipping – shortage, 92–3
Merchant ships stranded in north Russia, 61, 88, 171, 180
Miles, Admiral, Head of Naval Section, British Military Mission to Moscow June 1941–March 1943, 95, 116
Molotov, M., Soviet Foreign Minister, 5, 48, 59, 90, 124, 143, 166–9, 172–3, 175, 183–4, 194, 196, 200, 204–208, 242
Moore, Sir Henry, First Sea Lord & Chief of the Naval Staff, 33
Moscow Conference, 7–8, 10–12, 209
Moscow Protocol, 73, 75, 93

Niger, HMS (Minesweeper), 63
North Cape, 23, 28, 30, 39, 49, 137
  Battle of the, 210

Onslow, HMS (Destroyer), 105
Operations, Military,
  BOLERO, 38, 46, 79, 111
  BRIMSTONE, 96, 99–100
  FB, 83, 88, 246–7
  GRENADINE, 113–40

HUSKY, 111–13, 129–31, 138, 141, 143, 146–50, 152, 154, 156, 182, 185, 240, 247–8
JUPITER, 72, 78–80
NEPTUNE, 220, 242
ORATOR, 113, 116
OVERLORD, 187, 189, 220–3, 242, 248
  suspension of convoys before, 218
  plans for resumption after, 223
PARAVANE, 249
PUGILIST, 150, 152–3
ROUNDUP, 72, 78–9
TORCH, 67–9, 72, 77–86, 96–101, 110, 246

Pound, Admiral Sir Dudley, RN, First Sea Lord (died 21 October 1943), 24, 34–6, 38, 41, 82, 136
Press reports, 62, 231
Prince of Wales, HMS (Battleship), 4
Propaganda, 208, 227
Punjabi, HMS (Destroyer), 37

Raeder, Grand Admiral, 15, 17–18, 23, 50, 70, 141
RAF in North Russia, 91, 115–16, 118–19, 123, 136, 140, 161, 170, 175, 239, 248
Regulation of American shipments, 31–2
Resumption of convoys, 44, 59–60, 69, 96–9, 101, 153, 163–4, 173, 175, 177–9, 182–6, 188, 191–3, 205, 210, 221, 240–1
Retrospection and reflection, 238
Roosevelt, Theodore, US President, 1–2, 4, 6–9, 11, 23–4, 34, 37–8, 41–2, 45–6, 48, 51–2, 54, 59, 72, 78, 81, 83–8, 96–7, 109, 146–7, 149–53, 155–8, 177, 181, 189, 196, 202, 211, 218, 223, 238, 240

Scharnhorst, KMS (Cruiser), 15, 18, 55, 102, 141–2, 148, 153, 155, 210–11, 236
Sheffield, HMS (Cruiser), 105
Speedy, HMS (Minesweeper), 15
Shipment of supplies to Russia,
  problems with volume, 26
  bottleneck at Iceland, 27
  need for regulation of American shipments, 31

regulation of American shipments, 32
continuing debate over shipping
 backlog, 37
Russian pressure for clearance of
 backlog, 38
Stalin promised increase in deliveries, 41
Stalin, Joseph, Premier of the Soviet
 Union 1941–1943,
 demands second front, 3, 7–8, 56, 238
 correspondence on convoy programme,
  98, 101
 reaction to suspension of convoys, 157
 appreciation of convoy programme, 222
 final correspondence with
  Churchill, 224
Supply convoys – competing priorities in
 the future, 67–75, 245–6

Tirpitz, KMS (Battleship), 15, 17–19,
 22–5, 37, 39–40, 49, 55, 57, 62, 65, 82,
 97, 141–2, 144, 148, 153, 155, 158, 189,
 204, 206, 208, 210–11, 222, 226, 229,
 235, 239, 249
Treatment of British personnel in Russia,
 61, 89, 92
 restrictions on numbers, 90
 continuing restrictions, 123
 relaxation of restrictions, 137, 143
 continuing personnel problems, 162
 dismissal of Foreign Office
  representations, 165
 a measure of relief, 166

Russian reaction to accusations of
 mistreatment, 166
diplomatic negotiations in Moscow, 168
Anglo-Soviet perceptions, 169
review of numbers of personnel, 176
signs of progress in treatment of
 personnel, 180
Churchill threatens to withdraw
 personnel, 181
diplomatic relations in north Russian
 ports, 187
Trinidad, HMS (Cruiser), 37
Truman, Harry, US President, 236

U-boat Operations,
 U-boat deployments, shift in strategy, 30
 changes in tactics, 31
 review of deployments in Arctic, 42
 review of operations in northern
  waters, 48
 return of U-boat threat, 213
 attacks frustrated, 215
 review of effectiveness, 218
 deterrent effect of escort carriers, 222
United States enters war, 15

War Cabinet recognizes increasing enemy
 threat, 49
Waziristan – first convoy loss, 17

US/Soviet Mutual Aid Agreement, 48, 236